# Computational Models in Political Economy

# Computational Models in Political Economy

Edited by
Ken Kollman, John H. Miller,
and Scott E. Page

The MIT Press
Cambridge, Massachusetts
London, England

This book was set in Palatino on 3B2 by Asco Typesetters, Hong Kong, and was printed and bound in the United States of America.

Library of Congress Cataloging-in-Publication Data

Computational models in political economy / edited by Ken Kollman, John H. Miller, and Scott E. Page.
p. cm.
Includes bibliographical references and index.
ISBN 0-262-11275-2 (hc. : alk. paper)
1. Political science—Mathematical models. 2. Economics—Mathematical models.
I. Kollman, Ken, 1966– II. Miller, J. H. (John H.) III. Page, Scott E.
JA71.5.C66 2003
320′.01′51—dc21 2002040784

10 9 8 7 6 5 4 3 2 1

# Contents

# Acknowledgments

The editors acknowledge the generous financial assistance of the National Science Foundation, the Santa Fe Institute, and the following units at the University of Michigan: the Rackham School of Graduate Studies, the Center for the Study of Complex Systems, the College of Literature, Science, and the Arts, the Center for Political Studies, the Institute for Social Research, the Department of Political Science, the International Institute, and the Office of the Vice President for Research. These sponsors supported the conference at the University of Michigan on computational political economy that spawned the chapters of this book.

The editors also acknowledge participants at the conference in Michigan whose names do not appear as authors in this book but whose contributions, comments, and general support of the enterprise were instrumental: Greg Adams, Robert Axelrod, Robert Axtell, Jenna Bednar, D. Scott Bennett, Ravi Bhavnani, Lars-Erik Cederman, Kevin Esterling, Duncan Foley, Thomas Hammond, Matthew Hoffman, John Holland, Paul Johnson, Susanne Lohmann, Mark Lubell, Rebecca Morton, John Padgett, Philip Schrodt, Carl Simon, Pior Swistak, Charles Taber, and Richard Timpone. Finally, the editors thank John Covell for his support of the book project.

# Computational Models in Political Economy

# Introduction

Ken Kollman, John H. Miller,
and Scott E. Page

Increasingly, social scientists are using computational models to gain insight into important political and economic phenomena. Scholars have turned to such models in order to understand systems of diverse, interacting agents. Well-known examples in political economy include Axelrod's Prisoner's Dilemma tournaments (1984), Epstein and Axtell's sugarscape model (1996), Marimon, McGrattan, and Sargent's model of the emergence of money (1990), March's models of organizational innovation (1988), Padgett and Ansell's model of the rise of the Medici in Florence (1993), and Harrington's (1998) models of organizational hierarchies. Especially in the past decade, many papers in the social sciences have discussed computational models. As an indication, Arthur, Durlauf, and Lane (1997), Johnson (1999), Tesfatsion (2001), Judd (2001), Page (2000), Vriend (2002), and Rosser (1999) have all recently published survey articles on computational social science, each with many citations. Tesfatsion, meanwhile, maintains an up-to-date Web page with many connections to computational work in this area.

The subject of this book, political economy, naturally lends itself to a computational methodology. Much of political economy concerns institutions that aggregate the behavior of multiple actors, such as voters, politicians, organizations, consumers, and firms. Even when the interactions within and rules of a political or economic institution are relatively simple, the aggregate patterns that emerge can be difficult to predict and understand, particularly when there is no equilibrium. It is even more difficult to understand overlapping and interdependent institutions. Moreover, models in game theory and social choice often focus on the political while simplifying the economic, or vice versa. For example, many political economy models use the preferences of the median voter as a proxy for political outcomes, when political scientists are well aware that this may abstract too much from the interesting complexity of political institutions. And political scientists sometimes model political competition as though policymakers do not face budget constraints in making public spending decisions. Computational methods hold the promise of enabling scholars to integrate aspects of both political and economic institutions without compromising fundamental features of either.

The chapters in this book present diverse examples of research in computational political economy. The specific focus is on theoretical models that lend insight into traditional problems in the field. Contributors address important topics: government decentralization, status hierarchies, learning, voting systems, and agenda setting. Every chapter presents a different computational model. The methodological primitives, computational techniques, and role for the computer differ substantially across chapters.

To understand how the models in this book compare with one another and with other research in political economy, it will be helpful to consider a classification of types of computational models in the social sciences. We should be clear, however, that our views as presented in this introduction are our own and do not necessarily reflect a consensus view among all those who use computational models, and not even among all the contributors to this book.

We can divide computational social science models into three types: simulations, computations, and agent-based models. A simulation model is a numerical example, usually of an equilibrium outcome in a game or another kind of social system. The numerical examples help to explicate the logic of the model and, in some cases, to calibrate. For example, Baron and Ferejohn (1989) use simulations to show how bargaining agreements within legislatures vary with parameter choices. Simulations are not controversial and are not at odds with any fundamental premises of the major modeling approaches in the social sciences, such as game theory.

Computations are numerical approximations of equilibria that cannot be solved analytically. They are more commonly referred to as techniques in numerical analysis. Kenneth Judd's (1998) book on numerical techniques focuses on finding equilibria that cannot be solved for analytically. Whereas a simulation helps one to interpret or understand a derived functional form or solution, a computation uncovers relationships that may enable one to solve a problem analytically, posit a functional form, or see the relationship among variables in equilibrium. The computer helps one find equilibria when models are too difficult to solve analytically. It is a complement to mathematical theory.

Chapters 1 and 6 in this book describe such computations and are based on game theoretic reasoning. Baron and Herron (chapter 1) describe a sequential voting game with three players in a multidimensional issue space. Players are chosen randomly to set the voting agenda. The authors calculate mathematically the final stage-game proposal and the second-to-last stage-game proposal. However, as they remark, their model is "extremely poorly behaved." The value functions for the players and the trajectories of the majority-supported policies are discontinuous in both the policy space and the status quo location, and therefore the authors must use computational methods to calculate the outcomes for earlier rounds of voting. Note that an ill-behaved model is not necessarily a "bad" model. To the contrary, Baron and Herron suggest that the situation they model is inherently complex and that we should not expect a simple model to explain real-world outcomes. So, while their main result—that the more forward-looking voters are, the more power the agenda setter has in reaping immediate benefits by setting the agenda to its advantage—is similar to those from earlier, simpler models, the new model is more sophisticated and flexible for probing additional questions.

Bailey (chapter 6), in a related fashion, uses the computer to calculate the best response functions of candidates in a two-party political campaign. The computation extends a mathematical analysis of voters' decisions and the campaign spending decisions of the candidates. In the model, the candidates can spend money to inform specific groups of voters of candidate policy positions. Bailey finds that in equilibrium the candidates move their issue positions to attract diffuse groups of voters in anticipation of the other candidates' trying to mobilize (or inform) those same voters using money.

The third type of computational social science model, agent-based models, offers a different approach to modeling than traditional political economy approaches do. These models depart substantially from the focus in most political economy models on rational, optimizing agents and equilibrium outcomes. The models typically have four characteristics, or methodological primitives: agents are diverse, agents interact with each other in a decentralized manner, agents are boundedly rational and adaptive, and the resulting patterns of outcomes often do not settle into equilibria. Most of the chapters in this book present agent-based models.

The literature on agent-based modeling is vast, and as we indicated earlier, a number of excellent reviews have recently been published. Among agent-based models the computer can play two different roles. First, the computer can help to derive or solve reduced-form equations that aggregate either agent behavior or information. Or, second, the computer can be the platform for the analysis of artificial worlds. The purpose of using computer programs in this second role is to study the aggregate patterns that emerge from the "bottom up." The computer calculates each agent's behavior, and the overall behavior of the system is the aggregation of agent activity. Clearly, this second use of computers is more commonly associated with agent-based modeling.

One might ask, Why is the first-described use of the computer considered part of agent-based modeling? Note that an agent-based model does not have to be computational, although they almost always are. Schelling (1978) literally moved coins on a board to analyze his segregation model, which many consider to be the first well-known agent-based model. Furthermore, in the case where the computer solves reduced-form equations, it is the fact that the methodological primitives are the same as in other adaptive models that leads to the classification of a model as agent-based. The modeler has already aggregated agent behavior up to a point (thus the equations are reduced-form), and the computer picks up where the modeler left off.

The use of the computer to solve reduced-form equations in an agent-based model is evident in chapters 2–4. Harrington (chapter 2) analyzes a model of agents competing for promotion in a hierarchical society or organization, such as politicians rising to positions of prominence. In the political story told to motivate the model, candidates pair off against each other, and the winner goes on to compete again, while the loser leaves the population of competitors. The talent levels of the respective candidates and exogenous factors influence the election outcomes. Moreover, there are two types of candidates, those who adapt to their environment, and those who are rigid and do not adapt. The number of survivors gets smaller as competitors ascend up the hierarchy of political offices. Harrington analyzes which kinds of agents (or candidates) survive to higher office when the exogenous environment changes over time. In particular, he traces the proportion of rigid (versus flexible) agents in the top level of the hierarchy as competition unfolds and the population of surviving politicians evolves.

Hays and Richards (chapter 3) rely on computational methods to create a relatively simple way of analyzing learning in a stochastic environment. In their model, buyers and sellers of foreign currencies who can profit by predicting future exchange rates attempt to learn the true nature of the monetary regime by observing changes in the money supply. The currency traders use Bayesian reasoning to learn whether the regime is contractionary or expansionist, although the environment contains noisy information generated by the stochastic environment. The model indicates, surprisingly, that politically dependent central banks may benefit traders because learning the nature of the regime becomes easier. A dependent central bank produces politically motivated policies, and therefore traders can ascribe less of the variance in the money supply to stochastic variables than they can in the case of an independent central bank. The authors compare the results of their computational model to real data from Britain and Germany. The trajectories of excess returns from both countries differ in the predicted ways.

In chapter 4, Jackson describes a dynamic model of two-party electoral competition where both parties and voters adapt along a single ideological dimension. The parties adapt to the position of the median voter in trying to win elections, but the position of the median voter adapts to the positions of the parties. Voters who develop partisan attachments to the parties are influenced by the policy positions of the parties. The computer in this case solves a system of five equations that depicts the changing policy positions of the parties, the changing position of the median voter, and the changing levels of party loyalty present among the voters. Jackson finds that for reasonable ranges of parameter values, the model does settle into equilibrium party positions. Under many conditions, the fortunes of the parties, and their policy positions, fluctuate over time, with alternating stretches of one party's dominance followed by collapse and the emergence of the other party as the dominant force.

Three other chapters (5, 7, and 8) reside squarely in the emerging tradition of adaptive, agent-based models where the computer acts to create an artificial world from the "bottom up." In chapter 5, de Marchi analyzes the policy positions of adaptive parties in a two-dimensional issue space, where the parties respond to polls of voters on issues. The computer creates a population of voters and two political parties, endows them with characteristics, and then allows the voters and parties to interact according to a set of specified decision rules. The assumptions in the model incorporate widely accepted research findings on the distribution of information among mass electorates. This inclusion of empirically supportable assumptions of informational diversity among voters lends realism to the computational models and offers the potential for empirical testing. In the model, some voters have sophisticated ideologies and a good deal of consistency in their survey responses to pollsters. Other voters have little ideological "constraint," and their poll responses are highly variable. The author finds that the responsiveness of the adaptive parties to the voters is sensitive to the instability of voters' answers to pollsters about their favorite policy positions, and not so much to the levels of ideological sophistication.

Kollman, Miller, and Page (chapter 7) present a dynamic Tiebout model where citizens reside in towns, and the towns together make up a state or country. Each town uses a democratic process to choose multiple public policies. After these policies are chosen, citizens can move to the town that offers the best mix of benefits. The computer is used to model both the process of voting on public policies according to different voting systems and the process of the sorting and migration of the citizens among the towns. The authors find that those voting systems that offer the greatest utilitarian benefits in a single town when no one can migrate perform worst when citizens can migrate among multiple towns. This occurs because some citizens are spurred to migrate when their towns choose policies not in accord with their preferences. High levels of migration early on in the dynamic process lead citizens to sort into like-minded communities. The dynamic system eventually (and naturally) settles into a pattern of few migrations and well-sorted, relatively happy citizens, but only after an early period of unstable residential patterns.

Finally, the model by Bendor, Diermeier, and Ting (chapter 8), while undoubtedly agent-based, can be seen as a hybrid of adaptive and game theoretic modeling. Agents pair off and play one of a number of well-known games, such as Stag Hunt, Chicken, or Prisoner's Dilemma. However, instead of optimizing, agents "satisfice" according to an aspiration level. An agent's aspiration level adjusts in response to payoffs from previous games. Thus, the agents adapt their decision rules according to their experience. With this simple model, the authors examine a large number of questions, such as the amount of cooperation induced by agents with adaptive aspirations and the sensitivity of players' strategies to initial conditions (e.g., the initial aspiration levels). Among the many results in this chapter, they find that cooperation in games like Prisoner's Dilemma can occur even in one-shot settings. They also show by including trembles that the games have unique limiting distributions, a valuable "existence" result that allows for empirical applications of the model.

## The Use of Computational Models

Few social scientists dispute the usefulness of computational methods for generating examples or counterexamples, testing counterfactuals, and relaxing assumptions. Controversy arises when scholars rely solely on computational models to pose and analyze theoretical problems. The core of this criticism is that computational models are just examples and not representative of general phenomena. With computational models such risks exist if the outcome of a model is too closely tied to some specific assumption, or when outcomes are hard-coded into the "black box" of the computer. However, it is possible to construct simple, robust computational models that avoid these problems and that generate unanticipated but logically consistent findings.

To ensure robustness and relevance, and also to demonstrate the flexibility of computational techniques, many scholars build upon existing models in political economy. Not surprisingly, then, the models presented in this book combine, extend, and, in some cases, criticize previous theoretical research. This earlier research relied almost exclusively on mathematics, and although mathematics is often equated with theory in the study of political economy, it is important nevertheless to distinguish tools like mathematics and computation from the theories such tools help us generate. Tools should be evaluated based on how well they help us construct useful theories. Moreover, as several of the chapters show, the use of multiple tools may lead us to deeper insights than those gained by a reliance on a single methodology.

From our perspective, mathematics and computation complement one another. Computational models can serve as the foundation for a mathematical model by guiding intuition. They can also extend mathematical models when new assumptions threaten analytical tractability. Both tools require formally stated assumptions, and both rely on rigorous logic to derive results. In most applications, both approaches require explicit assumptions about the preferences of, and information available to, agents; about each agent's decision rules; and about the defining features of the relevant equilibrium or solution concept.

Overall, we see substantial advantages to a computational approach. First, computational models are flexible in their ability to encode a wide range of behaviors and institutions. Any set of assumptions about agent behavior or institutional constraints that can be encoded can be analyzed.

Second, as stated, computational models are rigorous in that conclusions follow from computer code that forces researchers to be explicit about assumptions. Of course, the fact that the code is explicit does not mean that it is understandable, and a high premium must be placed on simple coding. Computational models are a good middle ground between verbal theories that are flexible but have limited built-in checks on rigor and mathematical theories that are rigorous but demand extreme simplification for tractability.

Third, while most mathematical models include assumptions so that an equilibrium exists, a system of interacting political actors need not settle into an equilibrium point. It can also cycle, or it can traverse an unpredictable path of outcomes. Computational modeling allows for all three phenomena to be analyzed. For those systems that attain equilibria and have been analyzed mathematically, computational models can trace the paths to equilibria. Yet the great strength of computational models is their ability to uncover dynamic patterns. Computational models enable political scientists and economists to study characteristics of dynamic phenomena, including the length of electoral cycles, the frequency of uprisings and economic swings, and the formation and duration of strategic alliances under a variety of assumptions about information, incentives, rationality, and institutional constraints. Admittedly, in some cases, patterns can be considered as sequences of equilibria, but often that interpretation is forced, such as when a three-mile walk to work is interpreted as six thousand equilibria disrupted by six thousand random leg shocks.

Some patterns may not be understandable, even those generated by simple computational models. The possibility of perpetual novelty, where the system neither attains an equilibrium nor cycles, distinguishes a complex systems approach from most other mathematical and computational approaches. Consider that society is a complex social system containing citizens, organizations, firms, and institutions all responding to their environment and at the same time trying to anticipate future environments. On some dimensions, such as whether to drive on the left or right side of the road, we would expect the system to equilibrate. On other dimensions, including language, art, and culture, we might expect and even desire the system to change constantly and unpredictably. An explicit understanding of why some dimensions equilibrate and others do not would be invaluable not only in explaining data but also in designing political and economic institutions. Acquiring this knowledge would seem to require a methodology that allows for both equilibrium and disequilibrium.

## Standards

As the field of computational political economy advances, practitioners have come to agree upon certain standards of research. The flexibility of computational models demands that users construct models so that results can be communicated, evaluated, and if need be, replicated. Some of the requirements for computational models —clarity of assumptions, robustness of results, and relevance of findings—apply to all formal theoretical research. With reference to computational models more specifically, scholars seem to agree on these standards:

• *Explain the results.* The theoretical story should be transparent; the driving mechanisms should be analyzed, discussed, and verified. Results that appeal to black-box computations amount to nothing more than, "We ran the program and this is what came out."

• *Check robustness.* Key results should be robust to parameter and design choices. Researchers should search for the conditions under which their conclusions break down. Such searches can encompass not only possible parameters and distributions of random variables but also model process and timing, and agent information, ability and behavior. Increases in computer power call for better robustness checks. They do not mandate more complex models.

• *Build upon the past.* The model should be placed within its proper context and tied to existing work. Researchers should relate their work to other models and approaches, with a particular emphasis on comparing assumptions and conclusions. For example, within a computational model, one can often turn off components and compare the reduced computational model to an existing analytic one. The variety of computer programs and computational platforms on which to model social systems has allowed a proliferation of creations that would make Dr. Seuss proud. A tighter connection among new and past work promotes progress.

• *Justify the use of the computer.* Each theoretical tool has inherent comparative advantages. Computations often provide a convenient wedge into a problem, but then alternative tools may be better for ensuing analyses. Computations should be justified by the problem at hand and, where possible, be supplemented by more traditional analytical methods.

• *Question assumptions.* A standard behavioral assumption may exist for reasons of analytic tractability but may be neither descriptively accurate nor necessary. For example, suppose voters do not possess perfect information about the efficacy of crime policies but instead have local information about their town combined with information about national crime rates. Either assumption—perfect information or local information combined with a global signal—can be included in a computational model. If one is more descriptively accurate, it should be used. Or, at a minimum, if the other assumption is common in the literature, the effects of the two assumptions should be compared.

To summarize, models should be evaluated based on their ability to give insight and understanding into old and new phenomena in the simplest way possible. Good, simple models, such as the Prisoner's Dilemma or Nash bargaining, with their ability to frame and shed light on important questions, outlast any particular tool or technique.

To conclude our introduction, this book contains research that spans two fields, computational social science and political economy. Many readers will focus on the methodological innovations described here. We hope they will borrow and build upon these techniques. We believe, however, that the substantive contributions to political economy made by these authors deserve the bulk of the attention. The true test of the current computational methods is whether they and their successors can continue to aid our understanding of political and economic systems.

## References


Arthur, W. Brian, Steven Durlauf, and David Lane. 1997. "Introduction." In *The Economy as an Evolving Complex System II*, ed. W. Brian Arthur, Steven Durlauf, and David Lane. Reading, MA: Addison-Wesley.

Axelrod, Robert. 1984. *The Evolution of Cooperation*. New York: Basic Books.

Baron, David, and John Ferejohn. 1989. "Bargaining in Legislatures." *American Political Science Review* 83: 1181–1206.

Epstein, Joshua, and Robert Axtell. 1996. *Growing Artificial Societies: Social Science from the Bottom Up*. Cambridge, MA: MIT Press.

Harrington, Joseph. 1998. "The Social Selection of Flexible and Rigid Agents." *American Economic Review* 88 (March): 63–82.

Johnson, Paul. 1999. "Simulation Modeling in Political Science." *American Behavioral Scientist* 42 (Aug): 1509–30.

Judd, Kenneth. 1998. *Numerical Methods in Economics*. Cambridge, MA: MIT Press.

———. 2001. "Computation and Economic Theory." *Economic Theory* 18: 1–6.

March, James. 1988. *Decisions and Organizations*. New York: Blackwell.

Marimon, Ramon, Ellen McGrattan, and Thomas Sargent. 1990. "Money as a Medium of Exchange in an Economy with Artificially Intelligent Agents." *Journal of Economic Dynamics and Control* 14: 329–373.

Padgett, John, and Christopher Ansell. 1993. "Robust Action and the Rise of the Medici, 1400–1434." *American Journal of Sociology* 98: 1259–1319.

Page, Scott E. 2000. "Computational Economics from A to Z." *Complexity* 5: 35–40.

Rosser, Barkley. 1999. "On the Complexities of Complex Economic Dynamics." *Journal of Economic Perspectives* 13 (Fall): 169–192.

Schelling, Thomas. 1978. *Micromotives and Macrobehavior*. New York: Norton.

Tesfatsion, Leigh. 2001. "Introduction to the *Journal of Economic Dynamics and Control*: Special Issue on ACE." *Journal of Economic Dynamics and Control* 25 (March): 281–293.

Vriend, Nicolaas. 2002. "Introduction." *Computational Economics* (Special Issue on Evolutionary Processes in Economics) 19: 1–4.

# 1 A Dynamic Model of Multidimensional Collective Choice

David P. Baron and
Michael C. Herron

## 1.1 Introduction

This chapter presents a finite-horizon, game-theoretic model of the dynamics of multidimensional collective choice and a set of analytical and computational results characterizing those dynamics. The focus is on continuing collective goods programs that have the property that the current policy remains in effect until new legislation is passed. Continuing policies are at the center of government activity and include entitlements, regulations, antitrust law, tax policy, and international trade policy. One application of this model is to government formation and policy choice in parliamentary systems where the formateur changes as a function of elections or other factors such as confidence votes (Baron and Diermeier 1999; Diermeier and Merlo 1998). Another application is to the dynamics of entitlement programs, which constitute a majority of U.S. government expenditures. Changes in these program occur frequently, and the theory and computational results provide insights into those changes in the context of a simple game. Despite its simplicity, the game is remarkably poorly behaved.

Continuing collective goods programs have a number of common characteristics. First, they are typically multidimensional, since the programs have multiple components or parameters. For example, in an entitlements example presented in section 1.2, the two dimensions are the eligibility standard and the benefits provided to those eligible. Second, the policies that implement these programs are not particularistic, although the distributive effect need not be the same for everyone as with a pure public good. For example, an entitlement program cannot direct benefits to a named person, but it can direct benefits to people with impaired vision or low income. Third, the programs provide collective goods, so there is no participation condition, that is, no one can avoid the consequences of the programs. Fourth, many of the non–entitlement programs, such as regulation, do not have substantial budgetary impacts and hence do not require new legislation every year. Entitlement programs also do not require new legislation every year, although their expenditure requirements must be explicitly provided for in the budget.

The collective choice institution is assumed to be a majority-rule legislature that in each period has the opportunity to change the program. The sequential choice approach is used to model the legislature as a sequence of proposal-making and voting stages (Baron and Ferejohn 1989; Baron 1994). In the simplest sequential process, a legislator is recognized in a session to make a proposal, and that proposal is voted against the status quo, with the winner becoming the new status quo. In the next session, another legislator is recognized to make a proposal, and the process repeats. Arrow's (1951) theorem is not applicable in this setting, since in each session the institution chooses between only two alternatives. This approach thus avoids the intransitivities of collective choice in a multidimensional policy space (McKelvey 1976; 1979; Schofield 1983). A sequential choice approach is natural for the study of the dynamics of collective goods programs, where the dynamics studied are generated by random changes in which a player is selected to make a proposal.[1] This is intended to represent changes caused by elections, coalition formation, recognition of members to offer amendments, or other forms of the internal dynamics of a political system.

The strategic aspects of the dynamics of continuing collective goods programs are severalfold. First, in each legislative session members vote on an agenda that includes the status quo and a proposal to change it. This means that the proposer has an opportunity in the current period to set the agenda strategically, as in the Romer and Rosenthal (1978) model. This implies that the policy and the majority that supports it depend on the identity of the agenda setter as well as on the status quo. Second, under majority rule the proposer may select among various majorities, and the agenda setter chooses the most attractive majority, given the equilibria in the subsequent subgames. Third, the continuing nature of the policy implies that a proposal that defeats the status quo affects strategies and payoffs in future periods. The agenda setter thus has incentives to position the status quo to affect policy choices in future periods.

Fourth, since future payoffs depend on the current policy choice, time preferences matter. Intuition suggests that the more important is the future relative to the present, the stronger will be the incentives to position the status quo strategically to affect future actions.

In principle, future majorities can undo the policy a previous majority has enacted. This has been referred to as the durability problem.[2] The durability problem is mitigated, however, because a proposer can make a (successful) proposal that constrains the changes that can be made in the future. This is accomplished by positioning the status quo such that it affects the reservation values of the players in future periods. For unidimensional policies and single-peaked preferences Baron (1996) demonstrates that proposers take into account the durability issue by strategically positioning their proposals closer to the ideal point of the median voter so that future proposals will be closer to the median. The extension of this result to multidimensional policies is not straightforward and is one focus of this chapter. The principal difference between multidimensional and unidimensional choice problems is that in the former the agenda setter can choose among majorities, whereas in the latter the only real choice is the majority on the same side of the median as the agenda setter.

When agenda setters can choose among majorities, value functions for a finite-horizon, majority-rule game are discontinuous in the policy. In addition, in regions where the value function is continuous it can have flat spots making it nondifferentiable. Consequently, analytical results are limited, and computational methods are required to provide further insight into the dynamics of multidimensional collective choice. The results are developed for a symmetric, three-player game with two-dimensional alternatives, where the players have quadratic preferences. In the final period policies are on the single-period contract curves and tend to be closer to the centroid of preferences the more centrally located is the status quo. In choosing a majority partner an agenda setter always chooses that player who is disadvantaged by the status quo, that is, who has a lower reservation value at the status quo.

In the penultimate period, policies are strictly interior to the Pareto set so as to position the status quo to constrain the policies chosen in the final period. Those policies are closer to the centroid of the set of ideal points the higher is the discount factor. Computational results indicate that this property is characteristic of the equilibria in earlier periods as well. That is, the more important is the future, the more the agenda setter seeks to reduce the variation in future policies and can do so by making a (successful) proposal closer to the centroid.

The basic intuition, then, is that the more important is the future relative to the present, the greater is the incentive to constrain future policies. A conjecture based on the same intuition thus is that the longer the horizon, the closer the policies are to the centroid. The agenda setters, however, always choose policies closer to their ideal points than to their majority partner's ideal points.

This suggests that there are two reasons agenda setting is an important feature of collective choice in a dynamic model. First, the agenda setter always has an incentive to choose a policy closer to his ideal point than to the ideal point of his majority partner. Second, the agenda setter trades off that incentive against the incentive to position the status quo strategically to limit the changes that future agenda setters can make to the policy. The self-interest feature of politics is exhibited in the first effect, and the collective choice feature of politics is exhibited in the second effect. The more important is the future relative to the present, the more the collective choice considerations prevail.

## 1.2 An Example

To illustrate the substantive focus of the model, consider an entitlement program summarized by eligibility, which depends on the characteristics of recipients and the formula by which benefits are attached to those characteristics. For example, an eligibility standard may be a means test. Letting the $K$ characteristics of potential recipients be denoted by a vector $\bar{y} = (y_1, \ldots, y_K)$, where $y_i$ is the $i$th characteristic, a means test establishes a set $Y^E$ of eligible recipients. For example, eligibility for Supplemental Security Income (SSI) included those 65 years and older, those with 20/200 vision or less in their better eye when corrected or tunnel vision of 20 degrees or less, and disabled persons with certain medically determined physical or mental impairments (Ways and Means Committee 1993, 814). The benefits provided to an eligible recipient can be represented by a function defined on $Y^E$. For example, in 1993 SSI provided monthly benefits of $434 and $652 for individuals and couples, respectively. Congress chooses both the formula for eligibility and the amount of benefits.

An entitlement program with parameters $x$ provides benefits $B(x; \tilde{y})$, $\tilde{y} \in Y^E$, to eligible recipients. The benefits that accrue to the district of legislator $i$ will be denoted $B_i(x)$, where

$$B_i(x) \equiv \int_{Y^E} B(x; \tilde{y})\, dF_i(\tilde{y}),$$

and $F_i(\tilde{y})$ is the histogram of the characteristics of potential recipients in district $i$, $i = 1, \ldots, m$.

As an example of this formulation, suppose that eligibility is defined in terms of characteristics $\tilde{y}$ such as income, the number of children, disabilities, etc., and assume that those eligible satisfy $\tilde{y} \in Y^E$. For example, suppose there are two characteristics: income $y_1$ and whether the person has dependent children $y_2 = 1$ or not $y_2 = 0$. Eligibility is then an income no greater than $x_1$ and dependent children $y_2 = 1$. If benefits $x_2$ are paid to each eligible individual with dependent children, the total benefits $B_i(x_1, x_2)$ for district $i$ are

$$B_i(x_1, x_2) = \int_{\{y_1 \leq x_1\}} x_2 y_2\, dF_i(y_1, y_2).$$

If each district $i$ bears a share $C_i(x_1, x_2)$ of the total cost of the program, the net benefits $N_i(x_1, x_2)$ to district $i$ are

$$N_i(x_1, x_2) = B_i(x_1, x_2) - C_i(x_1, x_2).$$

This specification thus yields a two-dimensional collective choice problem in the policy $x = (x_1, x_2)$.

## 1.3 The Sequential Choice Game

### 1.3.1 *The Model*

The collective choice institution considered consists of a sequence of proposal and voting stages, as introduced in Baron and Ferejohn (1989), Harrington (1990), and Baron (1996). With this simple sequential structure, a theory of multidimensional collective choice can be developed. Although a general theory is not yet available, a simple example will be used to identify the nature of an equilibrium and develop the underlying intuition.

The finite-horizon model is intended to be a proxy for an infinite-horizon model with the same structure. Infinite-horizon sequential choice models with continuing programs have been studied by Baron (1996) for unidimensional policies. Infinite-horizon, multidimensional sequential choice models in which a legislature chooses a one-time policy, that is, there is no strategically chosen status quo, have been studied by Baron (1991), Banks and Duggan (1998), and Jackson and Moselle (1998). Baron (1991) provides a characterization of an infinite-horizon model of government formation with a preference configuration similar to that used here. In a general model Banks and Duggan (1998) prove the existence of a stationary equilibrium and show that if the discount factor is high, the equilibrium policy is close to the core, if the core exists. Jackson and Moselle (1998) consider a model with both a unidimensional policy space and a multidimensional transfer. They establish existence and use the model in a theory of political parties. These existence arguments should carry over to the infinite-horizon version of the model considered here. The expectation is that the qualitative properties of the infinite-horizon model will be similar to those of the finite-horizon model.

The example considered involves alternatives in $\Re^2$, three players, symmetry, complete information, and a finite number of periods. Each period has three stages. In the first or recognition stage, nature recognizes at random a player, $i = 1, 2, 3$, to be the proposer, that is, to have agenda-setting authority in the period. In the second or proposal stage, the player recognized makes a policy proposal $x \in \Re^2$. In the third or voting stage, that proposal is voted against the status quo under majority rule, and the winner becomes the policy implemented in the period and the status quo for the next period.

The policy $x(t) \in \Re^2$ implemented in period $t$ is thus either the policy $x$ enacted in period $t$ or the status quo $q^{t-1}$ entering the period, that is,

$$x(t) = \begin{cases} x & \text{if } x \text{ wins} \\ q^{t-1} & \text{if } q^{t-1} \text{ wins.} \end{cases}$$

The status quo $q^t$ entering period $t+1$ is thus $q^t = x(t)$. The initial status quo is denoted $q^0$.

Preferences are represented by a quadratic utility function with ideal point $z^i \in \Re^2$, $i = 1, 2, 3$, so the utility function $u_i(x)$ is

$$u_i(x) = -\sum_{j=1}^{2} (x_j - z_j^i)^2. \tag{1.1a}$$

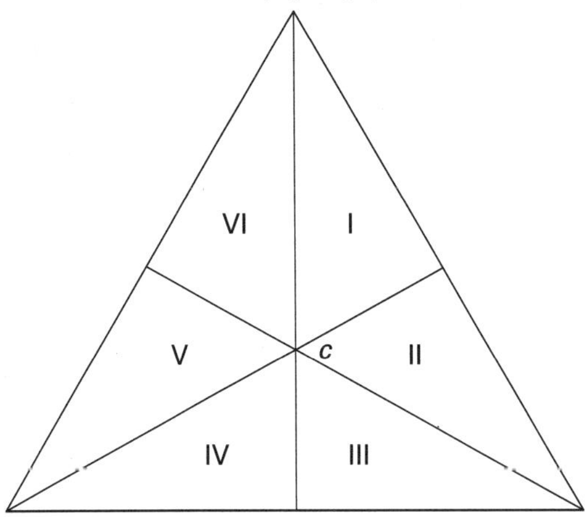


**Figure 1.1**
Ideal Points and Regions

The ideal points are assumed to be located at the vertices of an equilateral triangle, as illustrated in figure 1.1, with the distance between ideal points normalized to 1, that is, $z^1 = (0, 0)$, $z^2 = (1, 0)$, $z^3 = (\frac{1}{2}, \frac{\sqrt{3}}{2})$. Player $i$ maximizes the expected, discounted utility $U_i$ given by

$$U_i(x(1), \ldots, x(n)) = E \sum_{t=1}^{n} \delta^{t-1} u_i(x(t)), \tag{1.1b}$$

where $\delta \in [0, 1]$ is a common discount factor, $E$ denotes expectation with respect to which a player is recognized and any randomization in players' strategies, and $n$ is the number of legislative sessions or periods in the game.

Each player has two action sets. The proposal set $A_i^t$ in period $t$ for the recognized player $i$ is assumed to be the same in every period and the same for every player, so $A_i^t = A \subset \Re^2$, $i = 1, 2, 3$, $t = 1, \ldots, n$. For all players and periods, the voting set is $\Omega = \{0, 1\}$, where $\omega = 1$ is a vote for the proposal and $\omega = 0$ is a vote against the proposal and hence for the status quo.

The continuation value $v_i^{t+1}(q^t)$ summarizes the expected utility of player $i$ in the equilibrium in the subgame commencing in period $t + 1$ with status quo $q^t$. The continuation value is defined as

$$v_i^{t+1}(q^t) \equiv E\left[\sum_{\tau=t+1}^{n} \delta^{\tau-1} u_i(\hat{x}(\tau))\right], \tag{1.2}$$

where $\hat{x}(\tau)$ is the equilibrium policy in period $\tau$. The continuation value reflects the collective nature of choice in that it takes into account the policies chosen by other players if they are selected as the proposer in a future period.

Since each player is averse to variations in the policy, the *ex ante* expected utility of each player is maximized by proposals at the centroid of the (single-period) Pareto set. Once recognized to make a proposal, however, a player has an incentive to make a proposal closer to his ideal point. *Ex post* and *ex ante* incentives thus diverge, and this results in equilibrium proposals away from the centroid. Proposers thus must trade off the marginal utility of moving closer to their single-period ideal point against the marginal utility of moving toward the centroid to constrain the proposals of future proposers. That trade-off depends on the discount factor.

A player $i$ recognized to make a proposal in period $t$ chooses his proposal to maximize his expected utility. The optimal (and equilibrium) proposal $\hat{x}^i(q^{t-1}, t)$ is defined by

$$\hat{x}^i(q^{t-1}, t) \in \arg\max_x \; u_i(x) + \delta v_i^{t+1}(x), \tag{1.3}$$

subject to obtaining majority approval, that is,

$$u_k(x) + \delta v_k^{t+1}(x) \geq u_k(q^{t-1}) + \delta v_k^{t+1}(q^{t-1}), \qquad \forall k \in M, \tag{1.4}$$

where $M$ is a majority set of players. The right side of (1.4) is $k$'s reservation value. If in the majority condition (1.4) a player is indifferent between $x$ and $q^{t-1}$, she is assumed to vote for the proposal $x$. When a proposer is indifferent between proposals and their associated majorities, she is assumed to randomize between the two.

An optimal voting strategy $\hat{\omega}_k^t(q^{t-1}, x) \in \Omega$ for player $k$ is $\hat{\omega}_k^t(q^{t-1}, x) = 1$ (for $x$) if (1.4) is satisfied and $\hat{\omega}_k^t(q^{t-1}, x) = 0$ (for $q^{t-1}$) otherwise. The policy outcome is $x(t) = \hat{x}^i(q^{t-1}, t)$ if a majority votes for $\hat{x}^i(q^{t-1}, t)$ over $q^{t-1}$, that is, $\sum_{k=1}^{3} \hat{\omega}_k^t(q^{t-1}, \hat{x}^{ij}(q^{t-1}, t)) \geq 2$. Otherwise, $x(t) = q^{t-1}$.

A subgame perfect Nash equilibrium of this game consists of proposal strategies,

$$\hat{x}^i(q^{t-1}, t) : A \to A, \qquad i = 1, 2, 3,\ t = 1, \ldots, n,$$

and voting strategies

$$\hat{\omega}_i^t(q^{t-1}, x) : A \times A \to \Omega, \qquad i = 1, 2, 3,\ t = 1, \ldots, n,$$

such that for $t = 1, \ldots, n$,

$$\hat{x}^i(q^{t-1}, t) \in \arg\max_x \{u_i(\bar{x}(\xi)) + \delta v_i^{t+1}(\bar{x}(\xi)) \mid \hat{\omega}_k^t(q^{t-1}, x), k = 1, 2, 3\},$$

where

$$\bar{x}(\xi) = \begin{cases} x & \text{if } \xi \equiv \sum_{k=1}^{3} \hat{\omega}_k^t(q^{t-1}, x) \geq 2 \\ q^{t-1} & \text{if } \xi < 2 \end{cases}$$

and

$$\hat{\omega}_k^t(q^{t-1}, x)$$
$$\in \arg\max_{\omega \in \{0,1\}} \omega(u_k(x) + \delta v_k^{t+1}(x)) + (1 - \omega)(u_k(q^{t-1}) + \delta v_k^{t+1}(q^{t-1})).$$

### 1.3.2 *Discontinuities*

To identify the discontinuities resulting from the agenda setter's opportunity to choose among majorities, consider the final period $n$. The proposal by the player recognized will be on the contract curve with one other player. Suppose that player 3 is the proposer, and consider status quos with $q_2 = 0$. If $q_1 = 0$, player 3 proposes her ideal point, and player 2, who is indifferent between the proposal and the status quo, votes for the proposal, whereas player 1 votes against the proposal, since the status quo is his ideal point.[3] As $q_1$ increases toward one half, the constraint in (1.4), where $v_k^{n+1}(\cdot) \equiv 0$, is binding, and the proposals by player 3 move down the contract curve toward the ideal point of player 2, its majority partner, as illustrated in figure 1.2. As $q_1$ passes one half, player 3 switches from forming a majority with player 2 to forming a majority with player 1, so the optimal proposal jumps from the midpoint of the contract curve of players 2 and 3 to the midpoint of the contract curve of players 3 and 1.[4] As $q_1$ increases further, the proposals move up the contract curve toward player 3's ideal point. This discontinuity in the proposal mapping is a result of the fundamental property of majority rule—an agenda setter can choose among majorities. The proposer thus makes a proposal to obtain the vote of whichever other player is the more attractive in the sense of the utility the proposer

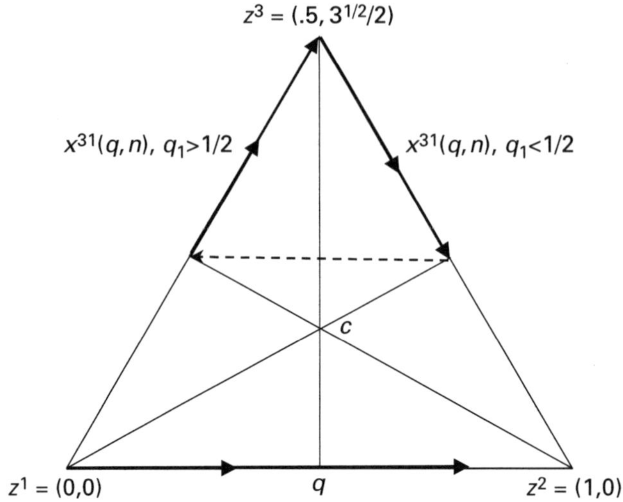


**Figure 1.2**
Optimal Proposals and the Status Quo

must give up to elicit the desired vote. The more attractive partner is the one who is farther from the status quo, since her reservation value (at the status quo) is lower. That is, the more attractive majority partner is the one who is disadvantaged by the status quo.

This property of majority rule also implies that if the status quo is to the left of the line $x_1 = \frac{1}{2}$ through player 3's ideal point $z^3 = \{\frac{1}{2}, \frac{\sqrt{3}}{2}\}$ and the centroid $c$, player 3 prefers to form a majority with player 2, and if it is to the right of that line, 3 prefers to form a majority with 1. Similarly, if $q$ is above and to the left of the line from $z^1$ through the centroid, player 1 forms a majority with player 2, and if the status quo is below and to the right of that line, with player 3. In the last period the proposer always forms a majority with the other player who is farther from the status quo. Because of these discontinuities, six regions $X_j$, $j = \text{I}, \ldots, \text{VI}$, of the Pareto set are identified in figure 1.1.

The discontinuities in the proposal mappings result in discontinuities in the continuation values for the players. For example, for players 1 and 2 there is a discontinuity at the line $q_1 = \frac{1}{2}$ as player 3 (when the proposer) shifts between forming a majority with player 2 and forming a majority with player 1. Player 1's continuation value jumps upward as $q_1$ passes from the left to the right of the line $q_1 = \frac{1}{2}$, since player 3 switches from forming a majority with player 2

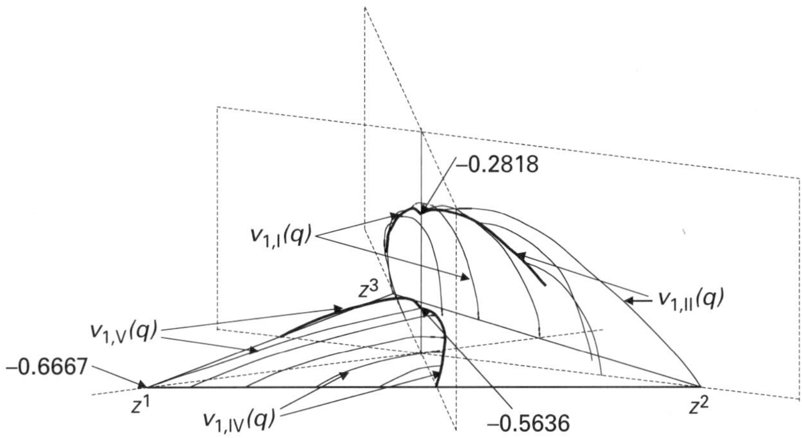


**Figure 1.3**
Continuation Value $v_1(q)$, Period $n$

to forming a majority with player 1. Player 1′s continuation value also jumps upward at the line from player 2′s ideal point through the centroid, since player 2 shifts from forming a majority with player 3 to forming a majority with player 1.

Figure 1.3 identifies the magnitude of the discontinuities in $v^n_{1,\ell}(x)$, $\ell \in \{\mathrm{I}, \mathrm{II}, \ldots, \mathrm{VI}\}$ between regions I and II and regions IV and V. For a policy $x = z^1$ at player 1′s ideal point, the continuation value is $v^n_{1,\mathrm{IV}}(z^1) = v^n_{1,\mathrm{V}}(z^1) = -0.6667$. The supremum in regions IV and V is at the centroid, where $\sup_{z \to c} v_{1,\mathrm{IV}}(x) = -0.5636$. The continuation value in regions IV and V is thus relatively flat. As the policy enters region I or II near the centroid, the continuation value jumps by nearly three times the magnitude of the increase from $z^1$ to $c$. That is, $\sup_{x \to c} v_{1,\mathrm{I}}(x) = \sup_{x \to c} v_{1,\mathrm{II}}(x) = -0.2818$.

These discontinuities imply that the indifference curves defined by (1.4) are as illustrated in figure 1.4 for player 3. The expected utility in the maximand in (1.3) for the proposer is continuous in the region around the line from her ideal point to the centroid but is discontinuous at the lines from the other players′ ideal points to the centroid.

### 1.3.3 *The Period n Equilibrium*

Provided that the status quo $q = q^{n-1}$ is not more than a distance of 1 from the ideal point of one of the other players, the optimal proposals $\hat{x}^{ik}(q, n)$ by proposer $i$ in the final period are given by

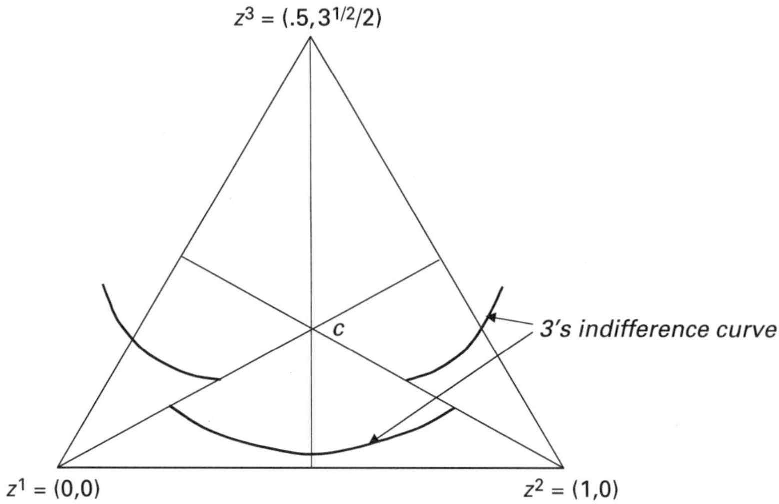


**Figure 1.4**
Player 3's Indifference Curve

$$\hat{x}^{ik}(q,n) = D(q,z^k)z^i + (1 - D(q,z^k))z^k, \qquad i = 1,2,3,\ k = 1,2,3,\ k \neq i, \tag{1.5}$$

where $k$ is the player whose vote is obtained by $i$, and $D(q,z^k)$ is the distance between $q$ and the ideal point $z^k$. If $D(q,z^k) > 1$, then $\hat{x}^{ik}(q,n) = z^i$. If the proposer $i$ is indifferent between obtaining either of the other two players' votes, then $i$ is assumed to randomize between the two proposals. Since the proposer always forms a majority with the other player who is the farther from the status quo, $D(q,z^k)$ is strictly greater than one half, so $i$'s proposals are always closer to her ideal point than to the ideal point of her majority partner.

The continuation value $v_i^n(q^{n-1})$ is well-defined, since the equilibrium proposals in (1.5) in period $n$ are unique. The continuation value can be determined by taking the expectation of the proposals with respect to the probability that a player is selected as the proposer. The discontinuities in the proposal mappings, however, imply that the continuation values of the players must be characterized for each of the six regions identified in figure 1.1. As indicated in the previous discussion, $v_1^n(q^{n-1})$ is discontinuous in going between regions I and VI, V and VI, II and III, and IV and III. It is continuous going between regions I and II and regions IV and V, since only player 1 switches majorities in moving between those regions. The nature and magnitude of the discontinuities are analyzed in the appendix. Despite the discontinuities, the proposals in (1.3) and (1.4) by player 1 are always in regions IV and V.

Since each player is equally likely to be selected in the recognition stage, the continuation value $v^n_{1,\mathrm{V}}(q)$ for player 1 for a status quo $q = q^{n-1}$ in region V, for example, is[5]

$$v^n_{1,\mathrm{V}}(q) = \frac{1}{3}[-(\hat{x}^{12}_1(q,n) - z^1_1)^2 - (\hat{x}^{12}_2(q,n) - z^1_2)^2 - (\hat{x}^{23}_1(q,n) - z^1_1)^2$$
$$- (\hat{x}^{23}_2(q,n) - z^1_2)^2 - (\hat{x}^{32}_1(q,n) - z^1_1)^2 - (\hat{x}^{32}_2(q,n) - z^1_2)^2].$$

In region V player 1 obtains the vote of player 2 by proposing $\hat{x}^{12}(q,n)$, and players 2 and 3 obtain each other's vote by proposing $\hat{x}^{23}(q,n)$ and $\hat{x}^{32}(q,n)$, respectively, when recognized as the proposer. Evaluating this using (1.5) yields

$$v^n_{1,\mathrm{V}}(q) = -\frac{1}{3}[2(1 - D(q,z^2))^2 + (1 - D(q,z^3))^2 + D(q,z^3)$$
$$+ D(q,z^2)]. \tag{1.6}$$

The continuation values for the final period can thus be expressed in terms of the distances between the status quo and the ideal points of the players whose votes are obtained. For example, if $q = z^1$, the player selected proposes his ideal point, and hence $D(q,z^1) = 0$ and $D(q,z^2) = D(q,z^3) = 1$ and $v^n_{1,\mathrm{V}}(z^1) = -\frac{2}{3}$.

The continuation values for the other five regions are

$$v^n_{1,\mathrm{IV}}(q) = -\frac{1}{3}[2(1 - D(q,z^3))^2 + (1 - D(q,z^2))^2 + D(q,z^3)$$
$$+ D(q,z^2)] \tag{1.7}$$

$$v^n_{1,\mathrm{III}}(q) = -\frac{1}{3}[2(1 - D(q,z^3))^2 + D(q,z^1)^2 + D(q,z^3)] \tag{1.8}$$

$$v^n_{1,\mathrm{VI}}(q) = -\frac{1}{3}[2(1 - D(q,z^2))^2 + D(q,z^1)^2 + D(q,z^2)] \tag{1.9}$$

$$v^n_{1,\mathrm{II}}(q) = -\frac{1}{3}[(1 - D(q,z^3))^2 + 2D(q,z^1)^2] \tag{1.10}$$

$$v^n_{1,\mathrm{I}}(q) = -\frac{1}{3}[(1 - D(q,z^2))^2 + 2D(q,z^1)^2]. \tag{1.11}$$

The continuation value $v_1^n(q)$ thus is defined by

$$v_1^n(q) = v_{1,j}^1(q), \qquad q \in X_j,\ j = \mathrm{I}, \ldots, \mathrm{VI}.$$

As noted, the discontinuities in the continuation values $v_1^n(q)$ occur for a status quo at which another player switches from forming a majority with one player to forming a majority with the other player. The continuation value is continuous, however, over regions IV and V, which are the regions in which player 1 makes proposals.

The continuation values $v_{1,\mathrm{IV}}^n(q)$ and $v_{1,\mathrm{V}}^n(q)$ increase as $q$ moves toward the centroid. This results because a status quo closer to the centroid constrains (through (1.4)) the proposals that can be made in the final period and hence reduces the variability in the possible period $n$ policies. The players are averse to variability, so the basic trade-off in period $n-1$ is between making a proposal closer to the centroid to reduce the variability of proposals in period $n$ and making a proposal closer to one's ideal point to increase period $n-1$ utility.

### 1.3.4 *Period $n-1$ Equilibrium*

Suppose player 1 is selected to make a proposal in period $n-1$, and assume that the status quo $q^{n-2}$ is far away, so all players would vote for any proposal in the Pareto set over the status quo. Player 1 thus could propose his ideal point, and both of the other players would vote for it. Player 1, however, has an opportunity to position the status quo $q^{n-1}$ for period $n$, and as noted, his continuation value increases as $q^{n-1}$ moves toward the centroid. Thus, player 1 finds it optimal to trade off a proposal closer to his ideal point, which yields a higher utility in period $n-1$, against a proposal closer to the centroid, which yields higher expected utility in period $n$. This trade-off depends on time preferences.

Player 1 will make a proposal to maximize $w_1^{n-1}(x)$, his period 2 utility plus his discounted continuation value, or

$$w_1^{n-1}(x) = u_1(x) + \delta v_1^n(x). \tag{1.12}$$

In contrast to the final period, the optimal proposal for each player is not on the single-period contract curve but instead is strictly interior to the (single-period) Pareto set.

To characterize the equilibrium in period $n-1$ when $q^{n-2}$ is far away from the Pareto set, first note that both $u_1(x)$ and $v_1^n(x)$ (which

**Table 1.1**
Equilibrium Period $n-1$ Proposals and Time Preference

| | Status Quo | | Equilibrium Proposal, Period $n-1$ | | | | Distance to |
|---|---|---|---|---|---|---|---|
| $\delta$ | $q_1$ | $q_2$ | $\hat{x}_1^{13}$ | $\hat{x}_2^{13}$ | $\hat{x}_1^{12}$ | $\hat{x}_2^{12}$ | Centroid |
| 1.0 | 1 | 0 | 0.1323 | 0.0969 | 0.15003 | 0.06609 | 0.4147 |
| 0.75 | 1 | 0 | 0.1121 | 0.0785 | 0.12406 | 0.05785 | 0.4412 |
| 0.50 | 1 | 0 | 0.0861 | 0.0572 | 0.09258 | 0.0460 | 0.4742 |
| 0.25 | 1 | 0 | 0.0509 | 0.0317 | 0.0529 | 0.02824 | 0.5174 |
| 0.0 | 1 | 0 | 0.0 | 0.0 | 0.0 | 0.0 | 0.5773 |
| 1.0 | 0.8 | $\frac{1}{\sqrt{3}}(1-q_1)$[a] | 0.1508 | 0.1401 | | | 0.3795 |
| 0.75 | 0.8 | $\frac{1}{\sqrt{3}}(1-q_1)$[a] | 0.1420 | 0.1441 | | | 0.3861 |
| 0.50 | 0.8 | $\frac{1}{\sqrt{3}}(1-q_1)$[a] | 0.1308 | 0.1498 | | | 0.3945 |
| 0.25 | 0.8 | $\frac{1}{\sqrt{3}}(1-q_1)$[a] | 0.1161 | 0.1567 | | | 0.4060 |
| 0.0 | 0.8 | $\frac{1}{\sqrt{3}}(1-q_1)$[a] | 0.0959 | 0.1660 | | | 0.4223 |

a. In region II.

is either $v_{1,\mathrm{IV}}^n(x)$ or $v_{1,\mathrm{V}}^n(x)$) are symmetric about the line from player 1's ideal point to the centroid. Consequently, $w_1^{n-1}(x)$ in (1.12) is symmetric about that line. The maximum of player 1's expected utility $w_1^{n-1}(x)$ thus is attained in both regions IV and V.

Optimization results presented in table 1.1 identify the equilibrium period $n-1$ proposals $\hat{x}^{1k} = \hat{x}^{1k}(q^{n-2}, n-1)$ for player 1 as a function of the discount factor and the status quo. The top panel corresponds to the case in which the status quo $q$ is not constraining in (1.4). In this case, there are two equivalent and symmetric equilibrium proposals as indicated in the table. The proposals in columns 4 and 5 result in a majority with player 3, whereas the proposals in columns 6 and 7 result in a majority with player 2. Note that the proposer does not make proposals on the line from her ideal point to the centroid, but instead responds to the preferences of her majority partner.

As indicated in table 1.1, the proposals by player 1 are in the interior of the Pareto set for $\delta \in (0,1]$. The top panel indicates that as the future becomes more important ($\delta$ increases) the equilibrium proposals move toward the centroid. That is, the more important is the future, the more a player prefers to position the status quo so as to constrain future proposals. This is the endogenous response to the durability problem.

The bottom panel of table 1.1 corresponds to a policy in which the status quo $q$ is located in region II (just to the right of the line from player 2's ideal point to the centroid). The equilibrium proposals by player 1 result in a majority with player 3 and are closer to the centroid the higher is the discount factor. Those proposals are uniformly closer to the centroid than are the proposals in the top panel, reflecting the constraining effect of the status quo.

Table 1.2 presents the equilibrium proposals for player 1 as a function of the status quo for two discount factors. As in the bottom panel of table 1.1, the status quos are in region II. For $\delta = 1$ the optimal proposals are unconstrained, that is, (1.4) is not binding, for the first two status quos. When (1.4) is binding, the closer the status quo is to the centroid, the closer the proposals are to the centroid, as expected from (1.5). As in table 1.1, the higher is the discount factor, the closer the equilibrium proposals are to the centroid, which is the endogenous response to the durability problem. When the status quo is positioned close to the centroid, the players in effect work the policy away from the status quo and closer to their ideal points.

### 1.3.5 *Period $n - 2$ Equilibrium*

As indicated in the first two rows of the top panel of table 1.2, there is a set of status quos such that the proposer makes the same proposal. There is a similar set for player 1 around the ideal points of each of the other players. Thus, viewed from period $n - 2$, the continuation value is constant on those sets, and outside those sets it increases as the status quo is closer to the centroid. This is illustrated in figure 1.5. Consequently, in period $n - 2$ the player recognized can make a proposal either in the region where the continuation value is flat or in the region where it is increasing (toward the centroid). Since a proposal in the flat region does not affect future proposals, the best proposal among those in the flat region is the proposer's ideal point. The proposer in period $n - 2$ thus will choose either a proposal at her ideal point or a proposal that will position the status quo to constrain at least one player's proposal in period $n - 1$.

**Table 1.2**
Equilibrium Period $n - 1$ Proposals and the Status Quo

| | Status Quo | | Equilibrium Proposal, Period $n - 1$ | | Distance to Centroid |
|---|---|---|---|---|---|
| $\delta$ | $q_1$ | $q_2$ | $\hat{x}_1^{13}$ | $\hat{x}_2^{13}$ | |
| 1.0 | 1.0 | $\frac{1}{\sqrt{3}}(1 - q_1)$[a] | 0.1323 | 0.0969 | 0.4147 |
| 1.0 | 0.9 | $\frac{1}{\sqrt{3}}(1 - q_1)$[a] | 0.1323 | 0.0969 | 0.4147 |
| 1.0 | 0.8 | $\frac{1}{\sqrt{3}}(1 - q_1)$[a] | 0.1509 | 0.1401 | 0.3794 |
| 1.0 | 0.7 | $\frac{1}{\sqrt{3}}(1 - q_1)$[a] | 0.1869 | 0.2194 | 0.3207 |
| 1.0 | 0.6 | $\frac{1}{\sqrt{3}}(1 - q_1)$[a] | 0.2190 | 0.2857 | 0.2810 |
| 1.0 | 0.5 | $\frac{1}{\sqrt{3}}(1 - q_1)$[a] | 0.2454 | 0.3364 | 0.2590 |
| 0.5 | 1.0 | $\frac{1}{\sqrt{3}}(1 - q_1)$[a] | 0.0861 | 0.0572 | 0.4742 |
| 0.5 | 0.9 | $\frac{1}{\sqrt{3}}(1 - q_1)$[a] | 0.0893 | 0.0638 | 0.4682 |
| 0.5 | 0.8 | $\frac{1}{\sqrt{3}}(1 - q_1)$[a] | 0.1308 | 0.1498 | 0.3945 |
| 0.5 | 0.7 | $\frac{1}{\sqrt{3}}(1 - q_1)$[a] | 0.1697 | 0.2275 | 0.3359 |
| 0.5 | 0.6 | $\frac{1}{\sqrt{3}}(1 - q_1)$[a] | 0.2046 | 0.2945 | 0.2955 |
| 0.5 | 0.5 | $\frac{1}{\sqrt{3}}(1 - q_1)$[a] | 0.2335 | 0.3479 | 0.2730 |

a. In region II.

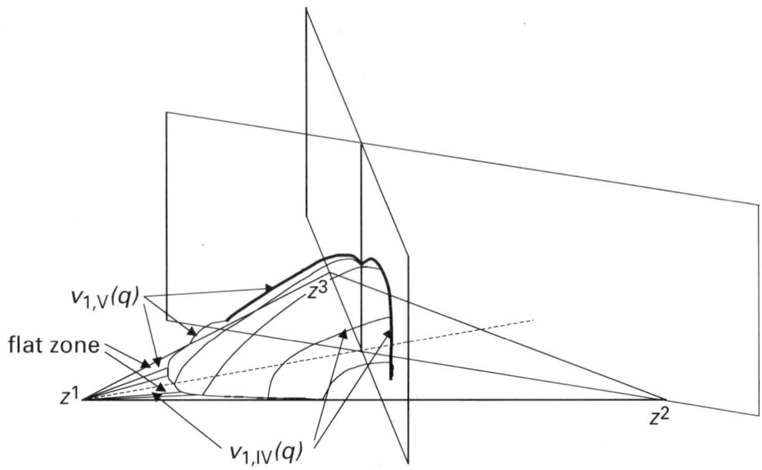


**Figure 1.5**
Continuation Value with Flat Zone

Computational results indicate that the optimal proposal is her ideal point for period $n-2$.

As viewed from period $n-3$, period $n-2$ equilibrium proposals at the players' ideal points yield a low continuation value $v_i^{n-2}(z^j)$ for each player. Depending on the discount factor, in some period the player recognized will prefer, as in the top panel of table 1.1, to constrain future proposals by making a proposal closer to the centroid. In the finite-horizon game, proposals, and hence the status quo, thus can be at the ideal points or strictly in the Pareto set, depending on the number of periods remaining in the game. To investigate the equilibrium in this game in more detail, it is necessary to take a computational approach.

## 1.4 A Computational Approach

The key to the numerical analysis of period $n-2$ is characterizing the players' value functions. If those functions can be calculated accurately, the optimal proposals for each player given any status quo can be determined. The players' value functions for period $n-1$ are, however, not continuous. Consequently, smooth functions such as polynomials cannot be used to approximate the value function. Moreover, it is not possible to use sets of locally continuous functions, since it is not known in advance where the value functions are continuous and where they are not. That is, although the regions of discontinuity for period $n-1$ can be characterized, it is impossible to know for earlier periods where the three value functions are discontinuous.[6] Therefore, the numerical approach to approximating the value functions is nonparametric. The value functions are approximated using a finite grid of points on the Pareto set.

The symmetry of the location of the players' ideal points implies that it is only necessary to approximate player 1's value function in regions I, V, and VI. For a point $q \in \Re^2$, let $r^1(q) : \Re^2 \rightarrow \Re^2$ be defined as the reflection of $q = (q_1, q_2)$ across the line $y_2 = (\frac{1}{\sqrt{3}})y_1$. This line connects player 1's ideal point to the centroid $c = (\frac{1}{2}, \frac{1}{2\sqrt{3}})$ of the (single-period) Pareto set. Then, given symmetry,

$$v_{1,\mathrm{II}}^{n-1}(q) = v_{1,\mathrm{I}}^{n-1}(r^1(q)) \tag{1.13}$$

$$v_{1,\mathrm{III}}^{n-1}(q) = v_{1,\mathrm{VI}}^{n-1}(r^1(q)) \tag{1.14}$$

$$v_{1,\mathrm{IV}}^{n-1}(q) = v_{1,\mathrm{V}}^{n-1}(r^1(q)). \tag{1.15}$$

The reflections used for player 1's value function reduce the number of calculations required to approximate this function. Once player 1's value function in regions I, V, and VI has been approximated, equations (1.13)–(1.15) can be used to identify the value function in regions II, III, and IV, respectively.

A similar argument can be used to show that in a symmetric equilibrium the value functions of players 2 and 3 can be obtained from player 1's value function.[7] For a point $q \in \Re^2$, define $r^2(q) : \Re^2 \rightarrow \Re^2$ as the reflection of $q = (q_1, q_2)$ across the line $y_2 = \frac{1}{\sqrt{3}}(1 - y_1)$, which connects player 2's ideal point $z^2 = (1, 0)$ with the centroid. Similarly, define $r^3(q) : \Re^2 \rightarrow \Re^2$ as the reflection of $q$ across the line $q_2 = \frac{1}{2}$, which connects player 3's ideal point $z^3 = (\frac{1}{2}, \frac{\sqrt{3}}{2})$ with the centroid.

For player 2 the reflections are

$$v_{2,\mathrm{I}}^{n-1}(q) = v_{1,\mathrm{I}}^{n-1}(r^2(r^1(q))) \tag{1.16}$$

$$v_{2,\mathrm{II}}^{n-1}(q) = v_{1,\mathrm{VI}}^{n-1}(r^3(r^2(q))) \tag{1.17}$$

$$v_{2,\mathrm{III}}^{n-1}(q) = v_{1,\mathrm{V}}^{n-1}(r^1(r^3(q))) \tag{1.18}$$

$$v_{2,\mathrm{IV}}^{n-1}(q) = v_{1,\mathrm{I}}^{n-1}(r^2(r^1(q))) \tag{1.19}$$

$$v_{2,\mathrm{V}}^{n-1}(q) = v_{1,\mathrm{VI}}^{n-1}(r^3(r^2(q))) \tag{1.20}$$

$$v_{2,\mathrm{VI}}^{n-1}(q) = v_{1,\mathrm{V}}^{n-1}(r^2(r^3(q))). \tag{1.21}$$

And, for player 3 the reflections are

$$v_{3,\mathrm{I}}^{n-1}(q) = v_{1,\mathrm{I}}^{n-1}(r^2(r^3(q))) \tag{1.22}$$

$$v_{3,\mathrm{II}}^{n-1}(q) = v_{1,\mathrm{VI}}^{n-1}(r^3(r^1(q))) \tag{1.23}$$

$$v_{3,\mathrm{III}}^{n-1}(q) = v_{1,\mathrm{V}}^{n-1}(r^1(r^2(q))) \tag{1.24}$$

$$v_{3,\mathrm{IV}}^{n-1}(q) = v_{1,\mathrm{I}}^{n-1}(r^2(r^3(q))) \tag{1.25}$$

$$v_{3,\mathrm{V}}^{n-1}(q) = v_{1,\mathrm{VI}}^{n-1}(r^3(r^1(q))) \tag{1.26}$$

$$v_{3,\mathrm{VI}}^{n-1}(q) = v_{1,\mathrm{V}}^{n-1}(r^1(r^2(q))). \tag{1.27}$$

This reduces the task of approximating three value functions on six regions to the problem of approximating one player's value function on three regions.

Player 1's value function is approximated on regions I, V, and VI as follows. First, place a grid $G_{\mathrm{V}}$ of $S$ points, $\{g_{\mathrm{V}}^1, \ldots, g_{\mathrm{V}}^S\}$, on region V. Second, using reflection functions $r^1(\cdot)$, $r^2(\cdot)$, and $r^3(\cdot)$, reflect the $S$ points in region V to create points $\{g_{\mathrm{I}}^1, \ldots, g_{\mathrm{I}}^S\}$ in region I and points $\{g_{\mathrm{VI}}^1, \ldots, g_{\mathrm{VI}}^S\}$ in region VI. With these reflections there are $3S$ points on three regions of the Pareto set. The full set of $6S$ points can be derived by additional reflections of the $S$ original grid points in region V.[8]

The period-$n$ analytical value functions in (1.6)–(1.11) are used for the values of $v_{1,j}^n(g_j^s)$, $j \in \{\mathrm{I}, \mathrm{V}, \mathrm{VI}\}$, $s = 1, \ldots, S$. Using (1.13)–(1.14), player 1's value function on all $6S$ grid points in the Pareto set is determined. Once player 1's value function is specified, the reflection equations (1.16)–(1.27) are used to evaluate player 2's and player 3's value functions on the Pareto set.

At this point, the approximation of player 1's value function—and, implicitly, players 2 and 3's value functions—is accurate, since the analytical solutions for period $n$ were used. However, the approximations lose some accuracy when the optimal period $n-1$ proposals are calculated, since the optimization is on a finite grid.

The optimal proposals for player 1 are determined by searching the grid points for the maximum in (1.3) subject to satisfying (1.4) for at least one other player. This is done for status quos in regions I, V, VI. The derivation of optimal proposals for the other regions uses symmetry in much the same way as the grid point reflections. Consider player 1. Once player 1's proposals when faced with status quo points in regions I, V, and VI are known, the reflections can be used to derive how player 1 proposes when the status quo is in regions II, III, and IV. For example, player 1's optimal proposal from a status quo in region V is a reflection of the optimal proposal for the reflected status quo in region IV.

Consider a grid point $g \in \{g_{\mathrm{V}}^1, \ldots, g_{\mathrm{V}}^S\}$. When player one is the proposer and the status quo is $q = g$, player 1's majority partner will be player 2, since $q$ is closer to player 3's ideal point than it is to player 2's ideal point.[9] Furthermore, player 1 will propose a point in region IV. Therefore, player 1's optimal proposal given a status quo $q$ is the grid point $x = g \in G_{\mathrm{IV}}$ in region IV such that player 2 weakly prefers $x$ to $q$ and player 1 weakly prefers $x$ to all other points in region IV.[10]

Note that player 1's optimal proposal is required to be a grid point in region IV; that is, $\hat{x}^1 \in G_{\mathrm{IV}}$. As the fineness of the grid increases ($S$ increases), the value function approximations improve. In fact, the only source of error in the approximations is the fact that optimal proposals have to lie on grid points.

Formally, for status quo points in regions I, V, and VI, player 1's optimal proposals are calculated as follows. Let $q = g_j^s \in G_j$, $j \in \{\mathrm{I}, \mathrm{V}, \mathrm{VI}\}$, $s \in \{1, \ldots, S\}$, denote a status quo. Player 2's reservation value for the status quo $q_j^s$ is

$$u_2(q_j^s) + \delta v_{2,\mathrm{V}}^{n-1}(q_j^s). \tag{1.28}$$

Player 1's optimal proposal $\hat{x}^{1k}(q_j^s, n-2)$ for status quo $q = g_j^t$ in period $n-2$ is the grid point satisfying

$$\hat{x}^{1k}(q_j^s, n-2) \in \arg\max_{x \in G_{\mathrm{IV}}} u_1(x) + \delta v_{1,\mathrm{IV}}^{n-1}(x), \tag{1.29}$$

subject to player 2 weakly preferring $\hat{x}^{1k}(q_j^s, n-2)$ to $q = g_j^s$. The proposal $\hat{x}^{1k}(g_j^s, n-2)$ is determined by considering all points in grid $G_{\mathrm{IV}}$.[11] Once player 1's optimal proposals for status quo points in regions I, V, and VI have been determined, all players' proposals are calculated for all grid points using reflections.

The final step is updating the value functions given the optimal proposals. With proposals for period $n-1$, define

$$v_{i,j}^{n-2}(q) \equiv u_i(\hat{x}^{i\ell}(q, n-2)) + \frac{\delta}{3}\sum_{k=1}^{3} v_{i,j}^{n-1}(\hat{x}^{k\ell}(q, n-2)), \qquad i = 1, 2, 3, \tag{1.30}$$

where $q \in G_j$, $j \in \{I, II, III, IV, V, VI\}$, and $\ell$ is the majority partner of $k$. Given approximations of the value functions for period $n-2$, the process can be repeated to produce value function approximations and equilibrium proposals for period $n-3$ and so forth.

The computational approach derives optimal proposals and continuation function values in period $n-2$ using a grid with 170,437 points in each region.[12] The main results are robust to the grid density as long as the density is sufficiently high. Extremely sparse grids lead to seemingly anomalous behavior, since a sparse grid generates a poor approximation of the value functions that causes optimal proposals to jump around the sparse grid.

## 1.5 Computational Results

### *1.5.1 The Flat Zone*

Table 1.3 identifies the effect of the flat zone on the calculated equilibria. The table presents the optimal proposal by player 1 in the first periods of games with horizons from 2 to 11 periods and in which the initial status quo is not constraining. With the exception of a game with 11 periods, for an even number of periods the first-period proposal is in the interior of the Pareto set, but with an odd number of periods it is at player 1′s ideal point. The results in the table suggest that the equilibrium proposals for an even number of periods

**Table 1.3**
Equilibrium Proposals with an $n$-Period Horizon, $\delta = 0.5$

| | Status Quo | | Equilibrium Proposal, $n-t$ | | |
|---|---|---|---|---|---|
| $t$ | $q_1$ | $q_2$ | $\hat{x}_1^{13}$ | $\hat{x}_2^{13}$ | Distance to Centroid |
| 1 | 1.0000 | 0.0000 | 0.0865 | 0.0571 | 0.4740 |
| 2 | 1.0000 | 0.0000 | 0.0000 | 0.0000 | 0.5773 |
| 3 | 1.0000 | 0.0000 | 0.1521 | 0.0969 | 0.3972 |
| 4 | 1.0000 | 0.0000 | 0.0000 | 0.0000 | 0.5773 |
| 5 | 1.0000 | 0.0000 | 0.1612 | 0.0976 | 0.3890 |
| 6 | 1.0000 | 0.0000 | 0.0000 | 0.0000 | 0.5773 |
| 7 | 1.0000 | 0.0000 | 0.1833 | 0.1260 | 0.3360 |
| 8 | 1.0000 | 0.0000 | 0.0000 | 0.0000 | 0.5773 |
| 9 | 1.0000 | 0.0000 | 0.0813 | 0.0606 | 0.4769 |
| 10 | 1.0000 | 0.0000 | 0.1229 | 0.0807 | 0.4307 |

are at the base of the continuation value hill illustrated in figure 1.5, and the coarseness of the grid results in the optimal proposal being either just on the hill or in the flat zone. If it is in the flat zone, the optimal proposal is at 1's ideal point. All the proposals that are not at 1's ideal point are in region V and are slightly above the line from 1's ideal point to the centroid.

The conjecture is that for an infinite horizon game the equilibrium proposals are near the base of the coninuation value hill. For a finite-horizon game, computations with a finite grid, however, cannot precisely locate the base, and hence the first-period proposal is either at the proposer's ideal point or on the hill. This feature is present in a game with 100 periods.

### 1.5.2 *Period $n - 2$*

Tables 1.4 and 1.5 present the period $n - 2$ equilibria in the formats of tables 1.1 and 1.2, respectively. When the status quo is not binding

**Table 1.4**
Equilibrium Period $n - 2$ Proposals and Time Preference

| | Status Quo | | Equilibrium Proposal, Period $n - 2$ | | Distance to Centroid |
|---|---|---|---|---|---|
| $\delta$ | $q_1$ | $q_2$ | $\hat{x}_1^{13}$ | $\hat{x}_2^{13}$ | |
| 1.0 | 1 | 0 | 0.0000 | 0.0000 | 0.5773 |
| 0.75 | 1 | 0 | 0.0000 | 0.0000 | 0.5773 |
| 0.50 | 1 | 0 | 0.0000 | 0.0000 | 0.5773 |
| 0.25 | 1 | 0 | 0.0000 | 0.0000 | 0.5773 |
| 0.0 | 1 | 0 | 0.0000 | 0.0000 | 0.5773 |
| 1.0 | 0.8 | $\frac{1}{\sqrt{3}}(1 - q_1)$[a] | 0.1710 | 0.1325 | 0.3642 |
| 0.75 | 0.8 | $\frac{1}{\sqrt{3}}(1 - q_1)$[a] | 0.1664 | 0.1325 | 0.3684 |
| 0.50 | 0.8 | $\frac{1}{\sqrt{3}}(1 - q_1)$[a] | 0.1385 | 0.1462 | 0.3886 |
| 0.25 | 0.8 | $\frac{1}{\sqrt{3}}(1 - q_1)$[a] | 0.1196 | 0.1555 | 0.4030 |
| 0.0 | 0.8 | $\frac{1}{\sqrt{3}}(1 - q_1)$[a] | 0.0995 | 0.1640 | 0.4195 |

a. In region II.

**Table 1.5**
Equilibrium Period $n-2$ Proposals and the Status Quo

| | Status Quo | | Equilibrium Proposal, Period $n-2$ | | Distance to Centroid |
|---|---|---|---|---|---|
| $\delta$ | $q_1$ | $q_2$ | $\hat{x}_1^{13}$ | $\hat{x}_2^{13}$ | |
| 1.0 | 1.0 | $\frac{1}{\sqrt{3}}(1-q_1)$[a] | 0.0000 | 0.0000 | 0.5773 |
| 1.0 | 0.9 | $\frac{1}{\sqrt{3}}(1-q_1)$[a] | 0.0520 | 0.0833 | 0.4928 |
| 1.0 | 0.8 | $\frac{1}{\sqrt{3}}(1-q_1)$[a] | 0.1709 | 0.1325 | 0.3642 |
| 1.0 | 0.7 | $\frac{1}{\sqrt{3}}(1-q_1)$[a] | 0.1931 | 0.2155 | 0.3156 |
| 1.0 | 0.6 | $\frac{1}{\sqrt{3}}(1-q_1)$[a] | 0.2366 | 0.2686 | 0.2642 |
| 1.0 | 0.5 | $\frac{1}{\sqrt{3}}(1-q_1)$[a] | 0.4914 | 0.2896 | 0.0086 |
| 0.5 | 1.0 | $\frac{1}{\sqrt{3}}(1-q_1)$[a] | 0.0000 | 0.0000 | 0.5773 |
| 0.5 | 0.9 | $\frac{1}{\sqrt{3}}(1-q_1)$[a] | 0.0546 | 0.0835 | 0.4904 |
| 0.5 | 0.8 | $\frac{1}{\sqrt{3}}(1-q_1)$[a] | 0.1385 | 0.1462 | 0.3886 |
| 0.5 | 0.7 | $\frac{1}{\sqrt{3}}(1-q_1)$[a] | 0.1729 | 0.2266 | 0.3329 |
| 0.5 | 0.6 | $\frac{1}{\sqrt{3}}(1-q_1)$[a] | 0.2074 | 0.2907 | 0.2927 |
| 0.5 | 0.5 | $\frac{1}{\sqrt{3}}(1-q_1)$[a] | 0.2347 | 0.3396 | 0.2702 |

a. In region II.

**Table 1.6**
Equilibrium Period $n-3$ Proposals and Time Preference

| | Status Quo | | Equilibrium Proposal, Period $n-3$ | | Distance to Centroid |
|---|---|---|---|---|---|
| $\delta$ | $q_1$ | $q_2$ | $\hat{x}_1^{13}$ | $\hat{x}_2^{13}$ | |
| 1.0 | 1 | 0 | 0.4349 | 0.3154 | 0.0704 |
| 0.75 | 1 | 0 | 0.2087 | 0.1406 | 0.3268 |
| 0.50 | 1 | 0 | 0.1521 | 0.0969 | 0.3972 |
| 0.25 | 1 | 0 | 0.0683 | 0.0440 | 0.4963 |
| 0.0 | 1 | 0 | 0.0000 | 0.0000 | 0.5773 |
| 1.0 | 0.8 | $\frac{1}{\sqrt{3}}(1-q_1)$[a] | 0.4349 | 0.3154 | 0.0704 |
| 0.75 | 0.8 | $\frac{1}{\sqrt{3}}(1-q_1)$[a] | 0.2087 | 0.1406 | 0.3268 |
| 0.50 | 0.8 | $\frac{1}{\sqrt{3}}(1-q_1)$[a] | 0.1606 | 0.1330 | 0.3734 |
| 0.25 | 0.8 | $\frac{1}{\sqrt{3}}(1-q_1)$[a] | 0.1242 | 0.1516 | 0.4001 |
| 0.0 | 0.8 | $\frac{1}{\sqrt{3}}(1-q_1)$[a] | 0.0994 | 0.1640 | 0.4195 |

a. In region II.

as in the top panel of table 1.4, the optimal proposals are in the flat zone and hence at player 1's ideal point. When the status quo is binding as in the bottom panel of table 1.4, the equilibrium proposals are all closer to the centroid than are those for period $n-1$. This suggests that with a longer horizon in which the future is more important, the equilibrium policies are closer to the centroid. Comparing table 1.5 with table 1.2 indicates that except for $q_1 = 1.0$ and $q_1 = 0.9$ for which the status quo is not restricting, the equilibrium proposals are also uniformly closer to the centroid for period $n-2$ than for period $n-1$. These results suggest that with a longer horizon the players choose proposals that are closer to the centroid so as to constrain the equilibrium proposals in future periods.

### 1.5.3 *Period n − 3*

Tables 1.6 and 1.7 present the equilibria for period $n-3$. As indicated in the top panel of table 1.6 the equilibrium proposals are

**Table 1.7**
Equilibrium Period $n-3$ Proposals and the Status Quo

| | Status Quo | | Equilibrium Proposal, Period $n-3$ | | Distance to Centroid |
|---|---|---|---|---|---|
| $\delta$ | $q_1$ | $q_2$ | $\hat{x}_1^{13}$ | $\hat{x}_2^{13}$ | |
| 1.0 | 1.0 | $\frac{1}{\sqrt{3}}(1-q_1)$[a] | 0.4349 | 0.3154 | 0.0704 |
| 1.0 | 0.9 | $\frac{1}{\sqrt{3}}(1-q_1)$[a] | 0.4349 | 0.3154 | 0.0704 |
| 1.0 | 0.8 | $\frac{1}{\sqrt{3}}(1-q_1)$[a] | 0.4349 | 0.3154 | 0.0704 |
| 1.0 | 0.7 | $\frac{1}{\sqrt{3}}(1-q_1)$[a] | 0.4349 | 0.3154 | 0.0704 |
| 1.0 | 0.6 | $\frac{1}{\sqrt{3}}(1-q_1)$[a] | 0.4349 | 0.3154 | 0.0704 |
| 1.0 | 0.5 | $\frac{1}{\sqrt{3}}(1-q_1)$[a] | 0.4349 | 0.3154 | 0.0704 |
| 0.5 | 1.0 | $\frac{1}{\sqrt{3}}(1-q_1)$[a] | 0.1521 | 0.0969 | 0.3972 |
| 0.5 | 0.9 | $\frac{1}{\sqrt{3}}(1-q_1)$[a] | 0.1521 | 0.0969 | 0.3972 |
| 0.5 | 0.8 | $\frac{1}{\sqrt{3}}(1-q_1)$[a] | 0.1606 | 0.1330 | 0.3734 |
| 0.5 | 0.7 | $\frac{1}{\sqrt{3}}(1-q_1)$[a] | 0.1814 | 0.2204 | 0.3259 |
| 0.5 | 0.6 | $\frac{1}{\sqrt{3}}(1-q_1)$[a] | 0.2119 | 0.2829 | 0.2882 |
| 0.5 | 0.5 | $\frac{1}{\sqrt{3}}(1-q_1)$[a] | 0.2574 | 0.3215 | 0.2448 |

a. In region II.

**Table 1.8**
Equilibrium Period $n-4$ Proposals and the Status Quo

| | Status Quo | | Equilibrium Proposal, Period $n-4$ | | Distance to Centroid |
|---|---|---|---|---|---|
| $\delta$ | $q_1$ | $q_2$ | $\hat{x}_1^{13}$ | $\hat{x}_2^{13}$ | |
| 1.0 | 1.0 | $\frac{1}{\sqrt{3}}(1-q_1)^{a}$ | 0.0000 | 0.0000 | 0.5773 |
| 1.0 | 0.9 | $\frac{1}{\sqrt{3}}(1-q_1)^{a}$ | 0.0495 | 0.0848 | 0.4945 |
| 1.0 | 0.8 | $\frac{1}{\sqrt{3}}(1-q_1)^{a}$ | 0.0983 | 0.1647 | 0.4204 |
| 1.0 | 0.7 | $\frac{1}{\sqrt{3}}(1-q_1)^{a}$ | 0.1425 | 0.2340 | 0.3608 |
| 1.0 | 0.6 | $\frac{1}{\sqrt{3}}(1-q_1)^{a}$ | 0.1793 | 0.3090 | 0.3214 |
| 1.0 | 0.5 | $\frac{1}{\sqrt{3}}(1-q_1)^{a}$ | 0.2123 | 0.3655 | 0.2978 |

a. In region II.

closer to the centroid the higher is the discount factor. Also, in the top panel the period $n-3$ equilibrium proposals are closer to the centroid than for period $n-2$. The equilibrium proposals are in Region V and are slightly above the line from player 1's ideal point to the centroid. In the bottom panel of table 1.6 the status quo is not binding for $\delta = 1$ and for $\delta = 0.75$, and the equilibrium proposals are closer to the centroid than for period $n-2$.

In table 1.7, when $\delta = 1.0$ as in the top panel, the period $n-3$ proposal is quite close to the centroid. Moreover, for all the status quos reported, the proposals are unconstrained. Comparing the bottom panels of tables 1.7 and 1.5 indicates that the equilibrium proposals are closer to the centroid in a game with three periods than in a game with two periods.

### 1.5.4 *Period n − 4*

Table 1.8 presents the equilibrium proposals for period $n-4$ as a function of the status quo. Comparing table 1.8 with table 1.5 indicates that the equilibrium proposals are farther from the centroid with $n-4$ periods than with $n-2$ periods remaining in the game.

This reflects the proposals reported in table 1.7 that indicate that the equilibrium proposal in the following period $(n-3)$ is near the centroid.

### 1.5.5 *Proposal Paths*

Figure 1.6 presents the paths of equilibrium proposals for discount factors $\delta = 0.5$ and $\delta = 0.25$ for a game with $n = 15$ periods. Each game begins at the ideal point of player 1, and the same sequence of random numbers is used to select the proposers in each game. As the figures indicate, most of the proposals made by each player are close to the lines from their ideal points to the centroid with the exception

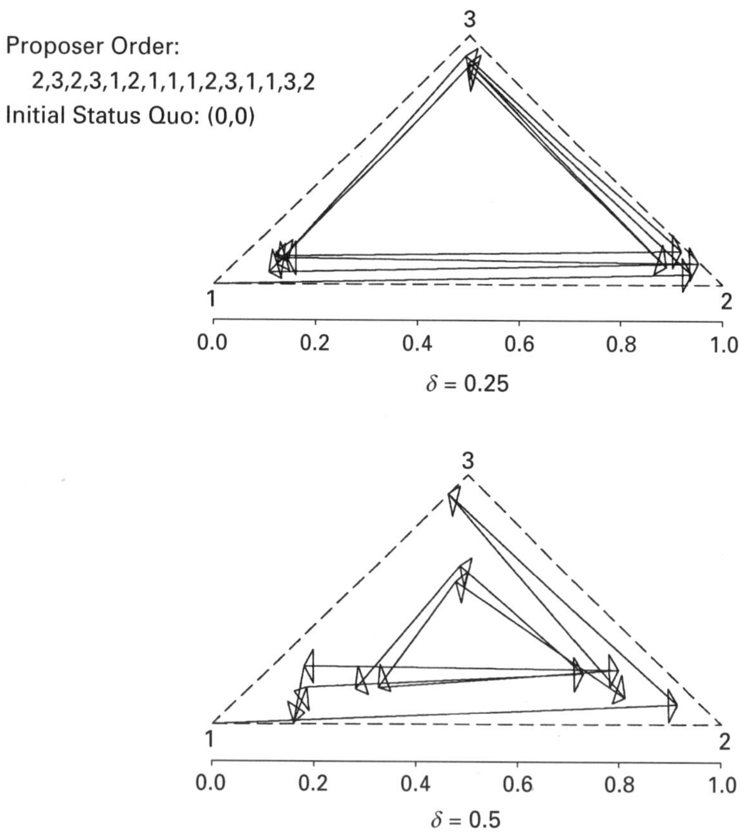


**Figure 1.6**
Proposal Paths for 15 Periods

of an occasional period in which a status quo is in a flat zone and leads the proposer to make a proposal on the (single-period) contract curve with its majority partner. The proposal is not at the proposer's ideal point because of the constraining effect of the status quo.

Comparing the two panels of figure 1.6 indicates that for higher discount factors the proposals tend to be closer to the centroid. This is consistent with the tables. The figures also suggest that there can be substantial change in the policies if the agenda setter changes from one period to the next. If the proposer remains the same, however, as in periods 7, 8, and 9, the proposals do not change substantially. The proposals, however, reflect the incentive of the proposer to form a majority with the player who is disadvantaged by the status quo.

## 1.6 Conclusions

A fundamental issue in collective choice is understanding the evolution over time of continuing policies—policies that remain in effect until changed by new legislation. Continuing policies typically have characteristics of public goods in the sense that they apply broadly. Even entitlement programs that deliver distributive benefits to eligible recipients take the form of local public goods in the sense that they are broadly applicable and their distributive benefits and costs can be expressed as functions of policy instruments. Most government policies and programs have these features, and many of them are changed frequently by legislative action. Despite their importance, little is known about the dynamics of such programs.

The model used to study the dynamics of continuing policies is a bargaining model of a majority rule legislature, and the focus is on characterizing the equilibrium in a finite-horizon model. The specific model studied is simple (three legislators, quadratic preferences), and the analysis utilizes symmetry to simplify the computations required to determine the equilibria. The assumption of quadratic preferences implies that the players prefer to avoid variation in the policy over time, and they can do so by positioning the status quo closer to the centroid, which affects the reservation levels of the players and can preclude large changes in the policy in the next period. The results obtained are intended to inform future computational and analytical research and to guide the design and interpretation of empirical studies of the dynamics of public policies.

The dynamics of continuing policies are best studied in the context of an infinite-horizon game, but characterization of equilibria in such games is elusive. For a finite-horizon game the analytical results indicate that the value functions in the game have discontinuities where the status quo is such that the proposer would shift from one majority partner to another. This complicates the analytical and computational analysis, and the hope is that with a sufficiently long horizon the discontinuities become negligible. A basic conjecture for an infinite-horizon game suggested by the analytical and computational results is that as the discount factor increases, the equilibrium proposals are closer to the centroid. In the finite horizon model, the higher the discount factor, the closer are the proposals to the centroid, unless the continuation value function has a flat zone.

The analytical and computational findings include the following. The more attractive majority partner for the proposer is the player who is the more disadvantaged by the status quo. Although the final-period policy is on the contract curve of the majority partners, the equilibrium proposals in earlier periods are typically interior to the (single-period) Pareto set unless the status quo is in a flat zone. When the status quo is not constraining, the proposal is close to the line from the proposer's ideal point to the centroid. The status quo can restrict the proposals the proposer can successfully make, and typically the closer is the status quo to the centroid, the closer are the proposals to the centroid. A proposer thus can limit the variation in future proposals by positioning the status quo close to the centroid. Nevertheless, a proposer has temporary agenda-setting authority, and it is always advantageous to move the policy toward his ideal point.

Future research on the dynamics of continuing programs should focus on the characterization of equilibria as a function of (1) the number and preferences of legislators, (2) the distribution of the consequences of policy alternatives, and (3) institutional factors. The principal institutional factors are the selection of the agenda setter, the extent to which the agenda setter is a temporary monopolist or agenda control is shared through amendment opportunities, the presence of veto players, and supermajority rule. In addition to these factors, uncertainty can play an important role in the dynamics of policies as the institution responds to exogenous shocks to the status quo.

## Appendix

To identify the magnitude of the discontinuities in the continuation values $v_i^n(q)$, consider status quos on the horizontal line through the centroid $c$. For points to the left of the centroid in region V, neither player 2 nor player 3 seeks player 1's vote. For points to the right of the centroid in region II, both players 2 and 3 seek player 1's vote. Consequently, the continuation value should jump up as it passes through the centroid from the left. The supremum of the continuation value in region V as $q_1 \to c_1$ is

$$\sup_{q_1 \to c_1} v_{1,\mathrm{V}}^n(q) = -\frac{4}{3}\left(1 - \frac{1}{\sqrt{3}}\right).$$

The supremum of the continuation value is region II is

$$\sup_{q_1 \to c_1} v_{1,\mathrm{II}}^n(q) = -\frac{2}{3}\left(1 - \frac{1}{\sqrt{3}}\right).$$

The jump is thus

$$\sup_{q_1 \to c_1} v_{1,\mathrm{II}}^n(q) - \sup_{q_1 \to c_1} v_{1,\mathrm{V}}^n(q) = \frac{2}{3}\left(1 - \frac{1}{\sqrt{3}}\right) = 0.2818.$$

Next consider moving from region VI to region I. Player 3 obtains 2's vote in region VI and obtains 1's vote in region I. Along a horizontal line corresponding to some $q_2 > c_2$, the limits are

$$\sup_{q_1 \to 1/2} v_{1,\mathrm{I}}^n(q) = -\frac{1}{3}\left(\frac{5}{4} + q_2^2\right).$$

$$\sup_{q_1 \to 1/2} v_{1,\mathrm{VI}}^n(q) = -\frac{2}{3}\left(\frac{5}{4} + q_2^2 - \left(\frac{1}{4} + q_2^2\right)^{1/2}\right).$$

The jump is then

$$\sup_{q_1 \to 1/2} v_{1,\mathrm{I}}^n(q) - \sup_{q_1 \to 1/2} v_{1,\mathrm{VI}}^n(q) = -\frac{1}{3}\left(-\left(\frac{5}{4} + q_2^2\right) + 2\left(\frac{1}{4} + q_2^2\right)^{1/2}\right).$$

This is positive for $c_2 \le q_2 < \frac{\sqrt{3}}{2}$ and equals zero at $q_2 = \frac{\sqrt{3}}{2}$, which corresponds to player 3's ideal point. For example, if $q_2 = c_2 + \varepsilon \approx \frac{1}{2\sqrt{3}}$, the difference in the limits is 0.0595. The magnitude of the jump is decreasing and strictly convex in $q_2$.

The continuation value of player 1 is continuous on regions I and II, since in both those regions the other two players seek the vote of player 1 when they are the proposer. The only difference in the strategies of the players in the two regions is that player 1 switches between obtaining the vote of player 2 and of player 3. The line from $z^1$ through the centroid is $q_2^c = \frac{1}{\sqrt{3}} q_1$, and the continuation values on that line for $q_1 \geq \frac{1}{2}$ are

$$v_{1,\mathrm{I}}^n(q) = v_{1,\mathrm{II}}^n(q) = -\frac{1}{3}\left[\left(1 - \left(\frac{4}{3}q_1^2 - 2q_1 + 1\right)^{1/2}\right)^2 + \frac{8}{3}q_1^2\right].$$

The continuation values $v_{1,\mathrm{I}}^n(q^c)$ and $v_{1,\mathrm{II}}^n(q^c)$ decrease along the line $q_2^c = \frac{1}{\sqrt{3}} q_1$ for $q_1 \geq \frac{1}{2}$, so their maxima are at the centroid $c$ and equal to

$$\sup_{x \to c} v_{1,\mathrm{I}}^n(x) = \sup_{x \to c} v_{1,\mathrm{II}}^n(x) = -\frac{2}{3}\left(1 - \frac{1}{\sqrt{3}}\right) = -0.2818.$$

The continuation value is also continuous and differentiable as $q$ moves between regions IV and V. Along the line from $z^1$ through the centroid, for $0 \leq q_1 \leq \frac{1}{2}$,

$$\begin{aligned} v_{1,\mathrm{IV}}^n(q) &= v_{1,\mathrm{V}}^n(q) \\ &= -\frac{1}{3}\left[3\left(1 - \left(\frac{4}{3}q_1^2 - 2q_1 + 1\right)^{1/2}\right)^2 + 2\left(\frac{2}{3}q_1^2 - 2q_1 + 1\right)^{1/2}\right]. \end{aligned}$$

At the centroid the continuation value jumps by $\sup_{x \to c} v_{1,\mathrm{I}}^n(x) - \sup_{x \to c} v_{1,\mathrm{IV}}^n(x) = \frac{2}{3}(1 - \frac{1}{\sqrt{3}}) = 0.2818 > 0$. Note that the continuation value increases as the status quo moves from region IV to region I and hence becomes farther from 1's ideal point. That is, when the status quo is farther from 1's ideal point, 1 is in a more advantageous position because he is more likely to have his vote sought by the other players. In addition, when 1 is selected as the proposer, he can still choose a proposal in region IV or V.

To compare regions II and III the value functions are

$$v_{1,\mathrm{II}}^n(x) = -\frac{1}{3}[(1 - D(x, z^3))^2 + 2D(x, z^1)^2]$$

$$v_{1,\mathrm{III}}^n(x) = -\frac{1}{3}[2(1 - D(x, z^3))^2 + D(x, z^1)^2 + D(x, z^3)].$$

The difference is

$$v^n_{1,\mathrm{II}}(x) - v^n_{1,\mathrm{III}}(x) = -\frac{1}{3}[-1 + D(x,z^3) - D(x,z^3)^2 + D(x,z^1)^2].$$

At a point $y$ on the line $(1 - x_1, x_2^c = (1 - x_1)\frac{1}{\sqrt{3}})$ to the centroid, the distance $D(y,z^3) = D(y,z^1)$, so

$$v^n_{1,\mathrm{II}}(y) - v^n_{1,\mathrm{III}}(y) = -\frac{1}{3}[-1 + D(y,z^3)] > 0.$$

Player 1's continuation value thus increases as the policy crosses the line from 2's ideal point to the centroid from region II to region III.

## Notes

This research has been supported by National Science Foundation grants SBR-9409559 and SBR-9809177.

1. Kramer (1977) presents a dynamic model in which voters are myopic and a single agenda setter chooses alternatives to be voted against the status quo.

2. See Weingast and Marshall (1988).

3. Weakly dominated voting strategies are assumed to be eliminated.

4. For $q_1 = \frac{1}{2}$, player 3 randomizes between the midpoints of the two contract curves.

5. If the players were not equally likely to be recognized, the continuation value would be

$$\begin{aligned} v^n_{1,\mathrm{V}}(q) = &-p_1[(\hat{x}_1^{12}(q,n) - z_1^1)^2 + (\hat{x}_2^{12}(q,n) - z_2^1)^2] - p_2[(\hat{x}_1^{23}(q,n) - z_1^1)^2 + (\hat{x}_2^{23}(q,n) - z_2^1)^2] \\ &- p_3[(\hat{x}_1^{32}(q,n) - z_1^1)^2 + (\hat{x}_2^{32}(q,n) - z_2^1)^2], \end{aligned}$$

where $p_i$, $i = 1, 2, 3$, is the probability that player $i$ is recognized.

6. In a computational approach that predates the method reported here, polynomial regressions were used to approximate the players' value functions in each of the six regions of the Pareto set. This approach had the advantage of allowing evaluation of the approximated value functions over the entire Pareto set. In contrast, the method described here evaluates the value functions only on a finite number of grid points. The drawback to the polynomial regression approach, however, was that it required value function continuity or, in a weaker sense, continuity in known areas of the Pareto set. Since at each iteration of the game the sets on which the value functions are continuous are not known, the computational analysis based on polynomial approximations of the players' value functions was infeasible. Moreover, estimating a polynomial value function over the Pareto set could not capture the discontinuities in the value functions.

7. This argument depends on the existence of a symmetric equilibrium. In an asymmetric equilibrium, the relations between the players' value functions may not be as simple as in the symmetric case.

8. There are no grid points on the three lines that connect ideal points to the centroid, since the computational analysis relies on reflecting grid points across these lines. Points on the lines would have ambiguous regions, and this could cause numerical complications.

9. In equilibrium, the majority partner of a proposer will be the player who has the lower reservation value at the status quo.

10. In the implementation of the algorithm described here, all weak inequalities are satisfied in a strict sense.

11. The number of comparisons required to determine an optimal proposal is of order $S^2$.

12. The horizontal and vertical distances between adjacent grid points are 0.00065.

## References


Arrow, Kenneth J. 1951. *Social Choice and Individual Values*. New Haven, CT: Yale University Press.

Banks, Jeffrey S., and John Duggan. 1998. "Stationary Equilibria in a Bargaining Model of Social Choice." Working paper, California Institute of Technology.

Baron, David P. 1991. "A Spatial Bargaining Theory of Government Formation in Parliamentary Systems." *American Political Science Review* 85 (March): 137–164.

———. 1994. "A Sequential Choice Theory Perspective on Legislative Organization." *Legislative Studies Quarterly* 19 (May): 267–296.

———. 1996. "A Dynamic Theory of Collective Goods Programs." *American Political Science Review* 90 (June): 316–330.

Baron, David P., and Daniel Diermeier. 1999. "Dynamics of Parliamentary Systems: Elections, Governments, and Parliaments." Working paper, Stanford University.

Baron, David P., and John A. Ferejohn. 1989. "Bargaining in Legislatures." *American Political Science Review* 83: 1181–1206.

Diermeier, Daniel, and Antonio Merlo. 1998. "Government Turnover in Parliamentary Democracies." Working paper, New York University.

Harrington, Joseph E., Jr. 1990. "The Power of the Proposal Maker in a Model of Endogenous Agenda Formation." *Public Choice* 64: 1–20.

Jackson, Matthew O., and Boaz Moselle. 1998. "Coalition and Party Formation in a Legislative Voting Game." Working paper, California Institute of Technology.

Kramer, Gerald H. 1977. "A Dynamical Model of Political Equilibrium." *Journal of Economic Theory* 16: 310–334.

McKelvey, Richard D. 1976. "Intransitivities in Multidimensional Voting Models and Some Implications for Agenda Control." *Journal of Economic Theory* 16: 472–482.

———. 1979. "General Conditions for Global Intransitivities in Formal Voting Models." *Econometrica* 47: 1085–1112.

Romer, Thomas, and Howard Rosenthal. 1978. "Political Resource Allocation, Controlled Agendas, and the Status Quo." *Public Choice* 33: 27–43.

Schofield, Norman. 1983. "Generic Instability of Majority Rule." *Review of Economic Studies* 50: 695–705.

Ways and Means Committee, U.S. House of Representatives. 1993. *1993 Green Book: Overview of Entitlement Programs*. Washington, D.C.: Government Printing Office.

Weingast, Barry R., and William Marshall. 1988. "The Industrial Organization of Congress." *Journal of Political Economy* 96 (February): 132–163.

# 2 Fluidity of Social Norms in a Hierarchical System

Joseph E. Harrington, Jr.

## 2.1 Introduction

Why do some governments fail to respond to large economic and social changes and ultimately lose power? Why are some elected officials unresponsive to their constituents? Why do some corporations remain rigid in their practices as market conditions change? Such ossification may reflect the embodiment of a norm of being resistant to change, of acting in the same manner regardless of the state of the environment. But what are the processes that would generate such a norm of behavior? Are certain features of the external environment conducive to people's being unresponsive to a change in circumstances? What about characteristics of the internal structure of the social system?

To gain some preliminary insight into these issues, a series of simple models have been developed that, while not yet accurate representations of governments, political systems, or corporations, do embody some essential features of those systems. One such feature is their hierarchical structure. Agents who hold important high-level positions are the product of an implicit selection process that chose them from the masses at the lower levels. A second feature is that, like any type of society, agents with status are imitated by young agents in their striving to succeed within the system. In the context of a hierarchy, status is closely related to rank. There is, then, social learning between new agents and high-ranking old agents. With these two dynamics—selection and social learning—a number of interesting insights have been derived.

In Harrington (1998), the social selection process is examined to understand what types of individuals are selected for advancement within a hierarchy. At each level, agents compete with one another for advancement with relative performance determining who advances. After observing the realization of a stochastic environment, each agent selects an action. Some agents are endowed with a flexible rule—choose the action that is best for that environment—while others follow a rigid rule—choose the same action irrespective of the environment. Performance depends on the appropriateness of one's actions for the current environment and how proficient one is with those actions. Proficiency is presumed to come from past experience as a result of such processes as learning-by-doing.[1] It is shown that if a hierarchical social system has sufficiently many levels, its highest levels are dominated by agents whose behavior is relatively unresponsive to the environment.[2]

The preceding analysis yielded some insight about the tendencies of those at high levels to be rigid. It cannot, however, help us understand how a mode of behavior can become ubiquitous throughout a society, in other words, become a social norm. To do that requires taking account of how rules get passed from agent to agent. This social learning feature is modeled in Harrington (1999a) along with social selection. In that setup new agents enter the system at the bottom rung. At that point, they make an initial adoption decision—whether to deploy a rigid rule or a flexible rule in trying to scale the hierarchy. This decision is determined by two factors: an innate tendency to be rigid or flexible, and imitation of those who have been successful. Specifically, a new agent randomly selects a mentor from the highest level and learns that mentor's history of actions and environments but does not observe his behavioral rule. He then attempts to draw inferences about his mentor's underlying behavioral rule and uses those inferences in deciding on a rule to adopt. After adopting behavioral rules, this population of new agents is subject to the social selection process. This is then a feedback system whereby new agents arrive and imitate old successful agents; out of that cohort of new agents comes a new set of role models, who are then imitated by the next generation of new agents; and the process continues. Agents at the top not only affect the rigidity of the system by themselves being rigid or flexible but may have a pervasive and lasting influence through what the next generation infers about "what it takes to move up." It is shown that a norm of being unresponsive to one's environment is more prevalent and robust than one of being adaptive. The reason is that it is easier for new agents to infer the mode of behavior of those agents who get to the top if they used a rigid rule than if they used a flexible rule. In the terminology of Boyd and Richerson (1985), a rigid rule is of "higher fidelity" than a flexible rule, and this makes it more imitable. The source of the lower fidelity of a flexible rule is that selection tends to promote those flexible agents whose history is consistent with their using a rigid rule, whereas it does not tend to promote those rigid agents whose history is consistent with their using a flexible rule. It is then easier for new agents to identify those role models who deployed a rigid rule, and this results in a higher fraction of new agents adopting a rigid rule. In brief, a rigid rule is more imitable than a flexible rule.

In the preceding model, an individual's environment was allowed to change stochastically. However, the aggregate environment was kept fixed in the sense that the frequency of environments for the population of agents did not change. Or, more to the point, what was the most common environment was fixed over time. As a result, the rigid rule that performed best on average did not change. This property would seem quite important for the stability of a rigid norm in that a rigid norm is always the rigid rule that performs best, on average. If the aggregate environment changes (and with it what is the best-performing rigid rule), then an existing rigid norm may become quite dysfunctional, and this could allow a successful invasion by a flexible rule. It is then not clear that we would observe a rigid norm if there are aggregate or large-scale changes. The objective of this chapter is to explore that issue.

While aggregate fluctuations do indeed make it more difficult for rigid norms to occur, a rigid norm is found to be capable of surviving such shocks. Under certain conditions, rigid norms are quite resilient. Though, when a rigid norm is in place, few agents may be deploying a flexible rule, those agents are shown to have a very important role in the persistence of rigid norms. Specifically, agents deploying a flexible rule are instrumental in transiting between rigid norms in response to changes in the aggregate environment. The analysis also shows that a rigid norm is more likely to occur when large-scale changes are less frequent, bigger in size, and more abrupt.

While, to my knowledge, this line of research is unique in asking how a norm of being resistant to change can develop in a social system, research on cultural transmission is similar in its interest in how behavioral norms develop. This work includes Cavalli-Sforza and Feldman (1981), Boyd and Richerson (1985), Harrison and Carroll (1991), Epstein and Axtell (1996), and Bisin and Verdier (2001). Relatedly, there has been considerable work in economics on social learning. The modeling approach here differs in both the space of traits over which learning occurs and in the transmission process. Previous work on social learning is concerned with learning about actions. This may involve agents' learning from the actions and associated payoffs of others, as in Ellison and Fudenberg (1993; 1995), Bala and Goyal (1998), and Rhode and Stegeman (2001), or agents' learning only from the population distribution of actions, as in Banerjee (1992; 1993), Bikhchandani, Hirshleifer, and Welch (1992), Bergstrom and Stark (1993), Kirman (1993), Vega-Redondo (1993), Banerjee and Fudenberg (1995), and Smith and Sørensen (1996). In contrast, the focus in this chapter is learning about rules, learning about how to respond to one's environment. This is a substantive difference in that rules are not directly observable; at best, one observes realizations of a rule as it interacts with the environment. In terms of modeling the transmission process, previous research has modeled *horizontal* transmission in that agents are learning from their peers. The transmission process here is *vertical* in that it is predicated upon a hierarchical society in which agents learn from those above them. Vega-Redondo (2000) also encompasses vertical transmission in an evolutionary-style model. I feel this is a critical and largely unexplored feature of such social systems as organizations and, more generally, ones in which status is important. In terms of the process by which traits are transferred between agents, it is standard in previous work to assume that imitation is perfect. A central assumption in the present model is that an agent's behavioral rule is private information, so imitation is problematic. In contrast with other social learning literature, this study endogenizes the imitability of an agent's trait.

## 2.2 A Dynamic Model of a Social System

The formulation in this chapter of the process determining behavioral norms in a social setting comprises four elements: a description of an agent's meta-environment and how it changes; the space of behavioral rules over which the population is evolving; the selection process by which agents compete and social status is determined;

and the social learning process by which traits are transmitted across generations.

### 2.2.1 *Structure of Society*

The most crucial element of the present conception of a society is that it is hierarchical. This means that it is composed of a set of $k$ ($\geq 2$) ordered levels that run from a "lowest" level, denumerated level 1, to a "highest" level, denumerated level $k$. At each level there is a large (countably infinite) population of agents. A key presumption is that agents strive to advance to higher levels. Whether it is a politician trying to advance from a state legislature to the House of Representatives, or a regional manager striving to become a vice president in a corporation, advancement typically requires performing relatively better than a subset of one's peers who face comparable circumstances. I model this process by assuming that, at each level, agents are randomly matched into pairs. Each of these matchings is faced with a stochastic environment. Once the environment is revealed to the agents, they choose actions. The agent with greater relative performance is promoted to the next level while the other agent is assumed to exit the system. Though this "up-or-out" structure is extreme, casual observation suggests that most candidates who lose do not run again, and those corporate employees who are passed over when their time has come may no longer be on the fast track, which makes them less likely to be considered for promotion.[3] Eventually, each agent "expires" in that agents are constrained to being in the system for at most $k$ periods, where a period is equal to the length of time spent at a level. A generation is equal to the length of a single lifetime (which is $k$ periods). The first generation of the model then encompasses periods $1, \ldots, k$, the second generation comprises periods $k+1, \ldots, 2k$, and so forth.

At each level, an agent faces two random events: the agent with whom he competes for advancement and the external environment. The latter is assumed to be of two possible types, $\{0, 1\}$, where the probability that an agent faces environment 1 in generation $g$ is denoted $b^g$. An agent's environment is assumed to be independently distributed across levels. Though there is individual uncertainty, there is no population uncertainty in the sense that, at every level, a proportion $b^g$ of all matchings have environment 1. This lack of population uncertainty greatly simplifies the analysis. In responding to her environment, an agent has two feasible actions at her disposal, $\{0,1\}$. In a manner to be described later, action 0 (1) is the best myopic response to environment 0 (1). When $b^g > (<)1/2$, action 1 (0) is then more frequently the appropriate response to the environment and, in that sense, is the best overall action.

The aggregate environment is subject to change in the form of movements of $b^g$, the frequency with which environment 1 occurs. This is modeled by assuming that it deterministically oscillates between $b \in (0,1)$ and $1-b$ with the switch occurring every $T$ generations:

$$b^g = \begin{cases} b & \text{if } g \in \{1,\ldots,T,2T+1,\ldots,3T,4T+1,\ldots\} \\ 1-b & \text{if } g \in \{T+1,\ldots,2T,3T+1,\ldots,4T,5T+1,\ldots\}. \end{cases}$$

Note that the time between changes in the aggregate environment is at least one generation. If change occurs within generations, imitation can be quite dysfunctional because new agents would be routinely imitating agents who were successful for a different aggregate environment. In that case, preliminary analysis suggests that a flexible rule prevails as a norm. Thus, I limit my attention to intergenerational changes where it is not so clear as to what norms will develop.

### 2.2.2 *Space of Behavioral Rules*

Associated with each agent is a behavioral rule. For simplicity, attention is limited to behavioral rules that condition only on the current environment. It is then the set of functions that map the set of environments, $\{0,1\}$, into the set of actions, $\{0,1\}$, with the exception that I exclude the pathological case of always choosing an action inappropriate for the current environment. I believe this simplifies the analysis without any loss of generality. A flexible agent is defined to be one who always selects the action best suited for the environment: he chooses action 0 (1) when the environment is 0 (1). A rigid agent chooses the same action irrespective of the environment. There are two types: those who always use action 0, and those who always use action 1.

As agents advance up through the system, they accumulate a personal history. Though there are many history-dependent types at any given level in the system, it is sufficient for present purposes to partition the population into the following five types: rigid agents endowed with action $i$ (denoted $R_i$), $i \in \{0,1\}$; flexible agents who have always chosen action $i$ (denoted $F_i$), $i \in \{0,1\}$; and flexible agents who have chosen both action 0 and action 1 (denoted $F_N$).

### 2.2.3 *Selection*

The process by which people advance in this social system and thereby gain social status is specified as follows. If the two matched agents choose distinct actions, then the agent whose action matches the environment survives and advances to the next level. If both agents select the action that matches the environment, the agent who has chosen that particular action more frequently in the past advances. If they have chosen that action equally frequently, an agent is randomly selected to survive. Who advances if both agents choose the less appropriate action need not be specified because the set of equations that describes the population dynamics is independent of it.

There are several notable features of this selection process. First, competition for advancement is local in that an agent competes with only one other agent (rather than competing with the population at large). Second, advancement depends only on an agent's current performance where, implicitly, an agent's current performance is determined by the current environment, his current action, and his proficiency with the action used. Third, proficiency comes from experience, from having done the same thing over and over. Note that survival depends lexicographically on one's current action and one's experience with that action, so the incremental effect from choosing a better action exceeds the incremental effect from more experience.[4]

### 2.2.4 *Social Learning*

The state of the social system is represented by $k$ populations, one at each of the system's $k$ levels. At the end of each period, those who were at the highest level are assumed to exit the system (there is "mandatory retirement" after $k$ periods in the system). For the population at level $h \in \{1, \ldots, k-1\}$, half of them advance to level $h+1$

according to the selection process described previously, and the other half exit the system. A fresh cohort of new agents is assumed to enter level 1.

The behavioral rule that a new agent adopts is determined by a confluence of two forces: imitation of those who were successful, and natural predisposition. There are two aspects to imitation: identifying who is worth emulating, and inferring their code of conduct. The former is relatively easy because it only requires identifying people with high rank. The latter is problematic. An agent does not wear her behavioral rule on her sleeve, and one cannot look into the heart of another. What an agent is presumed capable of doing is observing the past behavior of an agent and the context in which she had to act. The following imitation process is specified. Each new agent randomly chooses one agent from the current level $k$ population (those with the highest social status) to act as her role model or mentor. She does not observe the entire population because limited information seems more natural. An incoming agent observes his mentor's history in terms of the actions he selected and the environments he faced. If a new agent's mentor always chose the same action and, furthermore, chose this action when it was inappropriate for the environment, this would be unequivocal evidence that the mentor is rigid in that action. In that case, the new agent adopts that rigid rule. If a new agent's mentor chose both actions during his lifetime, then this is unequivocal evidence that he is flexible. A new agent then adopts the flexible rule. The problematic case is when a new agent's mentor always chose the same action but always faced the environment for which that action was appropriate. Such behavior is consistent with both flexible and rigid rules. I assume that new agents have natural predispositions to being flexible or rigid, and this predisposition breaks the indeterminacy. A proportion $w \in [0, 1]$ of new agents are predisposed to being rigid, which means that they adopt a rigid rule in that case. A proportion $1 - w$ are predisposed to be flexible, which means that they adopt a flexible rule in that case. A new agent then adopts the rule that he is predisposed to unless the behavior of his mentor is evidence to the contrary. One could imagine $w$ being determined by what types of norms are prevailing outside of this particular social system. Once a new agent adopts a rule, it persists with him throughout his time in the system.

This section has provided a narrative description of the dynamic system; the appendix provides a formal definition. Because of the system's complexity, numerical analysis is used. The model in Harrington (1999a) is a special case of this model when $T = +\infty$ so that the aggregate environment does not change.

## 2.3 Norms in a Fixed Aggregate Environment

Prior to examining the general model, results for the special case of a fixed aggregate environment are reviewed. Specifically, it is assumed that $T = +\infty$ and $b^g = b > \frac{1}{2}$ for all $g$. After reviewing what happens within the hierarchy during a single generation (Harrington 1998), social learning is introduced and the development of norms across generations is examined (Harrington 1999a).

### 2.3.1 *Selection of Rigid Agents*

The purpose of this section is to review briefly some properties of the selection process that operates within the $k$-level system and which was examined in Harrington (1998). To begin, the proportion of agents who are maximally proficient in action 0 (which means that either they are rigid in action 0 or they are flexible and have always faced environment 0) steadily and rather rapidly goes to zero after level 2. Since environment 0 occurs relatively infrequently, such agents are ill-suited for this meta-environment. All the meaningful dynamics then take place with respect to $F_1$s (flexible agents who are maximally proficient in action 1 because they have always faced environment 1), $F_N$s (flexible agents who are not maximally proficient in either action because they have faced both environments), and $R_1$s (agents who are rigid in action 1). At low levels, with agents having only faced a few environments, there will be a reasonable number of flexible agents who have only faced environment 1. Next, note that when an $F_1$ and an $R_1$ meet to compete for advancement, an $F_1$ advances with probability $\frac{b}{2} + (1 - b) > \frac{1}{2}$ because, when the environment is 1, he is equally proficient in action 1 to an $R_1$ and, when the environment is 0, he adapts and chooses action 0. This differential advantage provides a force by which the proportion of flexible agents can rise. However, as flexible agents rise through the hierarchy and face more environments, an increasing proportion of them will have faced environment 0 and thus be less proficient in the better action than $R_1$s. This lack of proficiency puts them at a disadvantage compared to those surviving agents who are rigid in action

1. Though $R_1$s may initially be driven down, their differential proficiency in action 1 becomes increasingly scarce among flexible agents, so that rigid agents eventually come to dominate.[5]

Using a phase diagram analysis, several possible paths for a population are derived. First, the proportion of flexible agents steadily rises as a cohort moves from the bottom to the top of the hierarchy. This requires that $k$ be sufficiently small. Second, the proportion of flexible agents rises as one goes from low to moderate levels but falls as one goes from moderate to high levels. This can occur when $k$ is sufficiently large. Third, the proportion of rigid agents (who use the action most appropriate for what is the most common environment) steadily rises as one moves up the hierarchy. This is not so much dependent on $k$ but rather on the initial population mix. While there are other possible paths, simulations show that these are by far the most common.[6]

Interpreting this model in the political context, let the environment be the policy preferences of voters, agents be politicians, and the action chosen be a politician's position on the issues. The hierarchy reflects the property that political aspirants might start by running for low-level office, and if they succeed by winning office, then they become eligible to run for the next-higher-level office. A rigid agent can be thought of as an ideologue in that her positions are unresponsive to voters' preferences, whereas a flexible agent is an office seeker as her positions are tailored to match those policies supported by voters (which also serves to maximize the probability of winning office). Given this interpretation, Harrington (1998) shows that ideologues can survive and dominate high-level offices. A closely related model in Harrington (2000) is specifically tailored to the political setting, and it shows how purely office-seeking politicians can end up looking like ideologues.

### 2.3.2 *Stability of Rigid Norms*

Let us now consider the development of stable norms when both selection and social learning are operative but when the aggregate environment is fixed. This is the special case of our model when $T = +\infty$ and was examined in Harrington (1999a). For our discussion, suppose $b^g = b > 0.5$ for all $g$ so that environment 1 is always the most frequent environment and thereby action 1 is always the best single action.

A behavioral rule is said to be a locally stable norm if there exists a local attractor for which a large fraction of agents use that rule. The key finding is that a rigid rule is more prevalent than a flexible rule as a locally stable norm. When enough new agents are predisposed to a particular mode of behavior, it is generally the case that that mode of behavior can dominate. In other words, for a wide range of values for $(b, k)$, it is a local attractor for a high fraction of agents to use a rigid (flexible) rule when enough incoming agents are predisposed to be rigid (flexible), that is, when $w$ is close to 1 (0). The more problematic and interesting case is when new agents are not predisposed to a rule. How likely is it that such a rule can dominate? Here I find a notable asymmetry: a rigid rule fares much better than a flexible rule when faced with an incoming population that is biased against it. It is common for a rigid rule to be a locally stable norm regardless of the value of $w$. Even when $w = 0$, so that all incoming agents are predisposed to be flexible, there is a local attractor with a high fraction of agents using a rigid rule for a wide range of values for $(b, k)$. In contrast, a flexible rule is generally not a locally stable norm when most incoming agents are predisposed to be rigid (that is, when $w$ is sufficiently close to 1).

Selection favors those agents who have always chosen action 1, for then they are maximally proficient in the action that is most frequently the best response to the environment. For agents who use a flexible rule, this implies that selection favors those who have always faced environment 1. Hence, many of those agents who use a flexible rule and rise to the top are indistinguishable from agents who use a rigid rule. This inability to differentiate themselves results in those new agents who have an innate bias to be rigid adopting a rigid rule and, in essence, hard-wiring their mentor's history of having always chosen action 1. When there are enough new agents predisposed to be rigid, a flexible norm is unlikely to develop. In contrast, since rigid agents (in action 1) are proficient in action 1 regardless of the history of their environments, selection does not favor those rigid agents who have exclusively faced environment 1. This allows them to differentiate themselves from agents who use a flexible rule and is why a rigid rule is a locally stable norm even when all new agents are predisposed to be flexible.

For a behavioral rule to thrive, it need not be sufficient that those agents deploying that rule rise to the top; what may also be required is that they have differentiated themselves from those who use other rules. A rigid rule does this more effectively than a flexible rule. In the terminology of Boyd and Richerson (1985), a rigid rule has "higher fidelity" than a flexible rule, and this makes it more likely to become ubiquitous.

## 2.4 Norms in a Changing Aggregate Environment

In this section, $T$ is finite so that what is the most common environment changes across generations. The main objective is to understand how such large-scale changes affect the stability of rigid norms. In conducting numerical analysis, values must be specified for the system's seven variables: the four parameters defining the meta-environment, $(b, k, w, T)$ and the three initial conditions, $(r_1, r_0, b^1)$, where, in the initial generation, $r_i$ is the proportion of agents using a rigid rule in action $i$ at the system's first level and $b^1$ is the frequency with which environment 1 occurs.[7] Without loss of generality, $b^1 = b$. Simulations were run for $(b, w, T) \in \{0.05, 0.10, \ldots, 0.95\} \times \{0, 0.1, \ldots, 1\} \times \{1, 2, \ldots, 20\}$, and: (1) $k \in \{5, 10, \ldots, 25\}$ and $(r_1, r_0) \in \{(0.25, 0.25), (0.33, 0.33)\}$; and (2) $k \in \{5, 10\}$ and

$$(r_1, r_0) \in \{(0.05, 0.05), (0.25, 0.25), (0.33, 0.33), (0.45, 0.45), (0.05, 0.45), (0.45, 0.05)\}.$$

In that qualitative results were independent of the initial population, results are reported only for $(r_1, r_0) = (0.25, 0.25)$. For reasons of visual presentation, results are reported for $T \in \{2, 3, \ldots, 20\}$.[8] When $T = 1$, so that what is the most common environment changes once every generation, a flexible rule prevails because social learning is dysfunctional; new agents are always imitating agents who were successful for when a different aggregate environment prevailed. Finally, note that the cases of, say, $b = 0.6$ and $b = 0.4$ both involve a cycle in which the frequency with which environment 1 occurs alternates between 0.6 and 0.4. What differs between them is the starting value, which is 0.6 when $b = 0.6$ and 0.4 when $b = 0.4$.

In that the aggregate environment (specifically, the frequency of environment 1) is subject to a cycle of length $2T$, a local attractor is defined to be a cycle of length $2T$. After specifying values for $(b, k, w, T, r_1, r_0)$, the system was run until convergence was achieved, where the criterion is that the state variables between the start of one cycle and the start of the next cycle are sufficiently close.[9] The system almost always converged to a cycle of length $2T$, though there were some incidents of a longer cycle.

To gauge the societal presence of a particular rule in a social system, the proportion of agents using that rule is calculated at each level and averaged across all levels. Let $\rho(Q,h,g)$ denote the proportion of agents using rule $Q \in \{R_1, R_0, Flexible\}$ at level $h$ in generation $g$. The presence of rule $Q$ in the social system in generation $g$ is measured by $\phi(Q,g) \equiv (\frac{1}{k}) \sum_{h=1}^{k} \rho(Q,h,g)$.[10] Assume the system has converged by generation $g'$. The presence of a rule at a local attractor is then measured by $\Phi(Q) \equiv (\frac{1}{2T}) \sum_{g=g'}^{g'+2T-1} \phi(Q,g)$, which is the proportion of agents using rule $Q$ averaged over all levels for a given generation and then averaged over the $2T$ elements of a cycle. Also reported is the range of values over a steady-state cycle:

$$Range(Q) \equiv [\min\{\phi(Q,g'),\ldots,\phi(Q,g'+2T-1)\},$$
$$\max\{\phi(Q,g'),\ldots,\phi(Q,g'+2T-1)\}].$$

### 2.4.1 *Properties of Attractors*

In figures 2.1–2.3 the height of a surface is $\Phi$ (*Flexible*). Its dependence on $T$ and $b$ is depicted. Figure 2.1 is for when the system has five levels, whereas figures 2.2 and 2.3 consider systems with ten and fifteen levels, respectively. First note that these figures appear symmetric around 0.5, which indicates that where one starts a cycle is not important for the long-run properties of the system. The following property is gleaned from these figures and the results for other values of $k$.

***Property 1*** When enough new agents are predisposed to be flexible ($w$ is sufficiently close to zero), a flexible rule is a locally stable norm and a rigid rule is not. When enough new agents are predisposed to be rigid ($w$ is sufficiently close to 1), a rigid rule is a locally stable norm when an individual's environment is relatively stable ($b$ is near 0 or 1) and a flexible rule is a locally stable norm when an individual's environment is relatively volatile ($b$ is near $\frac{1}{2}$).

When there are no aggregate fluctuations (that is, when what is the most common environment does not change over time), Harrington (1999a) found that a rigid rule could easily be the prevailing norm even when all incoming agents were predisposed to be flexible. By property 1, this does not occur when what is the most

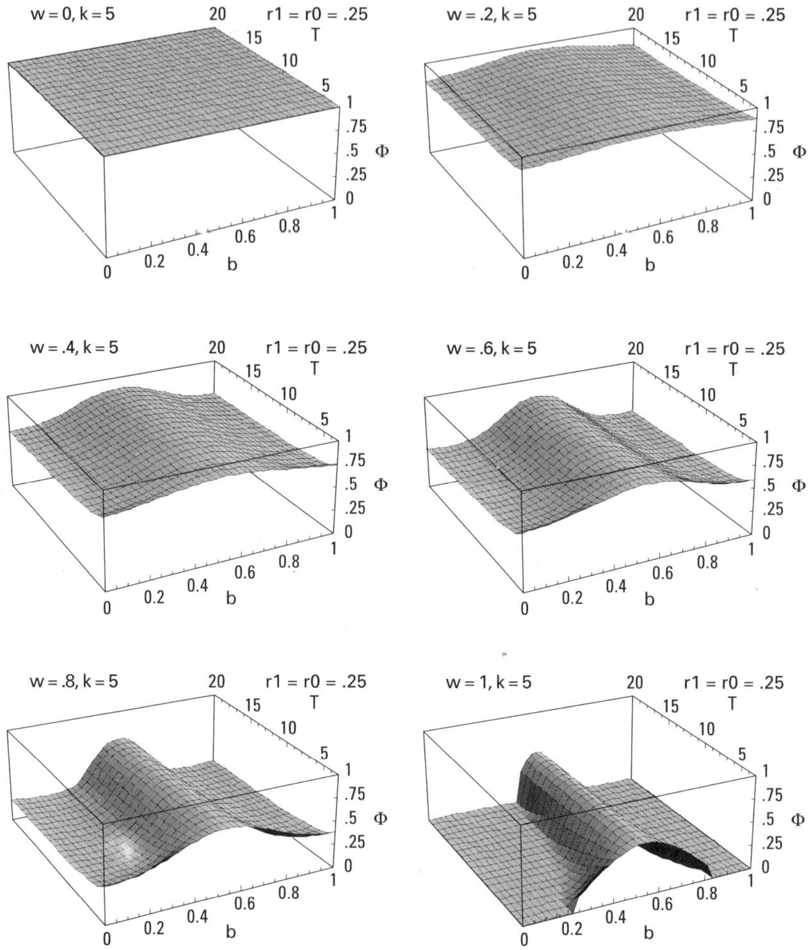


**Figure 2.1**
Average Proportion of Agents Using a Flexible Rule

common environment changes. In that case, the identity of the best rigid rule changes across generations. Hence, a rigid rule that became a social norm when, say, environment 1 was most common would be highly inadequate if environment 0 became most common. If sufficiently many new agents are biased to be flexible, a rigid rule would not survive such shocks and a flexible rule would be the locally stable norm. A necessary condition for a rigid norm to develop is that there be sufficiently many new agents whose inclination is to be rigid. Given that does hold, figures 2.1–2.3 show that it is quite

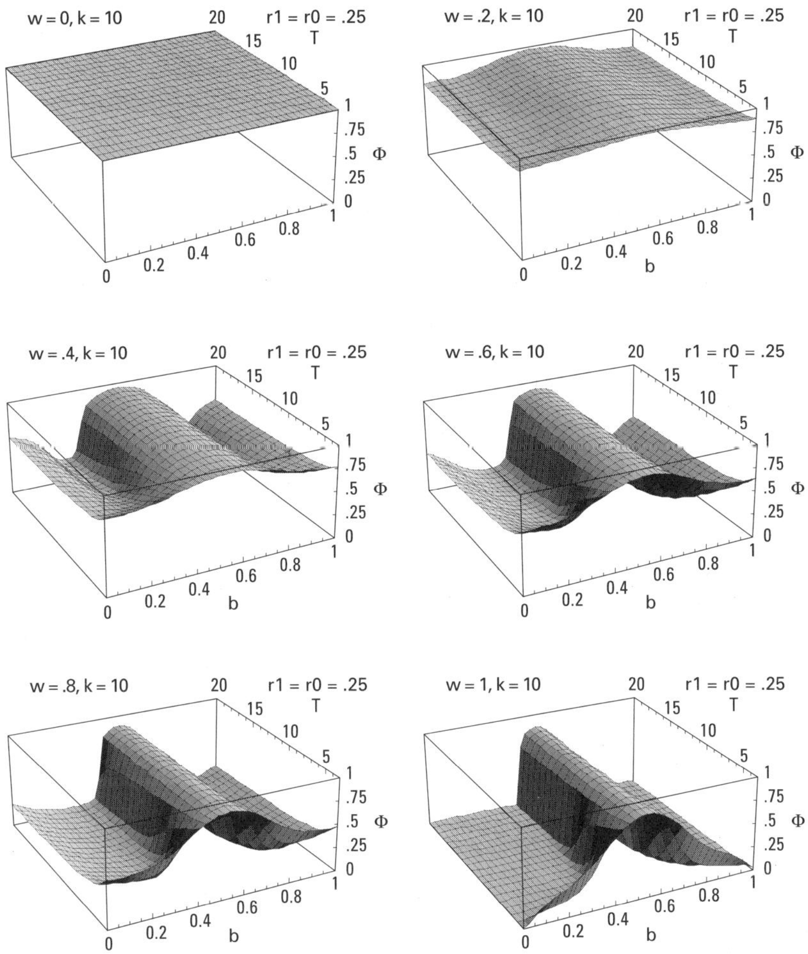


**Figure 2.2**
Average Proportion of Agents Using a Flexible Rule

common for most agents to be deploying a rigid rule, on average. Thus, a rigid norm can survive aggregate fluctuations.

What are the dynamics that allow a rule of being locked into a particular action to persist even when what is the appropriate action to be locked into changes over time? One possibility is the following. Suppose $b^g = b > \frac{1}{2}$, and further suppose that a rule of always choosing action 1 ($R_1$) is thriving. With environment 0 being relatively infrequent, those agents who use a rule of always choosing action 0 ($R_0$) do quite poorly in progressing up the hierarchy. Still,

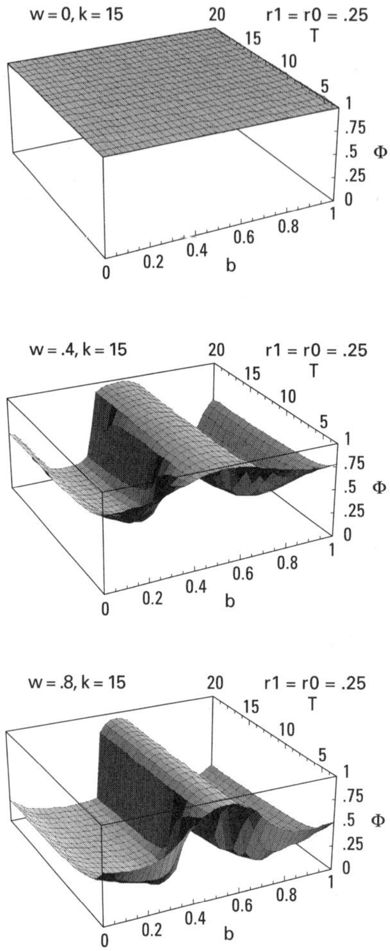


**Figure 2.3**
Average Proportion of Agents Using a Flexible Rule

there will be a latent population of such agents in that some agents at the top will either have used or look like they have used an $R_0$ rule. Some agents who use an $R_0$ rule will rise to the top because of either having always faced environment 0 or having always been matched with another agent using rule $R_0$. Some agents who use a flexible rule will rise to the top having always chosen action 0 because of having always faced environment 0. With agents who have always used action 0 as role models, some new agents will adopt an $R_0$ rule so that there are always such agents in the population. When $b^g$ switches to $1 - b$, so that the best action is action 0, one possibility is that the latent population of agents who use a $R_0$ rule thrives and ultimately dominates the set of agents at the top. In imitating them, the next generation would widely use an $R_0$ rule. However, all this does not happen.

While there is indeed a latent population of agents who use an $R_0$ rule, the latent population of agents who use a flexible rule is much larger because when environment 1 is more common, a flexible rule vastly outperforms a rule of always choosing action 0. When $b^g$ switches to $1 - b$, agents who use a flexible rule end up with a much greater share of the top level than agents who use an $R_0$ rule because, at the time of the change, their presence is proportionately so much bigger. This can be seen in figure 2.4a, which plots a cycle for $(b, k, w, T) = (0.65, 10, 0.7, 15)$. In the transitional generation (denoted generation 16), the fraction that uses an $R_1$ rule begins to decline. Even though the $R_1$ rule is quite ineffective, there are initially so many agents deploying such a rule that it has a substantive presence for two generations after the transition. During generations 16–18, the fraction using an $R_1$ rule shrinks and the fraction using a flexible rule grows (they are doing very well against agents who always play action 1). However, the proportion of agents using a flexible rule peaks in generation 18 with about half the population and steadily declines thereafter until the next large-scale change. The agents who are using a flexible rule are being replaced with agents using an $R_0$ rule. What is happening is that many of those agents who deploy a flexible rule and get to the top will have done so having always chosen action 0 because they have always faced environment 0. (Recall from section 2.3.2 the argument that selection tends to promote those flexible agents who have always faced the most common environment because they are then maximally proficient in what is most frequently the best action.) A new agent who is biased to be rigid and gets one of those agents as his role model will adopt a rule of always choosing action 0. When $w$ is close enough to 1, this results in a sizable fraction of new agents' deploying an $R_0$ rule even though almost all their role models use a flexible rule. It is this beachhead that allows rigid behavior to ultimately take over again.

This story is confirmed by examining the relationship between the average (figures 2.1–2.3) and the range (figures 2.5–2.7). When the average proportion of agents using a flexible rule is low, the range is often high. This high range reflects the large presence of flexible agents during the transitional generations and the small presence

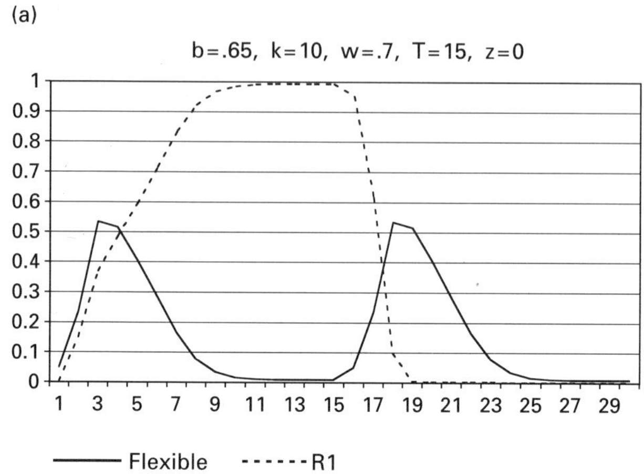


**Figure 2.4a**
Average Proportion of Agents over a Cycle

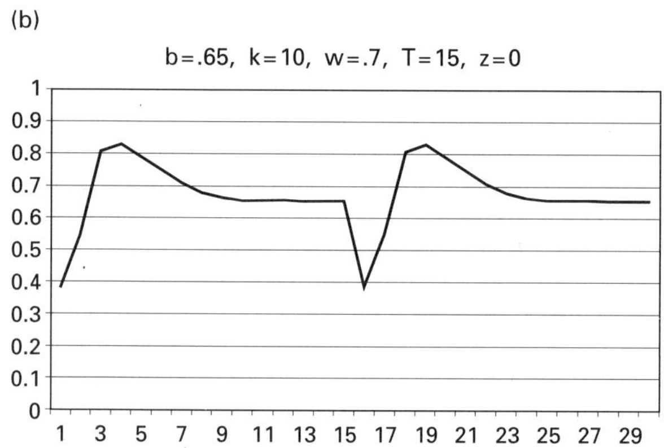


**Figure 2.4b**
Average Efficiency over a Cycle

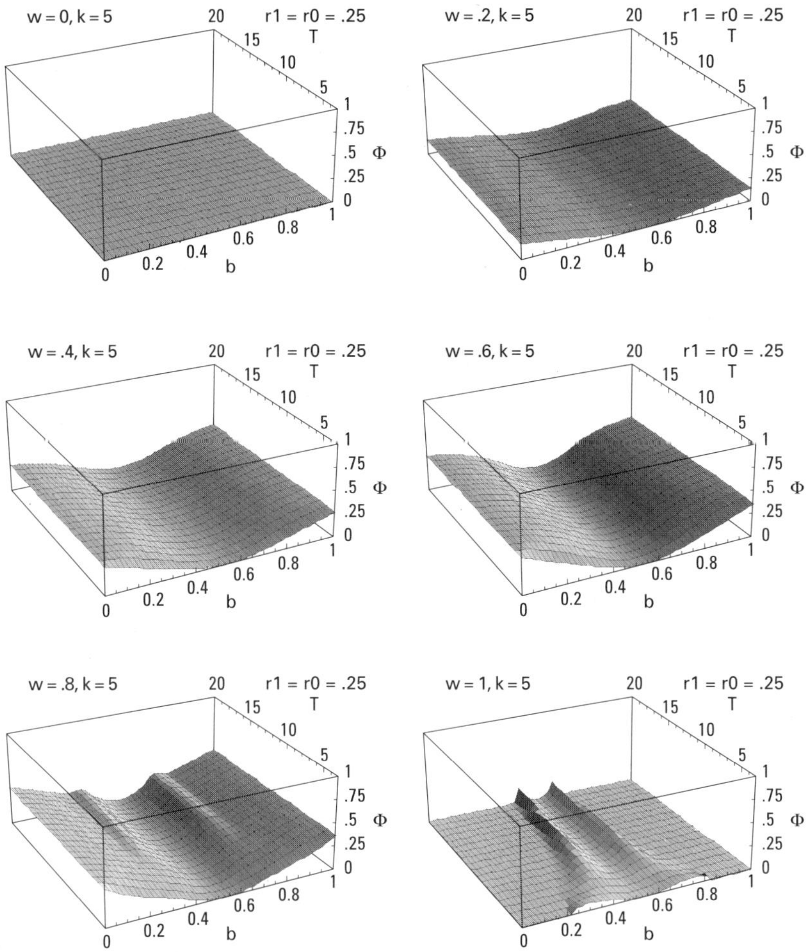


**Figure 2.5**
Range of Proportion of Agents Using a Flexible Rule

outside of that transition. This is strikingly clear when $k = 15$ and $w = 0.2$ (figures 2.3 and 2.7). The average is lowest when $b$ is between 0.15 and 0.3 (and 0.7 and 0.85) and this is also when the range is highest (thus generating these "cadillac tailfins"). This story also explains why a flexible rule prevails when a large fraction of incoming agents are predisposed to be flexible. Given a mentor who always chose action 0 (because she always faced environment 0), a large fraction of new agents will adopt a flexible rule rather than an $R_0$ rule, so flexibility begets flexibility.

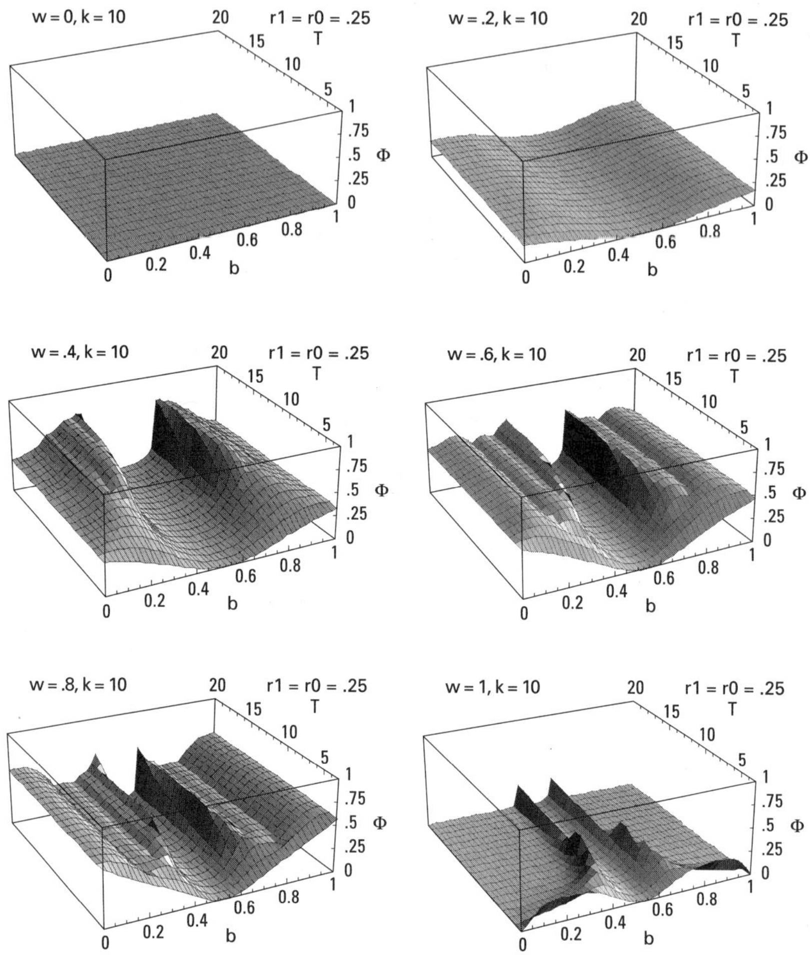


**Figure 2.6**
Range of Proportion of Agents Using a Flexible Rule

A QuickTime movie of figures 2.2, 2.3, 2.5, and 2.6 as $w$ is raised from zero to 1 is available at ⟨http://www.econ.jhu.edu/People/Harrington/Fluidity.htm⟩.

### 2.4.2 *Comparative Statics*

***Property 2*** Less frequent aggregate fluctuations and more severe aggregate fluctuations conduce a rigid rule to be a locally stable norm.

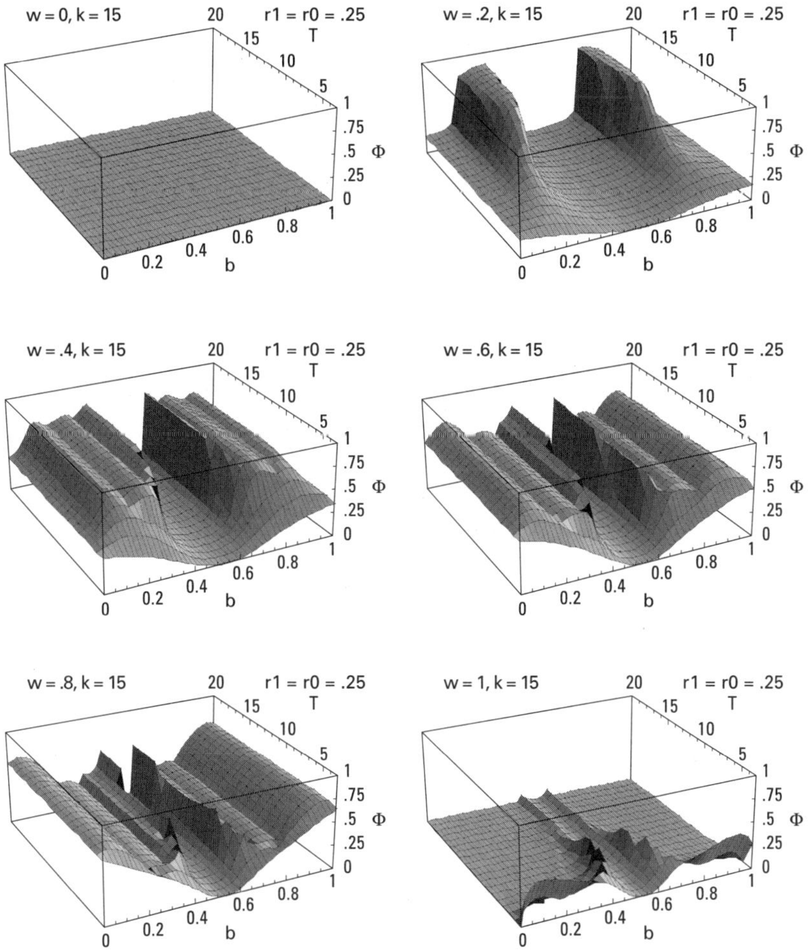


**Figure 2.7**
Range of Proportion of Agents Using a Flexible Rule

Figures 2.1–2.3 reveal that the prevalence of a rigid rule is increasing in both the size of the change, which is larger when $|b - \frac{1}{2}|$ is larger, and the infrequency of the change, which is increasing in $T$. The latter is most apparent for values of $b$ that lie at the cusp of a flexible rule being dominant and a rigid rule being dominant. For example, examine the contours around $(b, k, w) \in \{(0.4, 5, 1)(0.35, 10, 6), (0.35, 15, 0.6)\}$ that hold $b$ fixed. The reason is quite intuitive. Examination of figure 2.4a reveals that the proportion of agents using an $R_1$ rule is steadily growing with the number of generations for which environment 1 is most common. The more time until a transition, the more that agents deploying a rigid rule can grow.

A bit more interesting is the result that more severe aggregate fluctuations can lead to a prevalence of rigid norms. The prevalence of rigid behavior is not predicated upon the latent population of, say, $R_0$-using agents' thriving when the most common environment switches from 1 to 0. Rather, it is due to flexible-rule-using agents' thriving when the transition occurs and to many of those agents' getting to the top looking like they use an $R_0$ rule. A more extreme change then helps the cause of rigidity because it reduces the fidelity of a flexible rule; that is, it reduces the ability of agents who use a flexible rule and rise to the top to differentiate themselves from agents who use a rigid rule. The closer $b$ is to 1 (0), the more likely it is that flexible agents at the top will have only faced environment 1 (0) and have chosen action 1 (0) and thereby are observationally equivalent to an agent deploying a rigid rule. This means a higher fraction of new agents (who are predisposed to be rigid) adopt a rigid rule.

### 2.4.3 *Effects of Gradualism*

Thus far, the size and frequency of aggregate changes on social norms have been explored. In this section, the model is enriched to introduce a third characteristic of large-scale change—abruptness. Consider the following intertemporal path for the frequency of environment 1 over a single cycle:

$$b^g = \begin{cases} b & \text{if } g \in \{1, \ldots, T-z\} \\ b - (2b-1)\left(\dfrac{g-T+z}{1+z}\right) & \text{if } g \in \{T-z+1, \ldots, T\} \\ 1-b & \text{if } g \in \{T+1, \ldots, 2T-z\} \\ 1-b+(2b-1)\left(\dfrac{g-2T+z}{1+z}\right) & \text{if } g \in \{2T-z, \ldots, 2T\}. \end{cases}$$

This cycle repeats itself every $2T$ generations. The parameter space is now $(b, k, w, T, z)$, where $z \in \{0, 1, \ldots, T-1\}$ is the number of generations in the transition of $b^g$ from $b$ to $1-b$ (and similarly from $1-b$ to $b$). The preceding model is the special case of $z = 0$. For example, let $b = 0.8$ and $T = 10$. If $z = 1$, then a cycle has $b^g$ equaling

0.8 for nine generations, 0.5 for one generation, 0.2 for nine generations, and 0.5 for one generation. If $z = 2$, then $b^g$ equals 0.8 for eight generations, 0.6 for one generation, 0.4 for one generation, 0.2 for eight generations, 0.4 for one generation, and 0.6 for one generation. Raising $z$ then eases the transition.

I examined the dependence of $\Phi(Flexible)$ and $Range(Flexible)$ on $z \in \{0, 1, \ldots, T-1\}$ for $(b, k, w, T) \in \{0.05, 0.10, \ldots, 0.95\} \times \{5, 10, 15\} \times \{0, 0.1, \ldots, 1\} \times \{10\}$ and $(r_1, r_0) = \{(0.05, 0.05), (0.25, 0.25), (0.45, 0.45), (0.05, 0.45), (0.45, 0.05)\}$. I also considered $T \in \{5, 15\}$ and $(r_1, r_0) = (0.25, 0.25)$. The case of $(k, T) = (10, 10)$ is shown in figure 2.8 and is representative of the results. Flexible norms are more likely to develop when the transition is more gradual and less abrupt.

***Property 3*** A more abrupt transition conduces a rigid rule to be a locally stable norm.

This finding is consistent with preceding analysis, which established that more extreme changes in environmental frequency are conducive to a rigid norm. Figure 2.9 shows what a cycle looks like when $(b, k, w, T) = (0.7, 10, 0.5, 10)$ for $z \in \{0, 3, 6, 9\}$. When $z = 0$, so that the transition is maximally abrupt, the range of proportion of agents deploying a flexible rule is $[0.04, 0.65]$. When $z = 9$, so that the transition is very smooth, the range is instead $[0.67, 0.94]$ so that the minimum presence of agents using a flexible rule exceeds the maximum presence when $z = 0$.

### 2.4.4 *Efficiency of Norms*

While the model does not specify the performance of the social system (only the performance of individual agents as it pertains to their promotion within the system), some insight can be had into it if one supposes that an agent's contribution to the performance of the social system depends on the appropriateness of his action and his proficiency with that action. A flexible norm ensures that agents always respond appropriately to the environment. The cost, however, is that flexible rules involve lower proficiency. A rigid norm achieves proficiency, but then behavior may often be a poor response to the environment. Indeed, this cost could be quite substantial if the rigid norm involves an action that is infrequently a good match to the environment. In light of this trade-off, the best

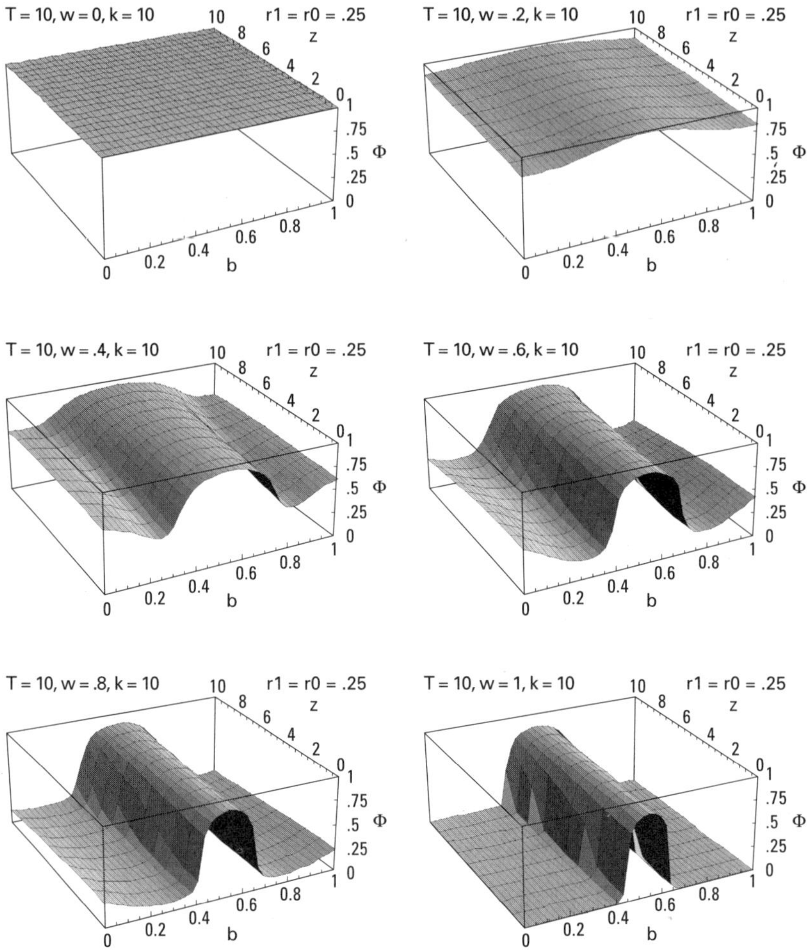


**Figure 2.8**
Average Proportion of Agents Using a Flexible Rule

solution might be to have an evolving rigid rule, where agents use a rule that is rigid in the action that is most frequently the best response to the environment. It must be evolving because what is the most common environment—and thereby what is most frequently the best response to the environment—changes over time.

The previous analysis showed that a rigid norm could persist over time, because it does evolve with the aggregate environment. However, the efficiency of a rigid norm will depend very much on how quickly it evolves. One that evolves slowly may entail extended

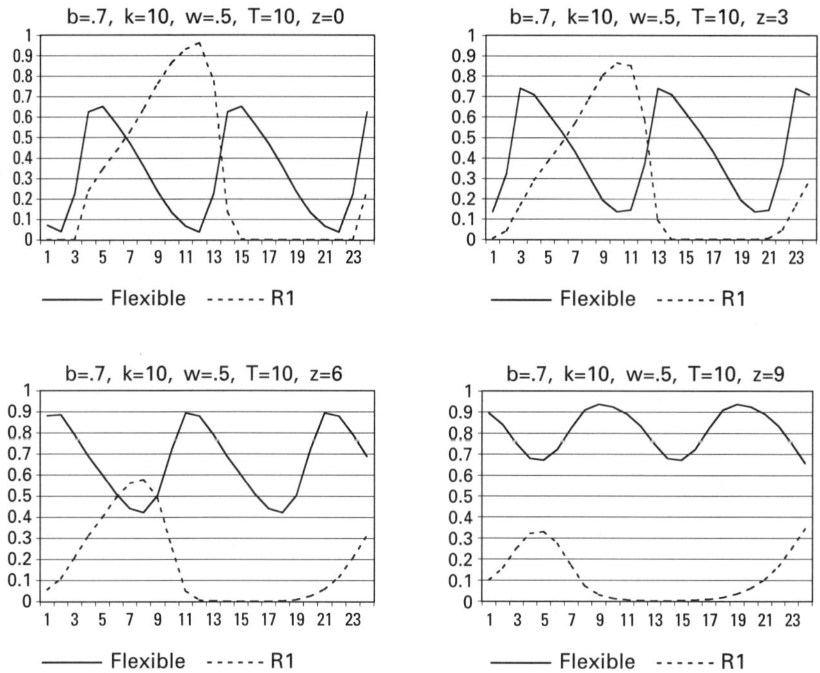


**Figure 2.9**
Average Proportion of Agents over a Cycle

periods of time in which agents are acting inappropriately for the environment at a high rate. To gain some insight into this issue, define $e^{h,g}$ as the proportion of agents at level $h$ in generation $g$ whose action matches the environment:

$$e^{h,g} = br_1^{h,g} + (1-b)r_0^{h,g} + (1 - r_1^{h,g} - r_0^{h,g}).$$

Next define $\theta(g)$ as that proportion averaged across all $k$ levels:

$$\theta(g) = \left(\frac{1}{k}\right) \sum_{h=1}^{k} e^{h,g}.$$

Finally, we define $\Theta$ to be this systemwide average after it is averaged across $2T$ generations (so that it encompasses an entire cycle):

$$\Theta = \left(\frac{1}{2T}\right) \sum_{g=g'}^{g'+2T-1} \theta(g),$$

where $g'$ is some generation for which the system has converged. $\Theta$ is said to be the *efficiency* of the system. However, recall that the measure is only the frequency with which the appropriate action was chosen; the proficiency of agents is not taken into account.

Figure 2.10 reports $\Theta$ for various values of $(b, w, T)$ where $(k, z) = (10, 0)$. Note that figure 2.10 corresponds to figure 2.2; for the same parameter values, the latter measures the presence of agents using a flexible rule, whereas the former measures the efficiency of the system. The first property to note is that efficiency can be high even if the proportion of agents using a flexible rule is not. Consider $w = 0.8$ and $b$ around 0.25 or 0.75 (the results are the same). The proportion of agents using a flexible rule is less than 0.5 and efficiency is around 0.75. This indicates that the rigid rule is evolving rather rapidly.

Next note that the efficiency of norms is nonmonotonic in the stability of the environment, as measured by $|b - \frac{1}{2}|$. Generally, efficiency is highest when the environment is very volatile ($b$ is close to $\frac{1}{2}$) or very stable ($b$ is close to 0 or 1). Since

$$\frac{\partial \Theta}{\partial b} = \left(\frac{1}{2Tk}\right) \sum_{g=g'}^{g'+2T-1} \sum_{h=1}^{k} (r_1^{h,g} - r_0^{h,g}),$$

if the population mix was fixed, then depending on the sign of $\frac{\partial \Theta}{\partial b}$, efficiency would either monotonically increase or decrease as, say, $b$ moves from $\frac{1}{2}$ to 1. Of course, the mix is not fixed and depends on the value of $b$. The nonmonotonicity follows from the property that there is a large presence of agents using flexible rules when the environment is very volatile and a large presence of agents using the appropriate rigid rule when the environment is very stable. Efficiency is lowest when the environment is moderately volatile because it allows for many agents to deploy a rigid rule but this results in the inappropriate action often being chosen, typically with a frequency of around $\min\{b, 1 - b\}$. The exception to this result is when $w = 1$ and $T$ is low (so that the aggregate environment changes rapidly), in which case efficiency is monotonically decreasing as the environment becomes more stable. This is due to the rigid rule's not evolving fast enough.

***Property 4*** Generally, the efficiency of the system is highest when the environment is very volatile ($b$ is close to $\frac{1}{2}$) or very stable ($b$ is close to 0 or 1). Efficiency is lowest when the environment is moderately volatile ($b$ is close to 0.25 or 0.75).

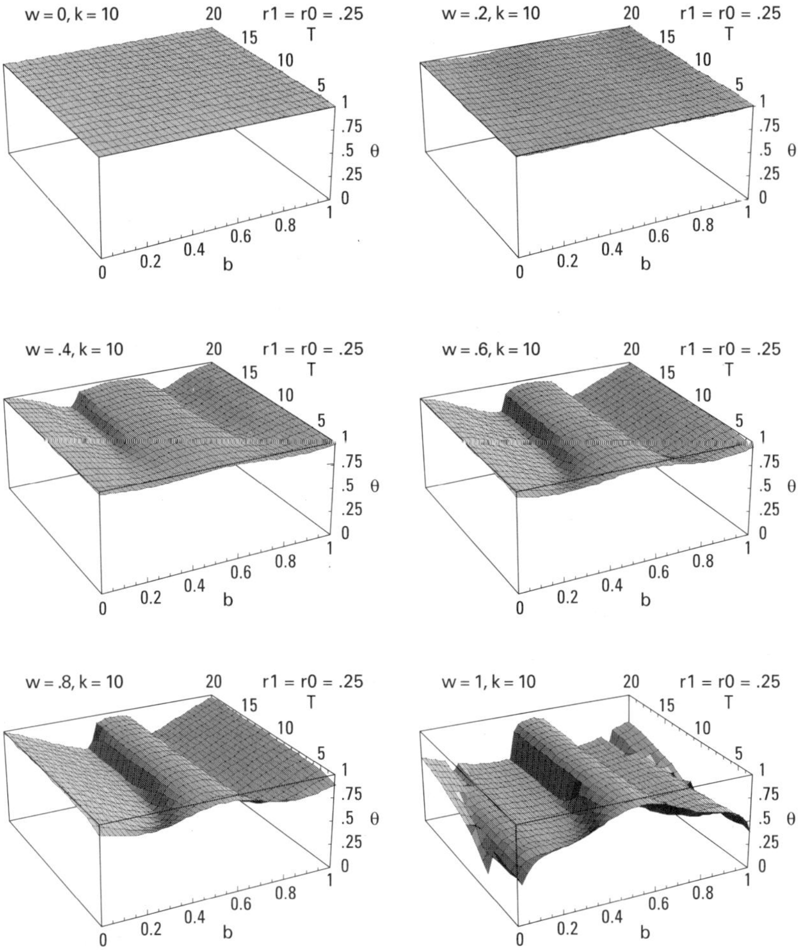


**Figure 2.10**
Average Efficiency

Figure 2.11 tracks efficiency over a cycle for various values of $b$ and $w$ with $(k, T, z) = (10, 10, 0)$. There are two distinct patterns. The first pattern occurs when the environment is sufficiently volatile and sufficiently many new agents are predisposed to be flexible; for example, $(b, w) = (0.6, 0.6)$. The efficiency of the system is quite high because of the high proportion of agents using a flexible rule. When the aggregate environment switches in generation 11, efficiency spikes up. Presumably, this is because there was a small proportion of agents using a rigid rule in the best action for generations 1–10.

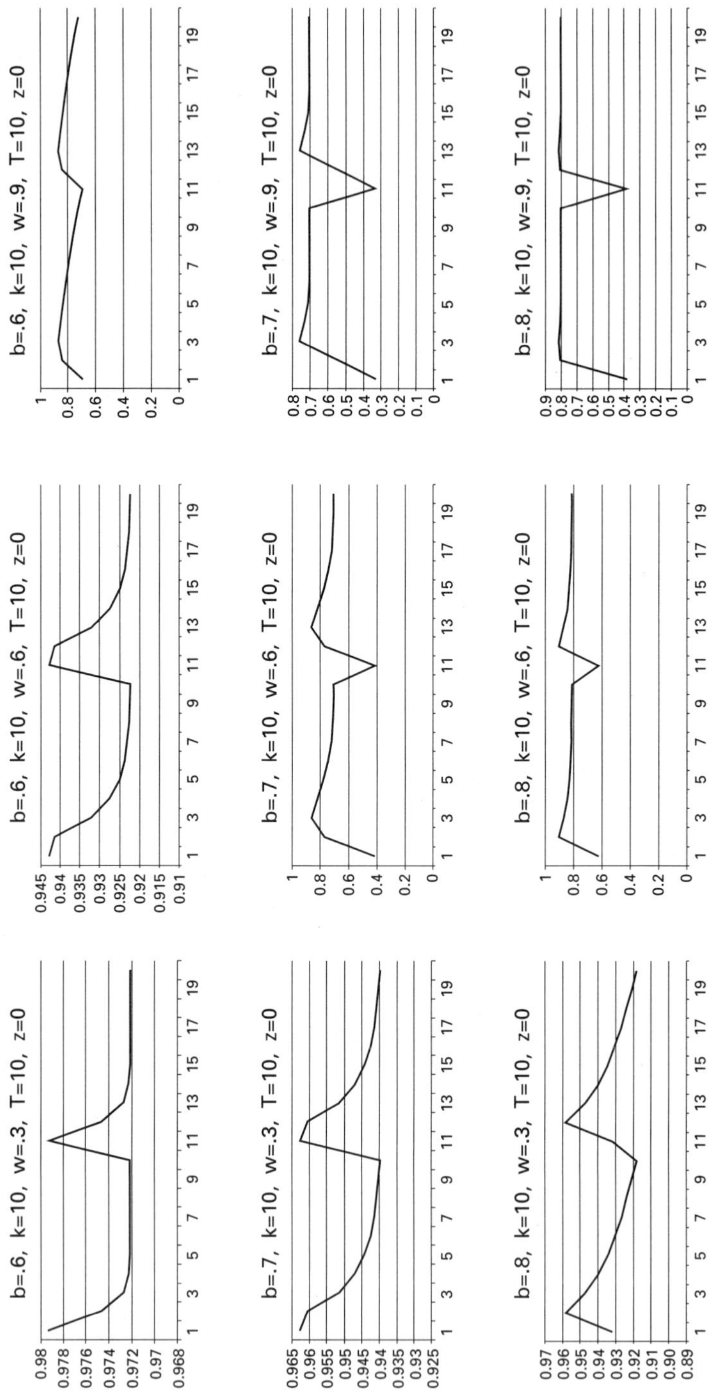


**Figure 2.11**
Average Efficiency over a Cycle

When what was the best action switches, these agents perform poorly and are replaced with agents using a flexible rule. Note that efficiency gradually declines after generation 11 as a rigid rule in what is the new best action has a small but growing presence. The second pattern occurs when the environment is relatively stable and sufficiently many new agents are predisposed to be rigid; for example, $(b, w) = (0.7, 0.6)$. Efficiency is noticeably lower because of a rigid rule's prevailing. Contrary to the first pattern, the efficiency of the system falls when what is the most common environment (and action) changes. When $(b, w) = (0.7, 0.6)$, efficiency drops from around 0.7 in generation 10 to about 0.4 in generation 11. Initially there are few flexible agents to replace these poorly equipped rigid agents, so the system is dominated by agents who most frequently choose the wrong action for the environment. As previously shown, the presence of flexible rules grows after such a switch, and this is reflected in the rise of efficiency after generation 11. However, agents deploying a flexible rule are gradually replaced with new agents who use a rule rigid in what is now the best action. At that point, efficiency falls and approaches the frequency with which that action is the best action. To more closely observe how the presence of a flexible rule corresponds with the efficiency of the system, see figure 2.4b.

## 2.5 Remarks

One of the more interesting insights is the role of those agents deploying a flexible rule in transiting the system from one rigid norm to another in response to a large-scale change. If one presumes, as modeled, that there are benefits from becoming good at one thing, then a rigid norm may be desirable. The trick is that, in response to large-scale changes, the properties of that rigid norm must adapt. There are two likely consequences if they do not. First, a rigid norm may become unstable and be replaced by a flexible norm. That is hardly disastrous and indeed may be best for certain contexts. However, for some situations, that may be less than best. Second, the social system persists with a rigid norm but one in which the action does not adapt. In that situation, the social system is periodically quite inefficient because agents are locked into the action that is inappropriate most of the time. However, the best of both worlds—specialization and adaptation to large-scale changes—can be achieved through the proper use of flexible agents. When a big change occurs, those few agents deploying a flexible rule in a population dominated by agents who are rigid (in what is now the inappropriate action) will quickly rise to the top. Some of them will have histories observationally equivalent to an agent deploying a rigid rule (in what is now the appropriate action). Those new agents who are predisposed to be rigid and have such agents as role models will hard-wire that behavior in the form of a rigid rule, and thus a new rigid norm develops.

Thinking about this issue more generally in the context of a corporation, the point is to have flexibility in promotion procedures, whereby someone who deviates from the norm but performs well in some objective sense is allowed to move up. In the model, advancement depends only on one's action, environment, and proficiency. However, in a corporation or a government, promotion is also likely to depend on the characteristics of one's superior and, in a system dominated by rigid behavior, one's superior is likely to deploy a rigid rule. It is not clear that an agent who deviates from the commonly accepted action will fare well compared to other agents who stick with the traditional action. An organizational design issue then is to put into place a structure that allows mavericks to succeed but balances this with the virtue of imitation—learning from the past experiences of others.

The force just described is not present in the model but is one I am currently attempting to encompass. The idea is to make performance depend not only on objective measures—how appropriate is one's action for the external environment and how proficient is one with that action—but also subjective measures—how well an action conforms with one's superior's notion as to what is a proper action. The twist is that the traits of one's superior are the product of selection and social learning, and thus the criteria for advancement deployed by superiors are evolving within the system. The performance criterion for advancement must then be allowed to evolve with the system. Rather than think of this criterion as something fixed and external to the model, like profit, it is instead the evolutionary product of the past.

This idea—that the criterion that determines success in a social system may itself be endogenous—has broad parallels with work on sexual selection in the evolutionary biology literature; see, for example, Andersson (1994) and Laland (1994). There it has been shown that a female preference for a male trait may emerge even if, putting that female preference aside, that trait is detrimental to the number of offspring produced. Thus, what types of traits enhance the rate of reproduction is not necessarily something exogenous (like strength, speed, smarts) but something that can evolve (perhaps to being red-headed, spectacled, and professorial!). While it is unlikely that this literature will provide any models appropriate for the evolution of social norms, it may offer some general insights that are applicable.

## Appendix

The initial population resides at the lowest level of the system and is composed of three types: rigid agents who use action 1, rigid agents who use action 0, and flexible agents. Agents accumulate a personal history as they advance through society. Though there are then many types after the population has a chance to interact with the environment, it is sufficient for our purposes to partition the population into the following five types. A hierarchy is composed of $k$ levels, and a generation is equal to the length of a single lifetime (which is $k$ periods).

$r_i^{h,g} \equiv$ proportion of the level $h$ population for generation $g$ that are rigid agents endowed with action $i$ ($R_i$), $i \in \{0, 1\}$

$f_i^{h,g} \equiv$ proportion of the level $h$ population for generation $g$ that are flexible agents who have always chosen action $i$ ($F_i$), $i \in \{0, 1\}$

$x^{h,g} \equiv$ proportion of the level $h$ population for generation $g$ that are flexible agents who have chosen both action 0 and action 1 ($F_N$).

The level $h$ generation $g$ state of the system is then $(r_1^{h,g}, f_1^{h,g}, r_0^{h,g}, f_0^{h,g}, x^{h,g})$. The initial population mix is generally assumed to satisfy: $r_1^{1,1} > 0$, $r_0^{1,1} > 0$, and $1 - r_1^{1,1} - r_0^{1,1} > 0$. Abbreviating $r_1^{1,1}$ with $r_1$ and $r_0^{1,1}$ with $r_0$, the initial condition of the system is $(r_1, r_0, b^1)$, where $b^1$ is the initial frequency with which environment 1 occurs.

Since agents do not have a history at level 1, the characterization of the dynamic process is different between level 2 and higher levels. The level 2 population is determined by the following system of equations:

$$r_1^{2,g} = (r_1^{1,g})^2 + 2r_1^{1,g}r_0^{1,g}b^g + r_1^{1,g}(1 - r_1^{1,g} - r_0^{1,g})b^g \tag{2.1}$$

$$f_1^{2,g} = b^g[(1 - r_1^{1,g} - r_0^{1,g})r_1^{1,g} + 2(1 - r_1^{1,g} - r_0^{1,g})r_0^{1,g} + (1 - r_1^{1,g} - r_0^{1,g})^2] \tag{2.2}$$

$$r_0^{2,g} = 2r_1^{1,g}r_0^{1,g}(1 - b^g) + (r_0^{1,g})^2 + r_0^{1,g}(1 - r_1^{1,g} - r_0^{1,g})(1 - b^g) \tag{2.3}$$

$$f_0^{2,g} = (1 - b^g)[2(1 - r_1^{1,g} - r_0^{1,g})r_1^{1,g} + (1 - r_1^{1,g} - r_0^{1,g})r_0^{1,g} + (1 - r_1^{1,g} - r_0^{1,g})^2] \tag{2.4}$$

$$x^{2,g} = 0. \tag{2.5}$$

The level $h+1$ population, for $h \in \{2\dots,k-1\}$, is determined by

$$r_1^{h+1,g} = (r_1^{h,g})^2 + 2r_1^{h,g}r_0^{h,g}b^g + r_1^{h,g}f_1^{h,g}b^g + 2r_1^{h,g}f_0^{h,g}b^g + 2r_1^{h,g}x^{h,g}b^g \tag{2.6}$$

$$f_1^{h+1,g} = r_1^{h,g}f_1^{h,g}b^g + 2r_0^{h,g}f_1^{h,g}b^g + (f_1^{h,g})^2b^g + 2f_1^{h,g}f_0^{h,g}b^g + 2f_1^{h,g}x^{h,g}b^g \tag{2.7}$$

$$r_0^{h+1,g} = 2r_1^{h,g}r_0^{h,g}(1 - b^g) + (r_0^{h,g})^2 + 2r_0^{h,g}f_1^{h,g}(1 - b^g) + r_0^{h,g}f_0^{h,g}(1 - b^g) + 2r_0^{h,g}x^{h,g}(1 - b^g) \tag{2.8}$$

$$f_0^{h+1,g} = 2r_1^{h,g}f_0^{h,g}(1 - b^g) + r_0^{h,g}f_0^{h,g}(1 - b^g) + 2f_1^{h,g}f_0^{h,g}(1 - b^g) + (f_0^{h,g})^2(1 - b^g) + 2f_1^{h,g}f_0^{h,g}(1 - b^g) \tag{2.9}$$

$$x^{h+1,g} = 2r_1^{h,g}f_1^{h,g}(1 - b^g) + (f_1^{h,g})^2(1 - b^g) + 2r_0^{h,g}f_0^{h,g}b^g + (f_0^{h,g})^2b^g + 2r_1^{h,g}x^{h,g}(1 - b^g) + 2r_0^{h,g}x^{h,g}b^g + 2f_1^{h,g}x^{h,g}(1 - b^g) + 2f_0^{h,g}x^{h,g}b^g + (x^{h,g})^2. \tag{2.10}$$

To see how these equations are derived, let us consider each term in (2.6). A proportion $(r_1^{h,g})^2$ of all matchings involve $R_1$s meeting, in which case an $R_1$ advances for sure. This gives us the first term in (2.6). A proportion $2r_1^{h,g}r_0^{h,g}$ of all matchings involve an $R_1$ and an $R_0$, in which case an $R_1$ advances only when the environment is 1 which occurs in a proportion $b^g$ of all such matchings, and thus we have the second term. A proportion $2r_1^{h,g}f_1^{h,g}$ of all matchings involve an $R_1$ and an $F_1$. An $R_1$ advances with probability $\frac{1}{2}$ when the environment is 1 and probability zero when the environment is 0. Since $2r_1^{h,g}f_1^{h,g}[b^g(\frac{1}{2}) + (1 - b^g)0] = r_1^{h,g}f_1^{h,g}b^g$, we have the third term. A proportion $2r_1^{h,g}f_0^{h,g}$ $(2r_1^{h,g}x^{h,g})$ of all matchings involve an $R_1$ and an

$F_0$ ($F_N$), and in those matchings $R_1$ wins for sure when the environment is 1 and loses for sure when the environment is 0. This gives us the final two terms.

Let $d_i^{h,g}$ denote the proportion of the level $h$ population for generation $g$ that have always chosen action $i$ and have faced at least one type $j$ ($\neq i$) environment. The following pair of equations determines the behavioral rules of the level 1 population of generation $g+1$:

$$r_1^{1,g+1} = w(r_1^{k,g} + f_1^{k,g}) + (1-w)d_1^{k,g} \tag{2.11}$$

$$r_0^{1,g+1} = w(r_0^{k,g} + f_0^{k,g}) + (1-w)d_0^{k,g}. \tag{2.12}$$

The complete dynamic system then involves the embedding of (2.1)–(2.10) in (2.11)–(2.12).

## Notes

This chapter has been improved by the extremely constructive comments of Scott Page and the participants of the 1997 Workshop on Social Learning and Institutions, in particular, Dilip Mookherjee and Fernando Vega-Redondo, and of the 2000 Academy of Management Meetings. I also gratefully acknowledge the very able research assistance of Jason Dulnev and Ron Taur and the financial support of the National Science Foundation under grants SES-9708910 and SES-0000649.

1. Another interpretation is that agents choose messages (for example, stances on political issues) and that consistency in one's messages (for example, with respect to a political ideology) lends advantage through enhanced credibility.

2. An equilibrium approach to these issues is examined in Harrington (1999b). Strategic behavior is shown to be a counteracting force because it results in agents' being more flexible as they approach the top level.

3. Schlesinger (1991) documents the progressive paths taken to higher office. Rosenbaum (1984) documents the fast-track feature of corporations.

4. There is presumed to be no cost to being flexible. There could be an *ex ante* cost to being flexible (for example, becoming familiar with both actions) or an *ex post* cost incurred whenever one switches actions. One way in which to model an *ex ante* cost is as follows. If a rigid agent and a flexible agent both choose the same action and have the same proficiency, then the rigid agent is promoted with probability $q \in (\frac{1}{2}, 1)$. In that the current model assumes $q = \frac{1}{2}$, this specification would seem to enhance the survivability of agents who deploy a rigid rule. In a sense, the model has an implicit *ex post* cost to being flexible in that an agent is less proficient with some actions.

5. It is shown in Harrington (1998): If $r_1^{1,g} > 0$ and $b^g > \frac{1}{2}$, then $\lim_{k \to \infty} r_1^{k,g} = 1$. The definitions of these variables are in the appendix.

6. As noted by Scott Page, this dynamic has the peculiar property that promotion may be *negatively* correlated with cumulative past performance; that is, agents whose cumulative performance is lower may be promoted at a higher rate. The argument is as follows. Promotion is based on current performance. Current performance is enhanced

through greater proficiency with action 1 (what is most frequently the best action). Proficiency with action 1 is enhanced through having chosen it more often in the past. This implies that current performance is maximized by having always chosen action 1 in the past. For the same history of environments (and where both environments are realized), cumulative past performance for an agent who always chose action 1 is lower than that of an agent whose action always matched the environment because the incremental value from choosing the best action is assumed to be infinitely larger than being more proficient with an action. We then find that agents with a history of having always chosen action 1 will (eventually) be promoted at a higher rate than agents with a history of having matched the environment even though the latter has higher past performance. This property is partly due to assuming that promotion is based only on current performance but also partly due to the simplifying assumption that choosing a better action is infinitely better than being more proficient with an action. If we made this effect finite, then eventually the past performance of rigid agents would overtake agents who deploy a flexible rule as rigid agents come to reap the benefits of investing in proficiency.

7. Actually, there are $k-1$ initial populations, because I start with an empty hierarchy. An exogenous population enters level 1 in period 1 with population mix $(r_1, r_0)$. In period 2, this cohort moves up to level 2 and a new population enters level 1. However, if $k \geq 3$, there is no level $k$ population for them to imitate so it is assumed that this new population is also exogenous with mix $(r_1, r_0)$ (though all results are robust to the mix being not too different from $(r_1, r_0)$). Come period $k$, the population that entered level 1 in period 1 will have reached level $k$, so the new population entering level 1 will have a level $k$ population to imitate. From period $k$ onward, the entering level 1 population will be endogenous because it is determined by the level $k$ population and $w$ through (2.11)–(2.12) (see the appendix).

8. Inclusion of $T = 1$ tends to obscure viewing portions of the three-dimensional surface.

9. The system is said to have converged by generation $g$ if $|r_1^{1,g} - r_1^{1,g+2T}| < 0.000001$ and $|r_0^{1,g} - r_0^{1,g+2T}| < 0.000001$, where the definitions for these variables are in the appendix.

10. Of course, $\phi(Q, g)$ is not the proportion of agents in the system using rule $Q$ because there are more agents at lower levels than at higher levels. This would argue for having a measure that gives more weight to lower levels. On the other hand, agents at higher levels have more power, so each high-level agent is equivalent to several low-level agents. Given these two countervailing forces, I chose to give all levels equal weight. I do not believe qualitative results are sensitive to the measure used.

## References

Andersson, Malte. 1994. *Sexual Selection*. Princeton, NJ: Princeton University Press.

Bala, Venkatesh, and Sanjeev Goyal. 1998. "Learning from Neighbors." *Review of Economic Studies* 65: 595–621.

Banerjee, Abhijit. 1992. "A Simple Model of Herd Behavior." *Quarterly Journal of Economics* 107: 797–817.

———. 1993. "The Economics of Rumours." *Review of Economic Studies* 60: 309–327.

Banerjee, Abhijit, and Drew Fudenberg. 1995. "Word-of-Mouth Learning." Manuscript, Harvard University.

Bergstrom, Theodore C. and Oded Stark. 1993. "How Altruism Can Prevail in an Evolutionary Environment." *American Economic Review* 83: 149–155.

Bikhchandani, Sushil, David Hirshleifer, and Ivo Welch. 1992. "A Theory of Fads, Fashion, Custom, and Cultural Change." *Journal of Political Economy* 100: 992–1026.

Bisin, Alberto, and Thierry Verdier. 2001. "The Economics of Cultural Transmission and the Dynamics of Preferences." *Journal of Economic Theory* 97 (April): 298–319.

Boyd, Robert, and Peter J. Richerson. 1985. *Culture and the Evolutionary Process*. Chicago: University of Chicago Press.

Cavalli-Sforza, Luigi L., and Marcus W. Feldman. 1981. *Cultural Transmission and Evolution: A Quantitative Approach*. Princeton, NJ: Princeton University Press.

Ellison, Glenn, and Drew Fudenberg. 1993. "Rules of Thumb for Social Learning." *Journal of Political Economy* 101: 612–643.

———. 1995. "Word-of-Mouth Communication and Social Learning." *Quarterly Journal of Economics* 110: 93–125.

Epstein, Joshua M., and Robert Axtell. 1996. *Growing Artificial Societies*. Cambridge, MA: MIT Press.

Harrington, Joseph E., Jr. 1998. "The Social Selection of Flexible and Rigid Agents." *American Economic Review* 88: 63–82.

———. 1999a. "Rigidity of Social Systems." *Journal of Political Economy* 107: 40–64.

———. 1999b. "The Equilibrium Level of Rigidity in a Hierarchy." *Games and Economic Behavior* 28: 189–202.

———. 2000. "Progressive Ambition, Electoral Selection, and the Creation of Ideologues." *Economics of Governance* 1: 13–23.

Harrison, J. Richard, and Glenn R. Carroll. 1991. "Keeping the Faith: A Model of Cultural Transmission in Formal Organizations." *Administrative Science Quarterly* 36: 552–582.

Kirman, Alan. 1993. "Ants, Rationality, and Recruitment." *Quarterly Journal of Economics* 108: 137–156.

Laland, Kevin N. 1994. "Sexual Selection with a Culturally Transmitted Mating Preference." *Theoretical Population Biology* 45: 1–15.

Rhode, Paul, and Mark Stegeman. 2001. "Non-Nash Equilibria of Darwinian Dynamics with Applications to Duopoly." *International Journal of Industrial Organization* 19: 415–453.

Rosenbaum, James E. 1984. *Career Mobility in a Corporate Hierarchy*. Orlando, FL: Academic Press.

Schlesinger, Joseph A. 1991. *Political Parties and the Winning of Office*. Ann Arbor, MI: University of Michigan Press.

Smith, Lones, and Peter Sørensen. 1996. "Rational Social Learning with Random Sampling." Manuscript, Massachusetts Institute of Technology.

Vega-Redondo, Fernando. 1993. "Competition and Culture in an Evolutionary Process of Equilibrium Selection: A Simple Example." *Games and Economic Behavior* 5: 618–631.

———. 2000. "Unfolding Social Hierarchies." *Journal of Economic Theory* 90: 177–203.

# 3 Learning, Central Bank Independence, and the Politics of Excess Foreign Returns

Jude C. Hays and Diana Richards

## 3.1 Introduction

When applied to international financial markets, the rational expectations paradigm implies that forward exchange rates will be unbiased predictors of future spot exchange rates. However, forward rates are in fact biased predictors of future spot rates, and consequently there are excess returns on foreign deposits relative to domestic deposits (Fama 1984; Lewis 1989; 1995; Evans and Lewis 1995; Isard 1995; Hallwood and MacDonald 1994). Many explanations have been put forth to account for what Lewis (1995) has called the "predictable excess return puzzle." One promising line of research focuses on the role of learning. For example, Lewis (1989) employs a model where currency traders use Bayes' law to learn about a shift in U.S. money demand. But these learning approaches are "institution-free" in that they do not consider how the learning process differs across institutional contexts.

This omission is problematic given the observed relations between political institutions and macroeconomic performance (Freeman 1989; Crepaz 1996; Garrett 1998). For example, central bank independence has been linked to lower inflation and lower money market volatility (Alesina 1988; Alesina and Summers 1993). If learning about money market equilibria is a cause of excess returns, then the institutional arrangements of the central bank should be related to the magnitude of excess returns. More specifically, combining the literature on learning and the "predictable excess return puzzle" with the political economy of money market volatility, one might expect greater excess returns for countries with dependent central banks.

However, a cross-national comparison of previously published regression results shows that excess returns are greater for countries with independent central banks. Politics seems to matter, but in an unexpected way. In this chapter, we present a model to explain this empirical puzzle. Like Lewis (1989), the agents in our model use Bayesian updating to learn about a shift in the money market equilibrium and thus are rational learners. We focus our attention on two countries over the period 1975–1990: the United Kingdom, with a highly dependent central bank, and Germany, with an independent central bank. We use a computational approach that allows us to take empirically estimated parameters from our two cases and generate "experimental data" by repeating the dynamics of the learning process for many separate trials. By doing this, we can examine whether there is a tendency in the aggregate for learning to generate excess foreign returns after a shift in monetary policy and how the learning processes differ across institutional contexts. A computational approach provides a relatively simple way to examine the tendencies of learning dynamics in a stochastic environment.[1]

## 3.2 Learning, Excess Returns, and Central Bank Independence

Empirical research has shown that there are predictable excess returns on foreign deposits. This means that the expected return from making a foreign deposit and then converting the proceeds back into the domestic currency is different from zero. Assuming that investors will arbitrage away profitable opportunities, this fact implies that they either demand time-varying risk premia or make systematic forecast errors. To outline why this is true, we need to consider the relation between forward exchange rates and spot exchange rates (e.g., Hallwood and MacDonald 1994, chs. 3 and 11). Forward exchange rates are prices for one currency in terms of another that are agreed upon today for delivery at some time in the future; spot exchange rates are prices for immediate currency purchases. If currency markets are informationally efficient and traders are risk-neutral, then forward exchange rates should be unbiased predictors of future spot exchange rates, and forward premia, which are defined as the difference between log forward exchange rates and log spot rates, should be unbiased predictors of future changes in exchange rates.

Buying and selling in forward exchange markets causes forward rates to equal expected future spot rates. Denote the log of the time $t$ forward rate for currency to be delivered at time $t+k$ as $f_{t,t+k}$

and the log of the time $t+k$ spot rate as $s_{t+k}$. Speculation in forward exchange markets ensures that

$$f_{t,t+k} = E_t s_{t+k}, \tag{3.1}$$

where $E$ is the expectations operator and $E_t$ is the time $t$ expectation. If the equality in (3.1) does not hold, for example, if the forward rate is less than the expected future spot rate, traders will buy foreign currency forward expecting to sell it at a higher price in the future.

If the expectations in (3.1) are rational and fully informed in the sense that they incorporate all the available information, then the forecast errors should be independent, identically distributed, and orthogonal to the information set:

$$s_{t+k} = E_t s_{t+k} + \varepsilon_{t+k}. \tag{3.2}$$

After substituting (3.1) into (3.2), we have

$$s_{t+k} = f_{t,t+k} + \varepsilon_{t+k}. \tag{3.3}$$

Finally, subtracting the current spot rate from both sides of (3.3) gives

$$\Delta s_{t+k} = (f_{t,t+k} - s_t) + \varepsilon_{t+k}. \tag{3.4}$$

Equation (3.4) says that the forward premium should be an unbiased predictor of future changes in the spot exchange rate. However, when Fama (1984) regressed realized changes in US$ exchange rates on the forward premia for nine different countries, he found overwhelming evidence against the theoretical presumption of unbiasedness. The condition that forward premia are unbiased predictors of future changes in exchange rates implies that the regression of realized changes in exchange rates on forward premia, namely,

$$\Delta s_{t+k} = \alpha + \beta(f_{t,t+k} - s_t) + \varepsilon_{t+k} \tag{3.5}$$

should have an estimate of $\beta = 1$. Yet, in each of the nine currency markets Fama examined, the estimates of $\beta$ were significantly different from 1 and negative. Lewis (1995) has called this finding of negative beta coefficients, which implies predictable excess returns, the Fama result.

The Fama result is robust across subsamples, currencies, and forecast horizons. In their review of foreign exchange anomalies, Froot and Thaler (1990) report that the average beta coefficient of 75 published estimates was $-0.88$. More recent studies, for example

Cavaglia, Verschoor, and Wolff (1994), provide similar results. Table 3.1 combines their results with the results of Fama (1984) for one, three, six, and twelve month US$ forward exchange rates. Thirty-three of the thirty-six beta estimates are negative, and the mean estimate is −3.73.

To see why the Fama result implies excess returns, consider first the covered interest parity condition (CIP), which equates the forward premium and the interest rate differential.[2] Let $i_t$ denote the time $t$ domestic interest rate on a $k$-period deposit and $i_t^*$ denote the interest rate on an equivalent foreign deposit at time $t$:

$$i_t - i_t^* = f_{t,t+k} - s_t. \tag{3.6}$$

If forward premia are unbiased predictors of future changes in exchange rates, then CIP implies that interest rate differentials are also unbiased predictors of future changes in exchanges rates. Assuming $k = 1$, the CIP condition allows (3.5) to be rewritten as

$$\Delta s_{t+1} = \alpha + \beta(i_t - i_t^*) + \varepsilon_{t+1} \tag{3.7}$$

or, after subtracting $(i_t - i_t^*)$ from both sides of (3.7),

$$i_t^* - i_t + \Delta s_{t+1} = \alpha + (\beta - 1)(i_t - i_t^*) + \varepsilon_{t+1}. \tag{3.8}$$

The left-hand side of (3.8) is the time $t+1$ return on investing in a foreign deposit. When the conditions $\alpha = 0$, $\beta = 1$ do not hold, there are predictable excess returns. Consider the simplest case where $\alpha, \beta = 0$. Under these circumstances, the expected change in the exchange rate is zero and the predictable component of the $t+1$ excess return is simply the time $t$ interest differential. If the interest rate on a foreign deposit is greater than the interest rate on a domestic deposit, it will be profitable to exchange domestic currency for foreign currency, invest in a foreign deposit, and then convert the return back into the domestic currency.

Why are there excess returns in international asset markets? One possibility is that there is a time-varying risk premium. If the risk premium on a domestic deposit rises with the interest rate differential, then $\beta < 1$. Another possibility, which is the focus of this chapter, is that traders make systematic forecasting errors. If the error term in (3.7) is negatively correlated with the interest rate differential, then $\beta < 1$. Learning can cause this to happen.[3] According to Lewis (1989), the market's underprediction of the dollar's strength

**Table 3.1**
Forward Discount Bias, $\Delta s_{t+k} = \alpha + \beta(f_{t,t+k} - s_t) + \varepsilon_{t+k}$

| US$ Exchange Rate | Term ($k$) | Dates | Beta Coefficient |
|---|---|---|---|
| Belgian franc | 1-month | 8/31/73–12/10/82 | −1.58 |
| Belgian franc | 3-month | 1/01/86–12/01/90 | −4.20 |
| Belgian franc | 6-month | 1/01/86–12/01/90 | −6.10 |
| Belgian franc | 12-month | 1/01/86–12/01/90 | −6.30 |
| Canadian dollar | 1-month | 8/31/73–12/10/82 | −0.87 |
| Canadian dollar | 3-month | 1/01/86–12/01/90 | 0.91 |
| Canadian dollar | 6-month | 1/01/86–12/01/90 | 0.86 |
| Canadian dollar | 12-month | 1/01/86–12/01/90 | 1.46 |
| French franc | 1-month | 8/31/73–12/10/82 | −0.87 |
| French franc | 3-month | 1/01/86–12/01/90 | −3.43 |
| French franc | 6-month | 1/01/86–12/01/90 | −2.80 |
| French franc | 12-month | 1/01/86–12/01/90 | −2.23 |
| Italian lira | 1-month | 8/31/73–12/10/82 | −0.51 |
| Italian lira | 3-month | 1/01/86–12/01/90 | −5.17 |
| Italian lira | 6-month | 1/01/86–12/01/90 | −4.81 |
| Italian lira | 12-month | 1/01/86–12/01/90 | −4.00 |
| Dutch guilder | 1-month | 8/31/73–12/10/82 | −1.43 |
| Dutch guilder | 3-month | 1/01/86–12/01/90 | −7.00 |
| Dutch guilder | 6-month | 1/01/86–12/01/90 | −6.24 |
| Dutch guilder | 12-month | 1/01/86–12/01/90 | −3.11 |
| British pound | 1-month | 8/31/73–12/10/82 | −0.90 |
| British pound | 3-month | 1/01/86–12/01/90 | −1.12 |
| British pound | 6-month | 1/01/86–12/01/90 | −2.58 |
| British pound | 12-month | 1/01/86–12/01/90 | −5.45 |
| German mark | 1-month | 8/31/73–12/10/82 | −1.32 |
| German mark | 3-month | 1/01/86–12/01/90 | −6.18 |
| German mark | 6-month | 1/01/86–12/01/90 | −5.64 |
| German mark | 12-month | 1/01/86–12/01/90 | −7.24 |
| Japanese yen | 1-month | 8/31/73–12/10/82 | −0.29 |
| Japanese yen | 3-month | 1/01/86–12/01/90 | −9.66 |
| Japanese yen | 6-month | 1/01/86–12/01/90 | −8.42 |
| Japanese yen | 12-month | 1/01/86–12/01/90 | −9.52 |
| Swiss franc | 1-month | 8/31/73–12/10/82 | −1.14 |
| Swiss franc | 3-month | 1/01/86–12/01/90 | −5.54 |
| Swiss franc | 6-month | 1/01/86–12/01/90 | −3.35 |
| Swiss franc | 12-month | 1/01/86–12/01/90 | −8.66 |

*Sources:* Fama (1984, table 2); Cavaglia et al. (1994, table 4).

from 1980 to 1985 was due to learning about a shift to a more contractionary monetary equilibrium. When agents do not anticipate shifts in economic policy, then they must learn about changes as information inconsistent with their expectations becomes available. If learning about money market equilibria is a cause of excess returns, then institutional arrangements affecting the extent of central bank independence should be related to excess returns.

Institutional arrangements have long been known to play a role in the stability of a country's money market. In particular, the degree of central bank independence is seen as a crucial link in the volatility of this market as it mediates both electoral and partisan politics. For example, according to traditional opportunistic models of monetary policy, where politicians are only motivated by reelection rather than their own partisan preferences, incumbents have an incentive to expand the money supply prior to an election and to contract it shortly after (Nordhaus 1975; Tufte 1978). In more recent extensions of this work, politicians expand the money supply prior to an election to show their competence and thus gain reelection (Persson and Tabellini 1990). Partisan politics also can be a source of volatility in money markets. According to both traditional and rational partisan models, left-wing governments prefer more expansionary monetary policy because it produces lower levels of unemployment, while right-wing governments prefer more contractionary monetary policy because it produces lower inflation (Hibbs 1977; Alesina 1988). Thus when institutional arrangements give politicians more control over the supply of money, both electoral cycles and changes in the partisan composition of the government are expected to produce more volatility in monetary policy.

Combining the research on learning with the research on central bank independence, one might expect greater excess returns for countries with dependent central banks. However, the opposite is true; excess returns are higher for countries with independent central banks. Alesina (1988) ranks the central banks of the nine countries in Fama's study on a scale from 1 to 4. Using this ranking to sort the currencies of table 3.1 according to central bank independence, we find that average beta coefficient is much lower (−5.58) for the countries with independent central banks than for the countries with dependent central banks (−2.81).[4]

How likely is it that this relation is due to the impact that central bank independence has on learning? As a quick plausibility check,

**Table 3.2**
Survey Expectations Bias, $\Delta s_{t+k} = \alpha + \beta \Delta s^{e}_{t,t+k} + \varepsilon_{t+k}$, February 1988–February 1991

| US$ Exchange Rate | Term ($k$) | Beta Coefficient |
|---|---|---|
| Belgian franc | 3-month | −0.01 |
| Belgian franc | 12-month | −0.42 |
| Canadian dollar | 3-month | 0.10 |
| Canadian dollar | 12-month | −0.56 |
| French franc | 3-month | 0.12 |
| French franc | 12-month | −0.40 |
| Italian lira | 3-month | 0.04 |
| Italian lira | 12-month | −0.43 |
| Dutch guilder | 3-month | −0.29 |
| Dutch guilder | 12-month | 0.47 |
| British pound | 3-month | −1.80 |
| British pound | 12-month | −1.37 |
| German mark | 3-month | −0.64 |
| German mark | 12-month | −0.45 |
| Japanese yen | 3-month | −1.09 |
| Japanese yen | 12-month | −1.17 |
| Swiss franc | 3-month | −1.03 |
| Swiss franc | 12-month | −0.89 |

*Source:* Chinn and Frankel (1994, table A1).

we can examine the expectational biases across the different markets. If the relation is partly due to learning, then expectational errors should be higher on average for countries with independent central banks. Table 3.2 presents the results of Chinn and Frankel (1994) who regressed observed changes in exchange rates on expected changes as measured by survey responses. Indeed, the size of the expectations bias seems to be related to central bank independence. In table 3.3 we present the average beta coefficients as measures of the forward and expectations biases respectively for countries with independent and dependent central banks.

One way that the impact of electoral and partisan politics on money markets has been demonstrated empirically is by showing the effects of central bank independence on inflation. Countries with independent central banks experience lower average inflation and lower variance in inflation rates than countries with dependent central banks (Alesina and Summers 1993). Figure 3.1 shows the empirical distributions of the logged changes in British-American and

**Table 3.3**
Central Bank Independence, Expectations and Excess Returns

| Central Bank | Average Beta Coefficient | |
|---|---|---|
| | Forward Discount | Survey Expectations |
| Dependent (Belgium, Canada, France, Italy, Netherlands, U.K.) | −2.81 | −0.38 |
| Independent (Germany, Japan, Switzerland) | −5.58 | −0.88 |

German-American money supplies for the period 1975 to 1990. Consistent with previous findings, the United Kingdom shows both a higher mean change in the relative money supply (0.449) and a greater variance (0.302) in changes than Germany, which has a mean change of −0.150 and a variance of 0.249.

If agents had to learn the means of these distributions, the task would be easier in the case of Germany because its relatively low variance makes the noise to signal ratio smaller. But this conclusion is based on the assumption that the data is generated by a single monetary regime. Because of the possibility of multiple regimes, we will refer to figures 3.1a and 3.1b as the unconditional distributions for our two cases. However, high unconditional variance may be caused by switching between multiple monetary regimes, which is affected by partisan and electoral politics (Freeman, Hays, and Stix 2000). Multiple monetary regimes imply very different learning dynamics. If high unconditional variance is caused by distinct and thus readily identifiable monetary regimes, learning may be easier in these cases.

Indeed, there is evidence of two monetary regimes: a contractionary regime and an expansionary regime, with a shift to the more expansionary regime occurring *circa* January 1987 in both cases (see figures in the appendix). We identify these regimes by estimating Markov regime-switching models using the data from figure 3.1 (details in appendix). For the United Kingdom, the ratio of British money to American money increases at an average of 0.252 percent per month in the contractionary regime and increases at 0.95 percent per month in the expansionary regime. For Germany, the ratio of German to American money decreases at 0.251 percent per month in the contractionary regime and increases at 0.10 percent per month in the expansionary regime.

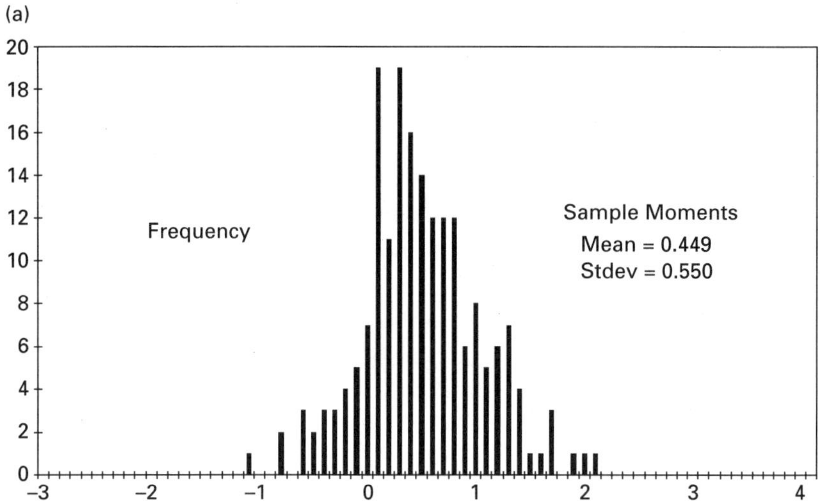


**Figure 3.1a**
Empirical Distribution of Log Changes in British-American Money Supply, 1975–1990

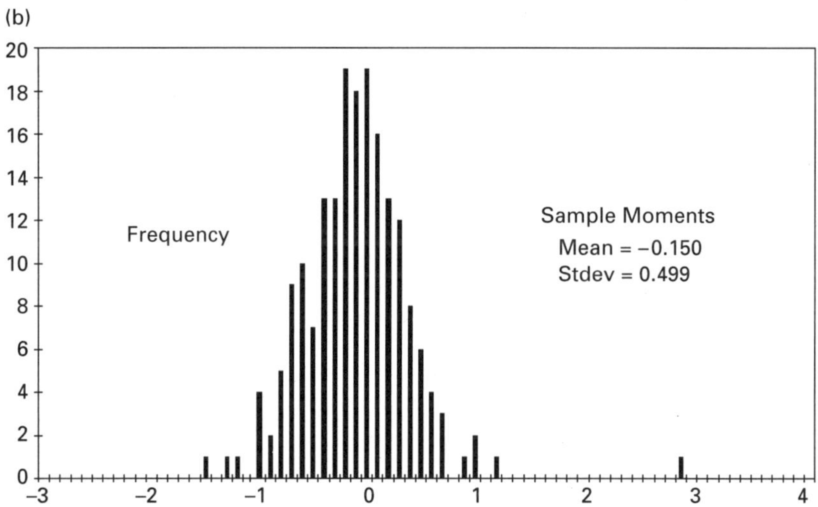


**Figure 3.1b**
Empirical Distribution of Log Changes in German-American Money Supply, 1975–1990

These results are summarized visually in figure 3.2, which shows the probability density functions of the two monetary regimes for the United Kingdom and Germany. While it is true that the unconditional variance of the change in relative money supplies is greater for the United Kingdom than for Germany (figures 3.1a and 3.1b), the two separate regimes underlying the British-American distribution are very distinct, as seen by the large difference in means. For example, the probability of observing a change in the relative money supplies in the contractionary regime that is greater than or equal to the expected change in the expansionary regime is extremely small at less than .07 (region A in figure 3.2a). For Germany, on the other hand, the probability of observing changes in the contractionary regime that are greater than or equal to the expected change in the expansionary regime is greater than .25 (region B in figure 3.2b).

If agents are aware of the characteristics of the two regimes, then one may hypothesize that learning would be much faster in the case of the United Kingdom and therefore excess returns would be smaller. However, large regime shifts also result in high *initial* excess returns. Therefore, the impact of regime switching on average excess returns is still uncertain. To more fully investigate the impact of learning dynamics on excess returns in the two institutional contexts, we turn to a more rigorous theoretical model.

### 3.3 The Model

We start with a two-country money market. Let $m^*$ and $m$ denote the log of the foreign and domestic money supplies, respectively, and $p^*$ and $p$ denote the log of the foreign and domestic price levels. For the sake of parsimony, we constrain the income elasticity to be zero,[5] so that

$$\Delta(m^* - m)_t + \Delta(p - p^*)_t = \theta\Delta(i - i^*)_t, \tag{3.9}$$

where $\theta$ is interest semielasticity of money demand. The change in the supply of money is

$$\Delta(m - m^*)_t = \mu + \sigma\varepsilon_t, \tag{3.10}$$

where $\mu$ is the mean change in the money supply, $\sigma$ is the volatility in monetary policy, and the errors $\varepsilon_t \sim N(0, 1)$. The equilibrium relative price level is determined by an exponentially weighted average of present and future money supplies (Mussa 1982):

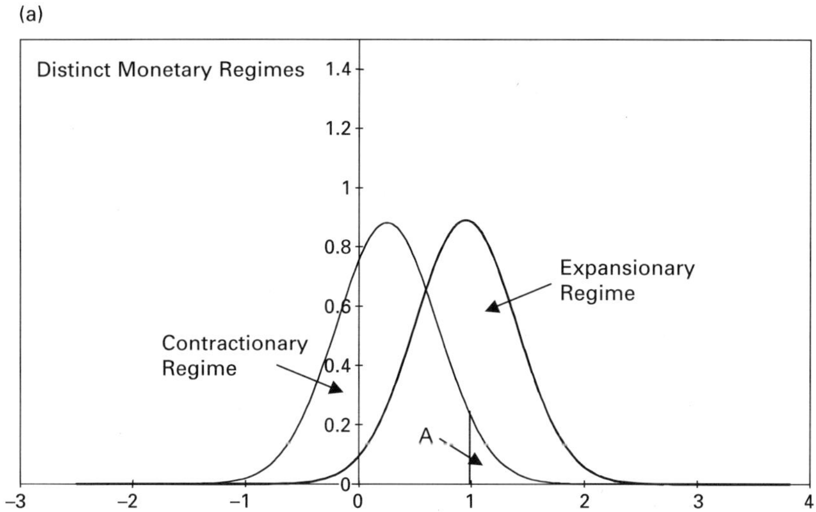


**Figure 3.2a**
Probability Density Functions for the Monetary Regimes (U.K.)

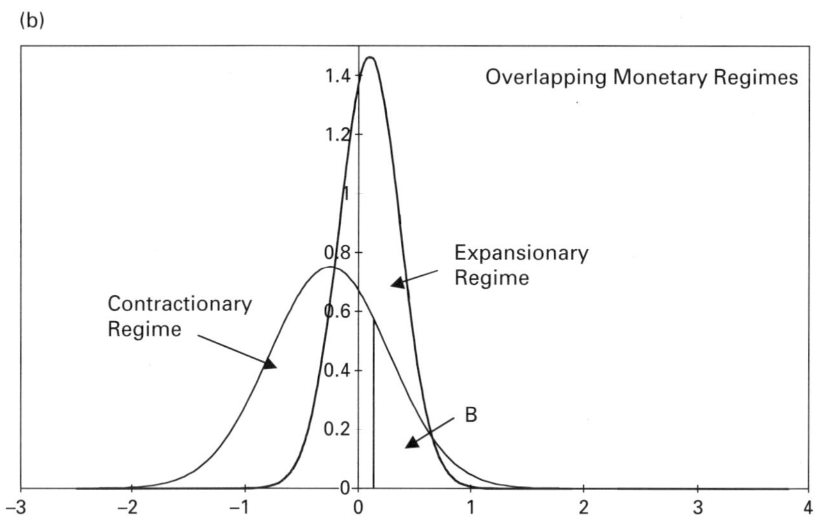


**Figure 3.2b**
Probability Density Functions for the Monetary Regimes (Germany)

$$(\bar{p} - \bar{p}^*)_t = \frac{1}{1+\theta} \sum_{k=0}^{\infty} \left( \frac{\theta}{1+\theta} \right)^k E_t(m - m^*)_{t+k}. \tag{3.11}$$

Equation (3.11) expands to

$$(\bar{p} - \bar{p}^*)_t = \frac{1}{1+\theta} \left[ (m - m^*)_t + \sum_{k=1}^{\infty} \left( \frac{\theta}{1+\theta} \right)^k (m - m^*)_t + \sum_{k=1}^{\infty} \left( \frac{\theta}{1+\theta} \right)^k k \cdot E_t \Delta (m - m^*)_{t+k} \right]. \tag{3.12}$$

Collapsing the two infinite series and substituting $\mu = E\Delta(m - m^*)$ gives

$$(\bar{p} - \bar{p}^*)_t = (m - m^*)_t + \theta\mu. \tag{3.13}$$

In our model there are two monetary regimes, which we label $r \in \{c, e\}$ for contractionary and expansionary. Agents are not certain about the current monetary regime and therefore assign a probability to each state, denoted $P_{c,t}$ and $P_{e,t}$ for the probability of being in a contractionary or expansionary regime, respectively. Using the probabilities, we can rewrite (3.13) as

$$(\bar{p} - \bar{p}^*)_t = (m - m^*)_t + \theta[P_{c,t}\mu_c + P_{e,t}\mu_e]. \tag{3.14}$$

We assume that prices and the exchange rate are sticky. Mussa's (1982) price adjustment rule gives

$$\Delta(p - p^*)_t = \Delta(\bar{p} - \bar{p}^*)_t + \Pi[(\bar{p} - \bar{p}^*)_{t-1} - (p - p^*)_{t-1}]. \tag{3.15}$$

The first term in (3.15) keeps relative prices from diverging from their expected equilibrium path; the second term drives the relative price level toward its expected equilibrium level at the exponential rate $\Pi$. In the long term, purchasing price parity (PPP) is assumed to hold; therefore the equilibrium exchange rate is equal to the equilibrium price level:

$$\bar{s}_t = (\bar{p} - \bar{p}^*)_t. \tag{3.16}$$

The adjustment of exchange rate gives

$$\Delta s_t = \Delta \bar{s}_t + \phi(\bar{s} - s)_{t-1}, \tag{3.17}$$

where $\phi$ is the rate at which exchange rates adjust. In sections 3.4 and 3.5, we explore the effects of learning on excess returns given a shift in monetary regime using simulations based on equations (3.9)–(3.17).

## 3.4 The Simulation

The simulation closely follows the model outlined in section 3.3. Market agents begin by believing they are in a contractionary monetary regime (with known mean and variance), although the regime has switched to a expansionary monetary regime that has a different mean and variance (as in figure 3.2). Agents must learn the "true" monetary regime through their observations of changes in the money supply, which consist of normally distributed random draws, $z_t$, where $z_t \sim N(\mu_c, \sigma_c)$ under a contractionary regime and $z_t \sim N(\mu_e, \sigma_e)$ under an expansionary regime (figure 3.2). The probability of being in a contractionary regime is updated according to Bayes' law:

$$P_{c,t+1} = \frac{P_{c,t} \cdot P(r = c \mid z_t)}{P_{c,t} \cdot P(r = c \mid z_t) + P_{e,t} \cdot P(r = e \mid z_t)}. \tag{3.18}$$

We are interested in the aggregate tendency of this learning process, in particular, the extent to which it generates excess foreign returns and, if so, how the learning process differs across the two cases.

The algorithm of the program is as follows.[6] Parameters were set based on empirically estimated values, including the estimates from our Markov-switching models, as summarized in table 3.4 (details in

**Table 3.4**
Estimated Simulation Parameters

| Parameters | U.K. | Germany |
|---|---|---|
| $\theta$ | 1.911 | 2.282 |
| $\phi$ | 0.014 | 0.009 |
| $\Pi$ | 0.004 | 0.006 |
| $\mu_c$ | 0.252 | −0.251 |
| $\mu_e$ | 0.950 | 0.100 |
| $\sigma_c$ | 0.453 | 0.531 |
| $\sigma_e$ | 0.448 | 0.272 |
| $(m - m^*)_0$, $(p - p^*)_0$ | −0.557 | 0.804 |
| $s_0$ | −0.491 | 0.586 |
| $(i - i^*)_0$ | 0.239 | −0.143 |

appendix). Market actors begin with a prior belief that they are in a contractionary regime of $P_{c,0} = 0.999$.[7] A learning time series of 48 iterations is generated. At each time period, a random variable $z_t$ is drawn from a normal distribution with mean and variance from the new (expansionary) monetary regime.[8] Market actors are unaware of the switch of monetary regime, but they observe the effect on the relative money supplies. They then update their beliefs about the regime that is currently determining monetary policy. These beliefs form the basis of their expectations about the future money supplies. The relative price level $(p - p^*)$ changes as a result of the new level of money and the agents' beliefs about the monetary regime (as in equation (3.11)). The interest rate differential $(i - i^*)$ and exchange rate are determined according to (3.9) and (3.17), respectively. Assuming CIP holds, these economic variables correspond to the variables in the Fama regression outlined in section 3.2. Specifically, the dependent variable in the Fama regression is the change in the exchange rate, and the independent variable is the interest differential. The simulation was run for 1001 trials, each using the estimated parameters for the United Kingdom and Germany. A separate Fama regression equation was estimated for each trial. Final results compare the distributions of the estimated $\beta$s in the Fama regressions for our two cases.

## 3.5 Results

A check on the model is the consistency of the computational estimates with empirical observations. The simulation did indeed result in negative $\beta$ estimates for both the United Kingdom and Germany, and the estimates are in the range of those found empirically by Fama (see table 3.1).[9] Table 3.5 shows the results of the simulation. The mean $\hat{\beta}$ from the simulation for the United Kingdom was −0.194 and for Germany the mean $\hat{\beta}$ was −0.235.

**Table 3.5**
Aggregate Simulation Results

| Beta Coefficient | U.K. | Germany |
|---|---|---|
| Mean | −0.19353 | −0.23527 |
| (Median) | (−0.1598) | (−0.2386) |
| [95% C.I.] | [−0.8029, 0.2903] | [−0.8865, 0.3222] |

The empirical observation of negative coefficients is often viewed as a "puzzle" (Lewis 1995) because traditional rational expectations models cannot account for it. Our model suggests that learning is a contributing cause of negative coefficients. An example makes clear why learning generates excess foreign returns in our model (namely, why learning generates negative beta coefficients).[10] Consider the simplest case where $\theta = 1$, $\phi = 0$, and $\Pi = 0$ so that (3.9)–(3.17) simplify to the two equations of the time $t$ change in the exchange rate:

$$\Delta s_t = \mu_e + \varepsilon_t + (\mu_c - \mu_e)\Delta P_{c,t}, \tag{3.19}$$

and the time $t-1$ interest rate differential:

$$(i - i^*)_{t-1} - (i - i^*)_0 + (\mu_c - \mu_e)\sum_{i=1}^{t-1} \Delta P_{c,i}. \tag{3.20}$$

The covariation between (3.19) and (3.20) is determined by the covariation between $\Delta P_{c,t}$ in (3.19) and $\sum_{i=1}^{t-1} \Delta P_{c,t}$ in (3.20). Both the change in the probability estimate, $\Delta P_{c,t}$, and the cumulative sum of previous changes in probability estimates, $\sum_{i=1}^{t-1} \Delta P_{c,i}$, are constrained by a combination of the normally distributed random draws and Bayes' law. Although both the stochastic element and Bayesian updating leaves much freedom as to the specific manifestations of any particular probability update and cumulative sequences, in the aggregate the covariation will be negative, regardless of the direction of the regime shift. Specifically, the plot of $\sum_{i=1}^{t-1} \Delta P_{c,i}$ versus $\Delta P_{c,t}$ from a set of updating trials given normal random variables results in a negatively sloped band of points.

The main purpose of the simulations is to compare the learning dynamics across institutional arrangements. When comparing the extent of excess returns in the two cases, our results show that excess returns tend to be greater for Germany. In the German case, the overlapping regimes resulted in a slower updating process, thereby generating greater excess returns. In contrast, the learning dynamics converged much more rapidly in the case of the United Kingdom because of its highly distinct regimes. This difference in learning dynamics is apparent in figure 3.3a, which plots the change in beliefs overtime about the underlying monetary regime for representative trials from our two cases.[11] Learning is much faster in the British case. After only seven iterations, the subjective probability that monetary policy is in the old regime is less than .20. After 14 iterations the probability has reached zero. In the German case, the

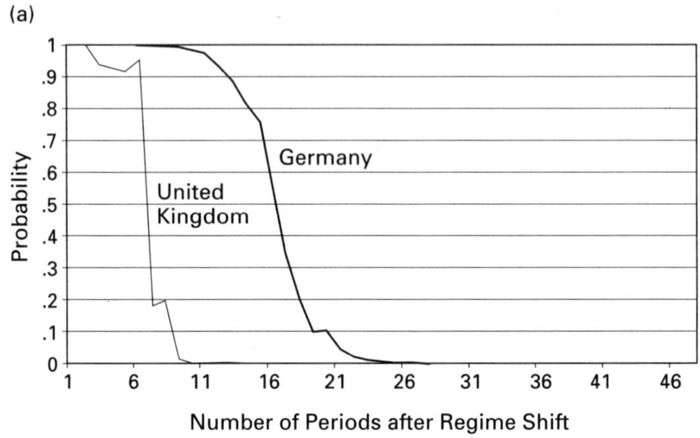


**Figure 3.3a**
Representative Simulations: Probability of Being in Contradictory Regime

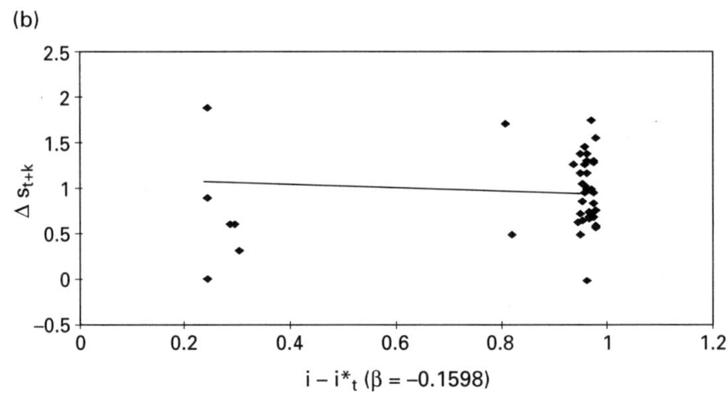


**Figure 3.3b**
Representative Simulation (U.K.): Fama Regression

subjective probability of being in the old regime remains near 1 for approximately 11 iterations before converging to zero after more than 25 iterations.

In the long run, the average change in the exchange rate should be equal to the average change in the money supply in the new expansionary regime. In the British case, there are a few extreme jumps in the exchange rate, but it quickly moves to a state of stochastic fluctuation around its long-term (new regime) equilibrium value (see figure 3.3b). The consequence of slow learning in the German case is

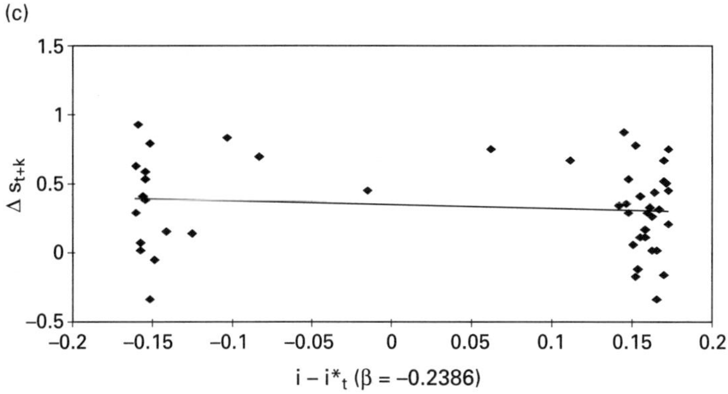


**Figure 3.3c**
Representative Simulation (Germany): Fama Regression

that many of the one-period changes in the exchange rate are above the long-term (new regime) equilibrium value (see figure 3.3c). In the end, slow learning in the German case has a larger impact on the slope of the Fama regression line than the few extreme changes in the British case.

## 3.6 Conclusion

It is well known that forward exchange rates are biased predictors of future spot exchange rates. As a result, there are predictable excess returns in international asset markets. One widely accepted explanation for excess returns is that they are caused in part by periods of learning, particularly learning about money market equilibria. Given the research in political science that argues central bank independence stabilizes money markets, one might expect excess returns to be smaller for countries with independent central banks. However, empirically this is not the case.

We present a model to account for this puzzle. In the simulations, learning generates excess returns in both our cases, but they are lower on average for the United Kingdom, which has a dependent central bank. The reason for the difference is that the high unconditional variance in monetary policy associated by Alesina and others with central bank dependence is caused by distinct monetary equilibria. Consequently, central bank dependence has the unexpected benefit of making it easier for traders to discern true regime shifts in monetary policy. This makes the expectational errors caused by such changes short-lived and, in turn, allows for quicker transitions between market equilibria. In contrast, central bank independence in Germany is associated with overlapping monetary policy regimes, which produce smaller shifts in monetary policy. As a result, the learning process in the German case is more difficult and protracted.

Learning is not the sole cause of excess returns, but it does contribute to them and therefore may be important to understanding the variation in excess returns that we observe across countries. Our simulations suggest that institutional arrangements affecting central bank independence contribute to the variation in excess returns and that the effect is due to differences in the learning environments associated with these two institutional contexts.

## Appendix

To estimate the monetary regime parameters, we fit Markov regime-switching models to the log difference in the relative U.K./U.S. and Germany/U.S. money supplies over the period 1975 to 1990. The starting point for this sample was determined by the availability of money supply data. The data are monthly and were taken from the International Monetary Fund's *International Financial Statistics*. The end point was chosen because Britain joined the Exchange Rate Mechanism (ERM) (albeit briefly) at the end of 1990; this also marks the time when the financial integration of East Germany and West Germany began. Both events produced significant changes in monetary policy.

The results are reported in table 3.6. In this table, $\mu_c$ and $\mu_e$ are the mean percentage changes in the relative money supplies in the contractionary and expansionary monetary regimes, respectively. The estimates for $\sigma_c^2$ and $\sigma_e^2$ are the variances of changes in each regime. Finally, the $\beta$ coefficients determine the probability of persisting in the two regimes from time $t$ to time $t+1$.

To test the null hypothesis of a single regime we rely on both Wald tests and Garcia's likelihood ratio test. Because there are unidentified parameters in the regime-switching model, if the null hypothesis is true, the likelihood ratio statistic does not have an asymptotic chi-square distribution. Garcia (1998) derives the asymptotic null distribution of the likelihood ratio statistic to obtain critical values.

**Table 3.6**
Markov Switching Models: Log Changes ($\times 100$) in Relative Money Supplies, 1975–1990

| Parameter | $\Delta(m - m^*)$ U.K./U.S. | $\Delta(m - m^*)$ Germany/U.S. |
|---|---|---|
| $\mu_c$ | 0.252 (.000) | −0.251 (.000) |
| $\mu_e$ | 0.950 (.000) | 0.100 (.000) |
| $\sigma_c^2$ | 0.201 (.000) | 0.282 (.000) |
| $\sigma_e^2$ | 0.206 (.000) | 0.074 (.000) |
| $\beta_c$ | 4.12 (.000) | 5.30 (.000) |
| $\beta_e$ | 3.22 (.000) | 4.78 (.000) |
| Log($L$): | −129.72 | −117.11 |
| Wald tests | | |
| $H_0$: $\mu_c - \mu_e$ | 88.82 (.000) | 35.24 (.000) |
| $H_0$: $\sigma_c^2 = \sigma_e^2$ | 0.009 (.925) | 6.670 (.010) |
| Garcia likelihood ratio test | 49.82[a] | 38.04[a] |

*Note:* $p$-values in parentheses.
a. $p$-value $< .01$.

In both cases, there is overwhelming evidence of two monetary regimes.

The Wald tests show that the distinctiveness of the two regimes is due primarily to differences in the mean change in the money supplies. In other words, one regime is more contractionary and the other is more expansionary. For the United Kingdom in the relatively contractionary monetary regime, the ratio of the British money supply to the American money supply increases at 0.252 percent per month. In the relatively expansionary monetary regime, the same money supply ratio increases at a much faster rate, 0.95 percent per month. For Germany, in the contractionary regime, the ratio of German to American money decreases at 0.251 percent per month. In the expansionary regime, it increases at 0.10 percent per month.

We can use our Markov regime-switching models to calculate the probability that monetary policy is in either the expansionary or contractionary regime at any point in time in our sample. The probabilities that the data are being generated by the expansionary regime are plotted against relative money supplies in figures 3.4a and 3.4b. In both cases, there is a switch from contractionary to expansionary monetary policy at or near the beginning of 1987. Given the timing of this switch, we use 1987 average values of relative prices,

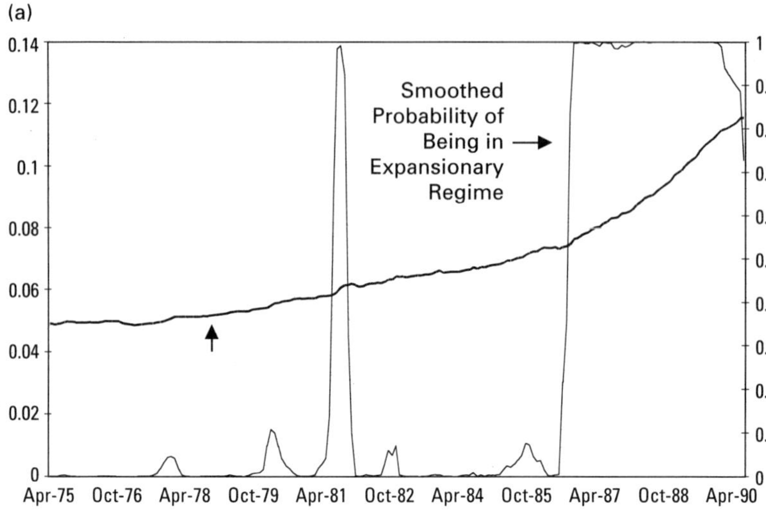


**Figure 3.4a**
Regime Switches in Relative Money Supplies, U.K.–U.S., 1975–1990

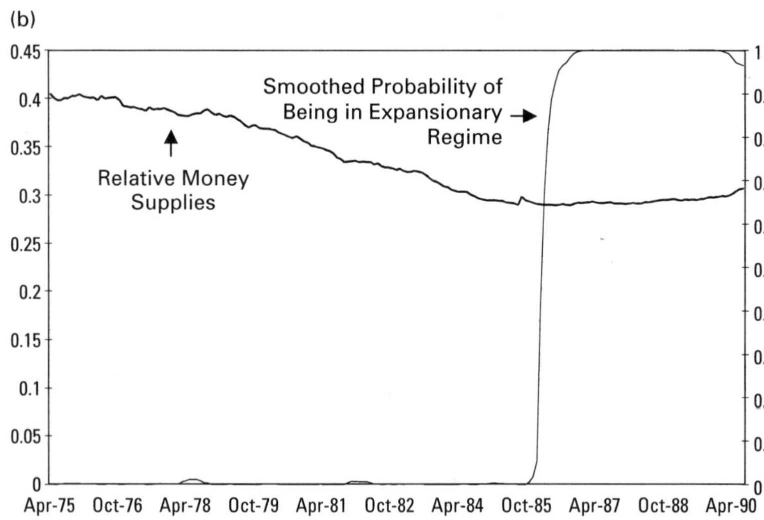


**Figure 3.4b**
Regime Switches in Relative Money Supplies, Germany–U.S., 1975–1990

exchange rates, and interest rate differentials as starting values for the simulation. The relative price and exchange rate data used are from the Penn World Table. To calculate our initial interest rate differential, we used the average 1987 hypothetical yield on a bond with a one-month maturity. The underlying yields were estimated using Nelson and Siegel's (1987) procedure.

To get estimates of $\phi$ and $\Pi$, we fit equations (3.21) and (3.22) as proxies for equations (3.15) and (3.17) using monthly data over the sample 1975–1990.

$$\Delta s_t = \alpha\Delta(p - p^*)_t + \phi[(p - p^*)_{t-1} - s_{t-1}] + \varepsilon_t \qquad (3.21)$$

$$\Delta(p - p^*)_t = \alpha\Delta s_t + \Pi[s_{t-1} - (p - p^*)_{t-1}] + \varepsilon_t. \qquad (3.22)$$

The exchange rate data are from *International Financial Statistics*. We used monthly inflation data from *International Financial Statistics* and 1975 price levels from the Penn World Table to construct a monthly price level series. To get an estimate of $\theta$, we fit the level version of equation (3.4) to monthly data from *International Financial Statistics*.

## Notes

We thank Helmut Stix for allowing us to use his GAUSS program to estimate the Markov switching models and for providing us with Nelson-Siegel parameter estimates for the United States, United Kingdom, and Germany.

1. Much of the research in this area relies on simulation methods. Lewis (1989) uses simulations to assess the impact of learning on the market's underprediction of the dollar's value in the early 1980s. Similarly, Evans and Lewis (1995) rely on simulations to examine the impact of "peso problems" on excess returns (i.e., the impact on the beta coefficient in the Fama regression).

2. The empirical support for CIP is strong (e.g., see the discussion in Hallwood and MacDonald 1994, 44). This is not surprising given that banks set forward exchange rates to equalize the interest rate differential (Llewellyn 1980). If CIP does not hold, then there are unexploited, risk-free profit opportunities.

3. We are not saying that learning alone accounts for excess returns. The Fama result is robust across subsamples; there are excess returns in periods when there are no shifts in economic policy. Both time-varying risk premia and expectational errors, some of which are caused by learning, account for the pattern of excess returns that we observe. But learning is clearly one of the causes and therefore, we believe, can help explain why excess returns are higher for some countries than for others.

4. Economists have noted an empirical connection between high inflation currencies, excess returns, and expectational biases. Froot and Thaler (1990, 187) point out that "tests of the [interest rate differential] bias during the buildup to hyperinflation, in which nominal interest rates move from being small to very large, show $\beta$s that are

positive and nearer 1." And Chinn and Frankel (1994, 763) write, "Exchange rate expectations appear much less biased when the high-inflation currencies (Argentina, Brazil, and Mexico) are included.... This is intuitive, since it is relatively easy to guess the direction of the changes in exchange rates when inflation is extremely high." But no one has yet connected these observations to central bank institutions.

5. Our money demand equation is standard. Overall, our model is similar to that used by Lewis (1989). She also constrains income elasticity to be zero. One important difference, however, is that we model a shift in money supply whereas she models a shift in money demand.

6. The program was written in Pascal and compiled using CodeWarrior. The time to run the program was negligible. The full program consists of a short (60-line) main program and four procedures ("compute mean," "generate normally distributed random variable," "Bayesian update," and "ordinary least squares"). The full program (~350 lines) is available from the authors.

7. We start with a strong prior because in our model agents learn the true regime quickly. For example, in our simulations (even with the strong prior) the subjective probability that policy is being determined by the contractionary monetary regime goes to zero on average in 12 periods after the regime switch in the United Kingdom and 24 periods after the regime switch in Germany. Since the results from the Markov switching model suggest that both countries were in the contractionary regime for 12 years prior to the switch in 1987, 0.999 is a reasonable prior. If we were to use a smaller prior, the subjective probability for the contractionary regime would go to zero even faster and the bias in the post-regime switch sample would be smaller. However, introducing uncertainty about the regime before the switch would create bias in the pre-regime switch sample that is not present in the strong prior case. Thus, the overall effects, when the appropriate samples are compared, are similar.

8. The choice of 48 iterations comes from the fact that there are four years of monthly data (January 1987–December 1990) in our empirical sample after the switch to the more expansionary monetary regimes. The normal random variable was simulated using the approximation based on the sum of uniformly distributed random variables (Ross 1984, 370). The cumulative density function of the normal distribution used for Bayes' law was done by numerical estimation using the equations in the *Mathematica* libraries.

9. Our purpose is not to precisely predict the values of the Fama coefficients but to examine how central bank independence affects learning. However, it is reassuring that the estimates have the correct sign and are relatively close in magnitude. The bias in our estimates is smaller than in Fama's, but this is to be expected. Learning alone produces our bias while a number of different factors are producing the bias in Fama's empirical estimates. We compare our simulation results to Fama's estimates because of his one-month forecast horizon. In the simulation, we regress the one-period change in the exchange rate on a one-period interest rate differential.

10. It is important to point out that the excess returns generated by the model are *ex post* realizations. It is relatively straightforward to show that the *ex ante* expected excess returns are zero. Hence, given the information set used by agents, there are no unexploited arbitrage opportunities.

11. These trials are representative in the sense that they produced the median $\hat{\beta}$ in our samples. If we want to know why learning tends to produce greater excess returns in Germany than in the United Kingdom, it is useful to compare these two trials.

## References


Alesina, Alberto. 1988. "Macroeconomics and Politics." *NBER Macroeconomics Annual*, ed. Stanley Fischer, 17–52. Cambridge, MA: MIT Press.

Alesina, Alberto, and Lawrence H. Summers. 1993. "Central Bank Independence and Macroeconomic Performance: Some Comparative Evidence." *Journal of Money, Credit, and Banking* 25 (2): 151–162.

Cavaglia, Stefano, Willem F. Verschoor, and Christian C. Wolff. 1994. "On the Biasedness of Forward Foreign Exchange Rates: Irrationality or Risk Premia?" *Journal of Business* 67 (3): 321–343.

Chinn, Menzie, and Jeffrey Frankel. 1994. "Patterns in Exchange Rate Forecasts for Twenty-five Currencies." *Journal of Money, Credit, and Banking* 26 (4): 759–770.

Crepaz, Marcus. 1996. "Constitutional Structures and Regime Performance in 18 Industrial Democracies: A Test of Olson's Hypothesis." *European Journal of Political Research* 29: 87–104.

Evans, Martin D., and Karen K. Lewis. 1995. "Do Long-Term Swings in the Dollar Affect Estimates of the Risk Premia?" *The Review of Financial Studies* 8 (3): 709–742.

Fama, Eugene F. 1984. "Forward and Spot Exchange Rates." *Journal of Monetary Economics* 14: 319–338.

Freeman, John R. 1989. *Democracy and Markets*. Ithaca, NY: Cornell University Press.

Freeman, John R., Jude C. Hays, and Helmut Stix. 2000. "Democracy and Markets: The Case of Exchange Rates." *American Journal of Political Science* 44 (3): 449–468.

Froot, Kenneth A., and Richard H. Thaler. 1990. "Anomalies: Foreign Exchange." *Journal of Economic Perspectives* 4 (3): 179–192.

Garcia, Rene. 1998. "Asymptotic Null Distribution of the Likelihood Ratio Test in Markov Switching Models." *International Economic Review* 39 (3): 763–788.

Garrett, Geoffrey. 1998. *Partisan Politics in the Global Economy*. New York: Cambridge University Press.

Hallwood, C. Paul, and Ronald MacDonald. 1994. *International Money and Finance*. Oxford, UK: Blackwell.

Hibbs, Douglas. 1977. "Political Parties and Macroeconomic Policy." *American Political Science Review* 71: 1467–1487.

Isard, Peter. 1995. *Exchange Rate Economics*. Cambridge: Cambridge University Press.

Lewis, Karen K. 1989. "Changing Beliefs and Systematic Rational Forecast Errors with Evidence from Foreign Exchange." *American Economic Review* 79 (4): 621–636.

———. 1995. "Puzzles in International Financial Markets." In *Handbook of International Economics III*, ed. G. Grossman and K. Rogoff, 1913–1971. New York: Elsevier.

Llewellyn, David T. 1980. *International Financial Integration*. New York: Wiley.

Mussa, Michael. 1982. "A Model of Exchange Rate Dynamics." *Journal of Political Economy* 90: 74–104.

Nelson, Charles R., and Andrew F. Siegel. 1987. "Parsimonious Modeling of Yield Curves." *Journal of Business* 60 (4): 473–489.

Nordhaus, W. 1975. "The Political Business Cycle." *Review of Economic Studies* 42: 169–190.

Persson, Torsten, and Guido Tabellini. 1990. *Macroeconomic Policy, Credibility, and Politics*. Chur, Switzerland: Harwood Academic Publishers.

Ross, Sheldon. 1984. *A First Course in Probability*. New York: Macmillan.

Tufte, Edward R. 1978. *Political Control of the Economy*. Princeton, NJ: Princeton University Press.

# 4 A Computational Theory of Electoral Competition

John E. Jackson

## 4.1 Introduction

This chapter presents a general model of electoral competition that integrates the propositions and empirical results from several different sets of literature. As such, it provides a flexible and rich framework within which to study elections and voter and elite behavior. The first literature is that describing electoral competition as a spatial contest between two parties. This work is the most basic model of electoral competition and forms the central piece of the computational model developed here. The basic two-party competition also becomes a special case of the model. The next literature comprises studies that model and empirically estimate the objectives of party elites in setting platforms as part of the parties' electoral strategies. These studies provide the basis for a broader conceptualization of party objective functions than that in the early spatial literature. Finally, the model includes propositions and empirical findings about individual policy preference formation and how the evolution of these preferences relates to the actions of party elites and their choices of platforms.

The key variables in the model are the means of the distributions of individual policy preferences, party affiliations, and vote choices, and party platforms. The special feature of the full model is that there are no exogenous or fixed variables. Only the lagged values of the variables can be treated as given at any point. Without any fixed variables the model might be metaphorically described as a dog chasing its tail, with each variable influencing and being influenced by all the other variables. Examination of the model addresses questions such as, Will an equilibrium exist and, if so, under what conditions? and If an equilibrium exists, what can be said about its spatial location given information about the initial conditions, any exogenous shocks, and party behavior? If an equilibrium exists and if it is possible to ascertain how different factors influence the equilibrium, it will then be possible to make predictive statements about the outcome of party competition under a wide range of different conditions and assumptions about voter and elite behavior.

The chapter begins with short summaries of the three election literature sets. The next section presents the explicit model and shows how it synthesizes these three different sets of propositions and how some become special cases within the full model. Once the model is presented and summarized, its equilibrium properties are explored. This is done using a computational model based on the analytical expressions. The last section uses this model to examine the outcomes under different assumptions and to explore different electoral scenarios.

## 4.2 Models of Elections and Electoral Behavior

### 4.2.1 *Spatial Models of Electoral Competition*

The model of two-party electoral competition and its predictions about individual choices, party strategies, and electoral outcomes is central to much work in political economy. This model was first outlined by Downs (1957) and then elaborated and extended in many directions by an impressive array of scholars. Davis and Hinich (1967; 1968) and Davis, Hinich, and Ordeshook (1970) show that Downs conclusion about the dominance of the median voter in single-dimensional elections can be extended to issue spaces with multiple dimensions, though Plott (1967) and Jackson (1973) show this conclusion requires voters with highly constrained utility functions. Subsequent work by Enelow and Hinich (1984a; 1984b; 1989) shows that if voters' decisions include a stochastic element, a weighted mean of the individual preferences, with the weights proportional to the salience of candidate issue differences, dominates the median. In all these models, some measure of the centrality of voters' preferences becomes the dominant position, with each party gravitating to that position. The less salient issue differences are to voters, or the larger the variance of the stochastic term, the more the mean dominates the median and vice versa for more deterministic and more issue-based voting.

Considerable work has been done exploring the robustness of the conclusion of the early work that the median, or mean, of voters' preferences constitutes a stable equilibrium that both competing parties adopt as their platforms. One extensive body of work begun by McKelvey (1976; 1979) and Schofield (1978) and summarized by Coughlin (1990) demonstrates that with more than one issue (dimension), the equilibrium results do not hold except under quite restrictive conditions. Furthermore, in these situations the top cycle set includes all possible positions. Recent work explores other types of constraints, such as limitations on parties' information and on their computational abilities, in an effort to find conditions that might produce an equilibrium or limit the probability of cycles (see Kollman, Miller, and Page 1992). This latter work is particularly important because it is the first to develop a computationally based model of electoral competition.

A second extensive area of scholarship explores situations in which an equilibrium might exist, but where the parties do not converge to the same platform. Two of these situations are particularly relevent for the model developed here. Erikson and Romero (1990) and Lindbeck and Weibull (1993) introduce a partisanship variable that relates to how people vote independently of their issue-based evaluations. Both assume, however, that this partisan advantage is exogenously determined and does not incorporate any issue considerations. Other factors that can be considered in the same way might be candidate attributes, valence issues such as honesty or competence where everyone agrees on the desired "location," or regional and ethnic allegiances. (On the role of the last two factors, see Cutler 2002.) Each of these factors gives a candidate or party an competitive advantage, so they can win without moving to the mean or median.

A very important reason why parties may not converge is that the leaders value certain policies, which they hope to pursue in office. This role for party policy preferences receives considerable theoretical and empirical attention, and is an important element of the model developed here. Aldrich (1983) presents a model that includes party activists and that identifies a party's positions by the mean (or median) of the party activists' preferences. Parties then compete to attract and hold activists as they also compete to win elections. Aldrich shows that in this setting an equilibrium exists but that both parties maintain distinct platforms that do not converge. Wittman (1983) presents a model in which candidates have policy preferences that are different from the mean or median of voter preferences. Candidates "prefer" to adopt a platform that matches their own preferences but must make a trade-off between the utility of such a platform and the expected utility once the likelihood of winning is considered. Wittman shows that candidates making these expected utility calculations will adopt platforms that are distinct from each other and from the mean (or median) of voters' preferences. Calvert (1985) questions Wittman's model and shows that divergence is likely only when parties have policy preferences and there is uncertainty about the distribution of voter preferences. Alesina (1988) extends this work to include the parties' degree of precommitment to their platform and whether it is a one-shot or a repeated game. He concludes that full convergence only occurs if parties are indifferent to the policies pursued after the election. The Kollman, Miller, and Page (1992; 1998) computational model considers two types of parties, ones that are only concerned with winning elections (ambitious parties) and ones that care about their platform as well as winning (ideological parties). In the Kollman, Miller, and Page model, convergence to an equilibrium is likely, even with a large number of issue dimensions and with few constraints on individual preferences. They also find that regardless of the search process, ideological parties are less likely to converge to a central point than ambitious parties. Morton (1993) reports results from a series of experiments in which participants' payoffs relate to how close outcomes are to their own preferences. Her results confirm the basic propositions about ideological parties, most notably that candidates do not converge. But she finds that they converge more than the utility-maximizing model predicts, which she attributes to the idea that participants also value winning, independent of the policy outcomes.

### 4.2.2 *Party Elite Preferences*

There is important empirical support for the proposition that party elites have strong policy preferences and that these preferences are part of any party objective function. Aldrich (1983) argues that his model's predictions are consistent with early studies of convention delegates. These studies show that each parties' delegates have preferences that differed significantly from those of the mass public and even from those of the mass members of their own parties

(McCloskey, Hoffman, and O'Hara 1960). Recent studies of convention delegates present similar findings (Miller and Jennings 1986; Kessel 1988). Kessel argues further that most delegates believe the parties ought to have policy and ideological motives in addition to the objective of winning elections. One may presume that convention delegates are typical of party activists who have a large influence on decisions about party strategy and platforms. These empirical findings argue for a utility function that includes the positions advocated by the party and the policies its leaders are likely to pursue once in office.

The proposition that party leaders have policy preferences and that these preferences are at least partly reflected in party platforms has important implications for the subsequent discussion of individual preference evolution. The likelihood that party platforms express, in part at least, the preferences of knowledgeable elites makes these platforms a credible information source for other individuals' own assessment of policies. If voters believed that party platforms solely reflect parties' vote-maximizing strategies, there would be no reason for them to treat these platforms as information that might help inform their own preferences. The empirical work and models just discussed, however, provide strong justification for the view that party platforms present information about how party elites evaluate policies and their likely outcomes. (For discussions about how self-interested elites provide information for voters, see Lupia 1994; Lupia and McCubbins 1998.)

### 4.2.3 *Preference Formation*

The final theme in the model uses the literature on individual preference formation and evolution to connect policy preferences to the parties' electoral strategies. There is a rich tradition of studies of opinions, attitudes, and preferences in the political behavior literature, but we are primarily concerned with the studies that connect the formation and evolution of individual preferences to the actions of parties, party leaders, or candidates.[1] Such connections make preference evolution an integral, or endogenous, part of models of electoral competition. This possibility has not yet been examined in the context of the spatial models.

Markus and Converse (1979) present empirical support for a model in which individuals' issue positions at time $t$ are a function of their positions at $t-1$ and any difference between those positions and the positions of the competing candidates at time $t$. The direction and magnitude of these latter relations are determined by peoples' evaluations of the candidates, so that respondents move their preferences toward the positions of favored, and away from the platforms of disliked, candidates. These results propose an electoral model in which preferences are not fixed but will under certain unspecified conditions evolve in response to positions taken by the competing parties and candidates. Markus and Converse do not, though, make this analytical connection.

Carmines and Stimson (1989) present an explicitly evolutionary model of issue preference formation. They show from a time series analysis that changes in the positions taken by Republicans and Democrats in the House and the Senate on civil rights legislation during the late 1950s and early 1960s led to changes in public opinion on that issue. They conclude that these shifts ultimately led to a substantial evolution in the structure and alignment of the parties, creating a new equilibrium in the link between issues and the mass public. They do not, however, speculate on the nature of that equilibrium or how it might be related to actions by the party leaders or the decisions of individual citizens.

Zaller (1991; 1992) develops a more elaborate model of preference formation in which political elites, which include but are not limited to party leaders, provide cues about policy positions that people use in developing or changing their own preferences. The major elaboration in his model is the proposition of a concave relation between information and knowledge and the amount of preference change that results from elite cues. The least and the most informed and knowledgeable individuals are the least likely to alter their preferences, though for quite different reasons. Zaller's propositions about the complexities of the relation between the actions of political leaders and individual preference formation are important and insightful, and clearly imply an endogeneity to preferences. He does not, however, draw a connection between this model of endogenous preference change and models of electoral competition.

Last, Gerber and Jackson (1993) develop and test a Bayesian model of preference formation based on an adaptive utility framework proposed by Cyert and DeGroot (1975; 1987) and by Cohen and Axelrod (1984). In this formulation, individuals are uncertain about how much they might like different policies or outcomes. People then treat changes in party positions as new information about how much they might like or not like policies, which enables them to update their preferences. Gerber and Jackson (1993) use data on civil rights preferences from the 1950s and 1960s and on Vietnam preferences from the 1960s and 1970s to provide empirical support for their model. This is the only work that begins to make a connection between the findings about preference formation and the nature of the electoral process. Gerber and Jackson argue that their description of preference evolution may lead to a "substantially" different model of electoral competition, and they offer some speculation about the nature of these differences.

Most of this empirical work examines preferences over policies, such as what actions the government should take in Vietnam, whether the federal government should integrate schools and workplaces, or whether the federal government should guarantee jobs and a good income. The information provided by the party platforms is of two types. The most prevalent is cues about the advisability of specific policies and whether they are likely to achieve the intended and desirable objectives. In these instances, individuals may have well-defined and informed preferences about outcomes but be uncertain about whether the proposed policies will achieve those outcomes and whether there are likely to be undesirable consequences associated with those outcomes. For example, most Americans in 1972 agreed that an end to the Vietnam war was desirable, but whether this would best be achieved by an immediate withdrawal of the troops or by increased bombing of North Vietnam was a topic of considerable debate, as were the likely global diplomatic consequences of each option. Similarly, people likely agree that unemployment should be low and that workers should have a good job and decent salary. Yet there is considerable disagreement over whether an increase in the minimum wage or a federal jobs program would achieve these goals or even whether it should be the federal government's responsibility to ensure those outcomes. When voters are uncertain about the consequences of alternative policies, the positions taken by party leaders will reduce that uncertainty because voters will believe that experienced leaders who share their objectives would be most likely to espouse policies that will achieve those ends. Shifts in party platforms would then signal a change in the views of the party leaders about the efficacy of different policies and lead the supports of each party to reassess their own policy preferences.

There is a second area of preference evolution that though less prevalent is nonetheless very important in a democracy. There are important instances when the debates associated with the adoption of a party's platform sends signals about preferences over outcomes as well as about the desirability of specific policies. The civil rights issues that are the focus of the Carmines and Stimson (1989) book and central to the Gerber and Jackson (1993) article provide a case in point. The debate was not just about whether federal efforts to guarantee the right to vote or to integrate schools (or public accommodations or housing) were the best or right way to achieve an integrated society, with the assumption that individual preferences on the value of integration were fixed. In addition to discussion on these points a significant part of the debate within and between the parties was about the value of an integrated society and how integrated our society should be, with the explicit intention of changing voters' preferences on these matters. The attitude shifts that Carmines and Stimson and Gerber and Jackson document are about preferences over outcomes in addition to changes related to preferences about policies.

The proposition that party platforms are an expression of the preferences of the party leaders as well as a strategic choice designed to garner votes becomes critical as one begins to consider preference evolution. Only if voters believe that party positions and any change in those positions reflect the views or changes in the views of policy experts will they treat this as information that should inform their own policy preferences. Platforms and policy changes that are perceived as only designed to attract voters are very unlikely to be treated as information about policy preferences and thus are unlikely to lead to changes in voters' preferences.

The empirical findings in this series of articles suggest that a model of electoral competition should be able to accommodate the idea of endogenous preferences. This model would then enable one to investigate the possible properties of such an electoral system and to explore how parties and voters are likely to behave in such an environment. The next step is to formulate a model that incorporates the main propositions of all three of these different literatures.

## 4.3 A Model of Electoral Competition with Endogenous Preferences

The two-party competition model presented here consists of two parts, a model of individual voter decisions that are aggregated into a model of the electorate, and a model of party behavior. The propositions about individual decisions are based on very standard models of individual electoral behavior, with the exception that in the general case preferences are related to party platforms as well as to exogenous factors. The model begins with the basic single-dimension spatial model in order to keep things simple and to focus on propositions about the evolution of individual policy preferences.[2] The model of party behavior includes the more elaborate propositions about party objectives, strategies, and decision making contained in the Aldrich (1983), Wittman (1983), and Kollman, Miller, and Page (1992) studies. The complete model of party competition and electoral outcomes follows from the integration of these two parts.

### 4.3.1 *Model of the Electorate*

The model uses the following notation:

$X_{it}$ = Policy preference of person $i$ at time $t$

$P_{it}$ = Party identification of person $i$ at time $t$

$V_{it}$ = Vote preference of person $i$ at time $t$

$V_{it}^{L}$ = Vote choice of person $i$ at time $t$

$R_t$ = Platform of Right party at time $t$

$L_t$ = Platform of Left party at time $t$

$D_t$ = Distance between parties' platforms at time $t$

$= R_t - L_t$

$\Delta_{L_t}$ = Change in Left party's position from $t-1$ to $t$

$= L_t - L_{t-1}$

$\Delta_{R_t}$ = Change in Right party's position from $t-1$ to $t$

$= R_t - R_{t-1}.$

The variables are arbitrarily defined so that the zero point defines pure indifference with respect to preferences, party identification (also called pure independence), and vote choice. Positive values of $P_{it}$ and $V_{it}$ are associated with increasing identification with, and preference for, party $R$, and negative values indicate the same for party $L$.

The basic deterministic equations are as follows (both the individual structural equations and the aggregate reduced-form versions are shown).

**Policy Preferences**

$$X_{it} = B_{3_t} X_{i,t-1} + (1 - B_{3_t}) B_4 (R_t - L_t) P_{it}.$$

$$\begin{aligned} \bar{X}_t = {} & [B_{3_t} \bar{X}_{t-1} + (1 - B_2) B_4 (1 - B_{3_t}) D_t \bar{P}_{t-1} \\ & - \alpha B_2 B_4 (1 - B_{3_t}) D_t (R_t^2 - L_t^2)] / \mathscr{D}. \end{aligned} \tag{4.1}$$

**Party Affiliation**

$$\begin{aligned} P_{it} & = (1 - B_2) P_{i,t-1} + B_2 \{-\alpha[(X_{it} - R_t)^2 - (X_{it} - L_t)^2]\} \\ & = (1 - B_2) P_{i,t-1} + 2\alpha B_2 D_t X_{it} - \alpha B_2 (R_t^2 - L_t^2). \end{aligned}$$

$$\bar{P}_t = [2\alpha B_2 B_{3_t} D_t \bar{X}_{t-1} + (1 - B_2) \bar{P}_{t-1} - \alpha B_2 (R_t^2 - L_t^2)] / \mathscr{D}. \tag{4.2}$$

**Vote Preference**

$$\begin{aligned} V_{it} & = (1 - B_1) P_{it} + B_1 \{-\alpha[(X_{it} - R_t)^2 - (X_{it} - L_t)^2]\} \\ & = (1 - B_1) P_{it} + 2\alpha B_1 D_t X_{it} - \alpha B_1 (R_t^2 - L_t^2). \end{aligned}$$

$$\begin{aligned} \bar{V}_t = {} & \{2\alpha B_{12} B_{3_t} D_t \bar{X}_{t-1} + (1 - B_2)[1 - B_1 + \alpha B_1 B_4 (1 - B_{3_t}) D_t^2] \bar{P}_{t-1} \\ & - \alpha B_{12} (R_t^2 - L_t^2)\} / \mathscr{D}, \end{aligned} \tag{4.3}$$

where $\mathscr{D}_t = [1 - 2\alpha B_2 B_4 (1 - B_{3_t}) D_t^2]$ is the determinant in the reduced-form expression and $B_{12} = (B_1 + B_2 - B_1 B_2)$.

The concern is with the properties of the electoral system as represented by the aggregate variables rather than with the behavior of individuals. Equations (4.1)–(4.3) give these aggregate properties of the electoral process at a given time as functions of the party strategies in that period and of the mean of the preference and party identification distributions in the previous period. This model follows quite standard forms (see Erikson and Romero 1990; Kollman, Miller, and Page 1992; Jackson 1996a) with the exception of the equations for individual and aggregate policy preferences.

The model for the evolution of preferences is derived from models of adaptive, or Bayesian, utility proposed by Cyert and DeGroot (1975; 1987) and by Cohen and Axelrod (1984). In these models, individuals' utilities consist of distributions of values over different outcomes, and decisions are based on expected utilities. These distributions are regularly updated on the basis of new information that suggests an individual might like a policy or an outcome more (or less) than previously believed. In the political model here, this new information comes from changes in the positions taken by the different parties, which provide information to voters about what policies they might or might not like. The specification here follows that in Gerber and Jackson (1993) and is consistent with the empirical studies previously cited.

The first element in the preference model is the cue about how different policies might be valued, as represented by the positions of the two parties and the terms $B_4(R_t - L_t)P_{it}$. Individuals are expected to shift their own preferences in the direction of the platform adopted by their own party and in the opposite direction of the platform of the opposing party.[3] The effect of this cue is related to the person's party identification, with strong identifiers shifting more than weak identifiers and nonidentifiers. The coefficient $B_4$ scales the magnitude of the cue provided by the party positions.

The second component in the preference equation assesses the value of this information cue in the updating process, indicated by the term $(1 - B_{3_t})$. Following the arguments of Cyert and DeGroot and Cohen and Axelrod, this term varies with the amount of new information, as measured by the changes in the party positions between time $t-1$ and $t$. The greater the amount of new information, the less weight given to previous preferences and the greater the amount of updating.[4] If there is no change in either party's position, then $B_{3_t} = 1$ and $X_{it} = X_{i,t-1}$. As changes in party positions become larger, $B_{3_t}$ becomes smaller, ultimately approaching zero, meaning that more weight is given to the new information, represented by the $B_4(R_t - L_t)P_{it}$ term. Obviously, $B_{3_t} = 1$ regardless of any change in party positions gives a model with fixed preferences, which makes that model a special case of the model presented here.

The model for current party identifications incorporates the recent treatments of party identifications as a running sum of past issue evaluations measured in spatial terms (Jackson 1975; Fiorina 1981; Franklin and Jackson 1983; Achen 1992). The coefficient $B_2$ measures the weight given to current policy evaluations relative to past partisanship. The issue evaluation term incorporates the traditional spatial quadratic loss function, though some recent work questions this assumption (Jackson 1992). The quadratic form is retained here because it makes partisanship a linear function of individual policy preferences. This linear form offers a substantial advantage in modeling aggregate partisanship (see next section). The coefficient denoted by $\alpha$ is an arbitrary parameter in the loss function, often referred to as a measure of issue salience.

Preferences and party affiliation are jointly determined during the current time period. The reduced-form expressions, which relate preferences and identifications at time $t$ to preferences and identifications at $t-1$ are shown. This model implies that changes in the party's positions induce shifts in both preferences and affiliations from what they were at $t-1$ and that there is a multiplier effect to these interactions. All the computational modeling is done here with the reduced-form expressions.

Three quite different models are nested within this structure. If $B_1 = 1$ and $B_{3_t} = 1$ for all $t$, one has the basic early spatial electoral model. Voting decisions are only a function of the relative distance between a person's preferred policy and the parties' platforms. Preferences are exogenously given and fixed. Party identifications play no role in the electoral process, so the value of $B_2$ is irrelevant.

The second model adds a role for party identifications. In this model, both $B_1$ and $B_2$ are less than 1 and greater than zero, but still $B_{3_t} = 1$ for all $t$. These specifications provide fixed preferences, party identifications that respond to party positions, and voting decisions that reflect both issue evaluations and party identifications. This model in the long run still resembles the basic spatial model in that the issue-based evaluations of the parties will dominate the outcomes but it will take longer for partisanship and vote choices to reach their long-run values. Reducing the values of $B_1$ and $B_2$ increases the lags in the process.

The third model allows $B_{3_t} < 1$, which creates a significantly different model than the previous two in that preferences now change over time in response to the sequence of party platforms. In this specification, party identifiers adjust their preferences toward whatever position is being advocated by their party relative to the position of the other party. The amount of the adjustment in individuals' preferences is related to the magnitude of the change in party positions, indicated by the size of $B_{3_t}$; to the strength of their party identification, $P_i$; to the cues provided by the parties' platforms, $(R_t - L_t) = D_t$; and to the scaling of these cues in developing preferences, $B_4$. This model, with endogenous preferences, is qualitatively different from earlier models and is the motivation for this chapter. With endogenous preferences, the preference mean may still be a key determinant of the equilibrium reached in the long run, but it is unlikely that this mean can be predicted from the initial conditions. Any equilibrium is likely to depend upon the sequence of platforms adopted by both parties as they move toward the equilibrium. Different sequences are likely to give different equilibria. This conjecture suggests a path-dependent process, such as the one described as an urn problem by Arthur, Ermoliev, and Kaniovski (1987) and explored in Jackson (1996b). The next part of the model develops expressions for party strategies, which are based on the aggregate properties.

### 4.3.2 *Party Strategies*

As in all electoral models, party strategies have a major influence on expected election outcomes and partisanship. What is different here is the possibly significant role that the sequence of platforms has on the distribution of preferences. The next question is how to model the parties' strategic decisions in choosing platforms. The model of party strategies is based on the presumption that parties have preferences for winning elections and possibly for their platforms themselves. Each party then pursues strategies that try to achieve its goals.

Development of the party strategy model starts with a representation of the parties' preferences, as represented by their respective utility functions. Following Aldrich's (1983) and Kollman, Miller, and Page's (1992) models and Morton's (1993) experimental result that candidates value winning per se, each party's utility is assumed to be a nondecreasing function of its probability of winning election, denoted by $\overline{V}_t$, and of the platform itself, denoted by $(R_t - R^*)$ and $(L_t - L^*)$, where $R^*$ and $L^*$ represent the parties' ideologically desired platforms.

The party utility functions can be written as,

$$U_t^R = U^R[\bar{V}_t, (R_t - R^*)] \quad \text{and} \tag{4.4}$$

$$U_t^L = U^L[\bar{V}_t, (L_t - L^*)], \tag{4.5}$$

where

$$\frac{\partial U_t^R}{\partial \bar{V}_t} > 0, \qquad \frac{\partial U_t^R}{\partial R_t} \geq 0 \quad \text{if} \quad R_t \leq R^*, \qquad \frac{\partial U_t^R}{\partial R_t} < 0 \quad \text{if} \quad R_t > R^* \quad \text{and}$$

$$\frac{\partial U_t^L}{\partial \bar{V}_t} < 0, \qquad \frac{\partial U_t^L}{\partial L_t} \leq 0 \quad \text{if} \quad L_t \geq L^*, \qquad \frac{\partial U_t^L}{\partial L_t} > 0 \quad \text{if} \quad L_t < L^*.$$

Parties are assumed to be utility maximizers that know their own preferences and the relation between their platforms and their utilities, given the opposing party's platform and the current distribution of voter preferences. They do not, however, know the opposing party's strategy or platform in the coming election. This model of party behavior implies that parties pick $R_t$ and $L_t$ such that

$$\frac{\partial U_t^R}{\partial R_t} = \frac{\partial U^R}{\partial \bar{V}_t}\frac{\partial \bar{V}_t}{\partial R_t} + \frac{\partial U^R}{\partial (R_t - R^*)} = U_v^R \frac{\partial \bar{V}_t}{\partial R_t} + U_R^R = 0 \quad \text{and} \tag{4.6}$$

$$\frac{\partial U_t^L}{\partial L_t} = \frac{\partial U^L}{\partial \bar{V}_t}\frac{\partial \bar{V}_t}{\partial L_t} + \frac{\partial U^L}{\partial (L_t - L^*)} = U_v^L \frac{\partial \bar{V}_t}{\partial L_t} + U_L^L = 0. \tag{4.7}$$

The terms $\partial U_t^{R/L}/\partial \bar{V}_t$, and $U_{R/L}^{R/L}$ indicate the relative importance each party gives to winning elections and to its platform. The ratio $\frac{\partial U^R/\partial R}{\partial U^R/\partial \bar{V}}$ indicates the utility of party platforms relative to winning elections for party $R$, and there is a similar ratio for party $L$. $\gamma_R$ and $\gamma_L$ denote the parameter for each party that reflects these ratios. A value of $\gamma = 0$ implies the party does not place a value on its own platform and only values winning elections. A more specific model of how parties might perform the utility-maximizing task is not important at this stage but is developed in a subsequent section.

### 4.3.3 *Summary of the Electoral Competition Model*

The model of electoral competition just developed is both simple and complex. It is simple in that it follows from the application of quite straightforward decision rules by voters and parties and relies on a small number of parameters. It is complex because the relations

**Table 4.1**
Parameters in Model of Electoral Competition

| Symbol | Role in Model | Value Range |
|---|---|---|
| $\alpha$ | Issue salience in utility function | Any value $> 0$ |
| $B_1$ | Amount of issue voting | $1 =$ Pure issue voting |
| | | $0 =$ No issue voting |
| $B_2$ | Rate of partisan adjustment | $1 =$ Instantaneous adjustment |
| | | $0 =$ No adjustment to issues |
| $B_{3_t}$ | Endogeneity of preferences | Any value $\leq 1$ |
| | | $1 =$ Fixed preferences |
| $B_4$ | Influence of party cues on preferences | Any value $\geq 0$, assumed to equal 1 |
| $\gamma^{R/L}$ | Party utility for platform | $0 =$ Only votes matter |

between party strategy and aggregate outcomes implied by these decision rules are nonlinear and likely dependent upon the sequence of party strategies. The simplicity is summarized in table 4.1, which shows the different coefficients in the model, their role in the decisions, and the values taken for special cases.

There are six parameters in the model, and of these only three, $B_{3_t}$, $\rho^R$, and $\rho^L$ are central to the story. The most interesting and theoretically important of these is $B_{3_t}$. If this term is less than 1, then preferences are endogenous and are subject to change as the parties adopt different platforms in the process of competing for votes. If $\rho \neq 0$ for either party, then that party values its platform as well as the election outcome. The objective here is to use this model to explore the properties of an electoral system with both endogenous preferences and ideological parties, to use Kollman, Miller, and Page's terminology.

## 4.4 Computational Model of Electoral Competition

The remainder of the chapter examines the electoral process and outcomes implied by this model through a computational model. The first part of the model uses equations (4.1)–(4.3) to predict the aggregate electoral properties, such as mean preferences and partisanship and electoral outcomes, based on the value of $\overline{V}_t$. For the purposes of this exercise the precise expression for $B_{3_t}$ is $e^{B_3(\Delta R^2+\Delta L^2)}$, so that fixed preferences is the special case where $B_3 = 0$.

The second part of the model is specific expressions for the party utility functions and explicit routines by which they choose platforms designed to maximize these utilities. The selection of a form for the utility functions is arbitrary, within certain constraints. The first constraint is that the function be concave, implying decreasing marginal utilities as parties get closer to their desired outcomes. A second is that it be relatively easy to solve the first-order conditions for a desired platform.

In this model, parties value their probability of winning election and their platform. The probability of $R$ winning election follows a logistic distribution, $P^R = (1 + e^{-\bar{V}})^{-1}$, and the probability of $L$ winning is $P^L = 1 - P^R = (1 + e^{\bar{V}})^{-1}$; the parties' utility is related to the log of each probability. The desired platforms are fixed and denoted by $R^*$ and $L^*$. The parties' utility functions are arbitrarily selected and contain a single parameter, $\gamma_R$ and $\gamma_L$, respectively, that measures the importance of the desired platform relative to the probability of winning. The precise utility functions are

$$U^R = -\gamma_R(R^* - R)^2 - (1 - \gamma_R)\log(1 + e^{-\bar{V}}) \quad \text{and} \tag{4.8}$$

$$U^L = -\gamma_L(L - L^*)^2 - (1 - \gamma_L)\log(1 + e^{\bar{V}}). \tag{4.9}$$

For a given $\overline{X}$ and $\bar{V}$ the utility maximizing platforms are

$$R^{\ddagger} = \frac{\alpha(B_1 + B_2 - B_1B_2)(1 - \gamma_R)\overline{X} + \gamma_R R^*(1 + e^{\bar{V}})}{\alpha(B_1 + B_2 - B_1B_2)(1 - \gamma_R) + \gamma_R(1 + e^{\bar{V}})} \quad \text{and} \tag{4.10}$$

$$L^{\ddagger} = \frac{\alpha(B_1 + B_2 - B_1B_2)(1 - \gamma_L)\overline{X} + \gamma_L L^*(1 + e^{-\bar{V}})}{\alpha(B_1 + B_2 - B_1B_2)(1 - \gamma_L) + \gamma_L(1 + e^{-\bar{V}})}. \tag{4.11}$$

Parties are assumed to adjust their platform toward the utility-maximizing position, if they are not already there. The adjustment parameter for each party is denoted by $\delta_R$ and $\delta_L$, so that

$$R_{t+1} = (1 - \delta_R)R_t + \delta_R R_t^{\ddagger} \quad \text{and} \tag{4.12}$$

$$L_{t+1} = (1 - \delta_L)L_t + \delta_L L_t^{\ddagger}. \tag{4.13}$$

The addition of (4.12) and (4.13) describing party behavior and (4.1)–(4.3) describing mean preferences, partisanship, and vote evaluations creates a dynamic system with five nonlinear first-difference equations. These are relatively easy to program, and provide a computational model by which we can examine the properties of this electoral system. A previous paper (Jackson 1996a) conducted sensitivity tests to ascertain the parameter ranges within which the model easily reached and maintained an equilibrium. The results indicated that the model behaved well over a wide ranges of values for the key parameters. Only for extreme values for the parties' ideological preferences ($R^*$ or $L^* \geq 2.5$), high utilities for that position ($\gamma \geq 0.5$), and large values for $B_3$ were there problems. For all the simulations here, relatively small values for all the parameters are selected, so there is no doubt about working in a range where the model is well behaved. (The selected values are $B_1 = B_2 = \alpha = 0.5$; $B_3 = 1$; $R^* = 2$; $L^* = -2$; $\gamma = 1/3$; and $0.5 \leq \delta \leq 1$. These values are also consistent with empirical work that shows a significant lag in partisan adjustments and a significant role for partisanship in voting decisions.) This means that the variations in electoral results are a consequence of the model's basic properties and not from some unfortunate choice of parameters near an unstable range.

The assumption of fixed party preferences is overly rigid in two ways. One rigidity is that, as Aldrich (1983) points out, the composition and preferences of each party's activists will determine the party's preferred policies. Thus, in a proper dynamic model this term would evolve over time as the composition of the party and of its activists change.[5] The second condition maintained is that voters do not know the parties' ideological preferences but only know the announced platforms. (In game theory parlance, $R^*$ and $L^*$ are private information.) This condition is plausible in that there will be many voices speaking within the party, thereby concealing the true preferences. The only revealed information is the announced platform, which is what voters use to update their own preferences.

### 4.4.1 *Basic Simulations*

The first simulations repeat ones done in Jackson (1996b) but are included here to demonstrate the characteristics of the model, including its path-dependent nature. The simulations start with the system in equilibrium with $\overline{X} = 0$ and the parties located at $\pm 1.4545$, respectively. At election (iteration) 4, preferences experience a shock of $+0.75$. The parties then adjust their positions in response to this shock. The first simulation was with $B_3 = 0$, meaning there is no further change in mean preferences—the traditional case. In subsequent simulations $B_3 = 1$, so that preferences change as the parties' platforms change. The differences in these simulations are that the rate of party adjustment, $\delta$, varies from 0.5 to 1. These variations imply a different sequence of party platforms following the initial shock. The path-dependent nature of the process will be evident, as each of these simulations reaches a different equilibrium despite the fact that the starting conditions, shock, and parameters other than $\delta$ are identical.

The simulation with fixed preferences performs as expected. After the shock to preferences, it takes three iterations to reach the new equilibrium (defined as being less than 0.001 from the final result). The parties are located at 1.793 and −1.022, respectively, and mean partisanship and vote evaluations are 1.025, which strongly favor party *R*, as would be expected with a preference shift of +0.75. None of this is surprising, and only serves to confirm that the simulation functions as it should for the standard case.

Figure 4.1 shows the sequence of party positions and mean preferences and vote evaluations for the case with endogenous preferences and $\delta = 0.9$. Mean preferences continue to shift in the positive direction following the shifts in the party positions. An equilibrium is reached with $\overline{X} = 1.12$, with each of the parties further to the pos-

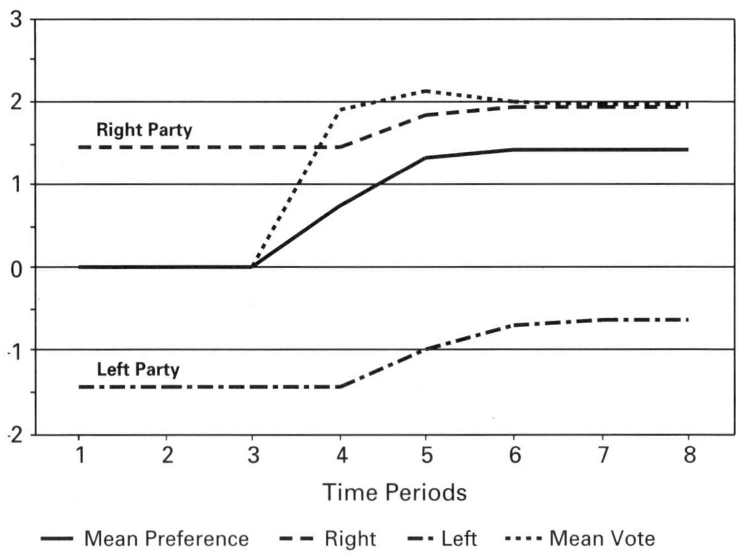


**Figure 4.1**
Two-Party Electoral Competition, Endogenous Preferences: $\delta = .09$

itive side and with $R$ having an even larger vote advantage than in the fixed-preference case.

Figure 4.2 plots the sequence of preference means for the simulation with fixed preferences and for the ones with endogenous preferences with different values for $\delta$. The different values for $\delta$ imply different histories in the form of different sequences of party platforms in reaching a new equilibrium in response to the preference shock. Each of these histories reaches a substantially different equilibrium, despite the same initial conditions and shock. This is graphic evidence of the path-dependent nature of the model.

### 4.4.2 *Adaptive Party Utility and Electoral Cycles*

The next set of simulations builds from the results in the basic case. One obvious consequence of the preference shift in the previous scenario is to leave one party as the permanent minority and the other party winning all the elections and able to pursue its ideological preferences. This new scenario alters the model by allowing party utilities to shift slightly in response to election outcomes. Specifically, each party's utility for the probability of winning the election relative to ideology shifts to put a greater weight on elections each

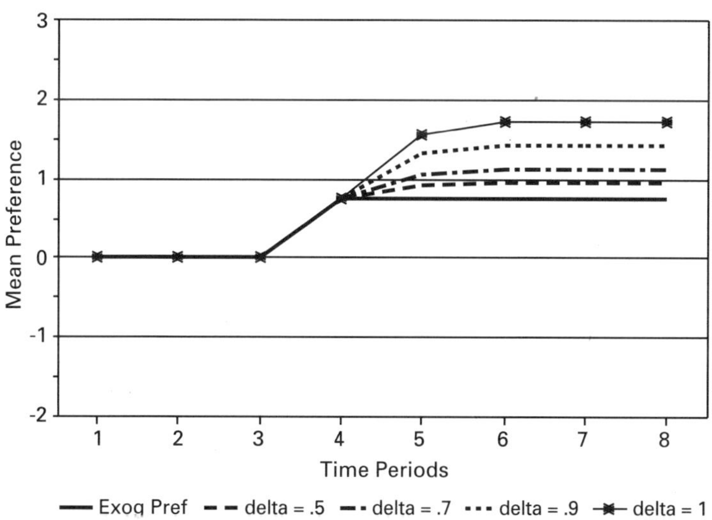


**Figure 4.2**
Two-Party Electoral Competition, Mean Preference Equilibria

time they lose an election. Conversely, the winning party shifts its preference to give a greater weight to its policy preferences. The proposition in the former case is quite straightforward: the losing party will become less ideological in order to capture the election. The proposition for the winning party is that, once in office, it can and will pursue its policy preferences. The expectation is that this behavior will induce electoral cycles.

The preference adjustment equation, (4.1), is altered slightly to accommodate the proposition here that small shifts in party positions reflect attempts to win elections, not a possible change in party preferences. The longer a party is out of office, the less credible are changes in its platform as cues about changes in preferences. To accommodate this proposition, the expression for $B_{3_t}$ is altered so that shifts in party platforms have to exceed some threshold before $B_{3_t} < 1$. Further, this threshold increases the longer a party is out of office.

The simulation with $\delta = 0.9$ is used to examine these propositions about adaptive utilities. To incorporate the adaptive utilities, with each successive election lost the minority party's weight for elections increases by 0.03, and the weight given to policy preferences by the incumbent party increases by the same amount. Simultaneously, the threshold that changes in party platforms must exceed to alter preferences is initialized at 0.02 and is increased by 0.03 each year the party is in the minority. The process is started at its equilibrium values, and then mean preferences receive a shock of +0.5 to create the disequilibrium.

Figure 4.3 shows the sequence of party platforms, mean vote preferences, and mean policy preferences during the series of election cycles induced by this shock and the changes in party utilities. As before, a new equilibrium is reached, with mean preferences even further in the positive direction than the initial shock. What is particularly remarkable here is that subsequent to reaching equilibrium, the relatively small changes in the utility function parameters produced noticeable cycles. The frequency of the cycles is a function of how adaptive are the parties' utilities. The larger the change in the relative value of winning, the higher the frequency of the cycles. The idea of adaptive utilities, and their implications for the sequence of electoral outcomes, becomes more important in subsequent sections.

The cycles in electoral outcomes, denoted by $\bar{V}_t$ being greater than or less than zero, and in the platforms of $L$, are quite evident. The

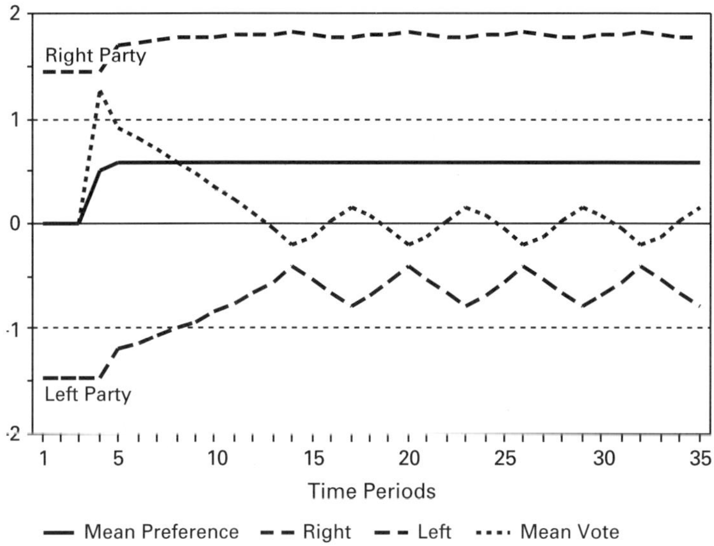


**Figure 4.3**
Two-Party Electoral Competition, Adaptive Party Utility

cycles in the positions of party $R$ are far less evident. The positive shift in voter preferences greatly advantages $R$ in that members can much more easily accommodate their policy preferences and compete for votes. Because $L$'s activists' ideological preferences are much further from the voter's preferences, they face a starker trade-off between satisfying their preferences and trying to win elections, which leads to larger fluctuations in positions.

### 4.4.3 *Stochastic Platforms*

The next scenario changes the structure substantially by introducing a small random element into the parties' platform decisions. This extension is done by adding a random element to (4.12) and (4.13), so that

$$R_{t+1} = (1 - \delta_R)R_t + \delta_R R_t^{\ddagger} + \varepsilon_{R_{t+1}} \quad \text{and}$$

$$L_{t+1} = (1 - \delta_L)L_t + \delta_L L_t^{\ddagger} + \varepsilon_{L_{t+1}}.$$

This is another way to illustrate the path dependency, as different sequences of random elements in the party platforms are expected to lead to different sequences of results. With fixed preferences, there should be relatively little difference in outcomes for different random sequences.

The $\varepsilon$ for each time period and for each party are drawn independently from a normal distribution with a mean of zero and a standard deviation of 0.1. In order to adjust for the possibility that voters would perceive this random variation as exactly that and only treat large shifts in platforms as true signals of a change in party preferences, only shifts greater than 0.2 (two standard deviations in the random element) are treated as information. Any shifts smaller than this do not lead to any updating of individual preferences.

Ten different simulations are conducted, each with 100 iterations. The seeds for the random number generator in each simulation are selected from a uniform random distribution. The different seeds will guarantee different sequences, or a different history of party platforms. All simulations are started in equilibrium and there are no external shocks to either preferences of platforms, other than the random component to party platforms, which begin at iteration 4. Table 4.2 shows the values of the mean preference and the party positions at iteration 100. It also shows the number of elections won by each party.

There is one notable result here. The different sequences of random platforms clearly generate quite different electoral histories, as one would expect. What might be a surprise, however, is that each simulation generates an electoral sequence that strongly favors one of the parties. One party wins nearly 80 percent or more of the elections

**Table 4.2**
Simulations with Random Platforms

| Seed | $\bar{X}$ | $N_R$ | $N_L$ |
|---|---|---|---|
| 225 | −1.277 | 10 | 90 |
| 19 | −0.203 | 35 | 65 |
| 945 | −0.382 | 21 | 79 |
| 127 | 1.354 | 96 | 4 |
| 177 | −0.229 | 37 | 64 |
| 585 | −0.084 | 50 | 50 |
| 983 | −0.522 | 13 | 87 |
| 705 | 0.710 | 92 | 8 |
| 93 | 1.253 | 98 | 2 |
| 215 | 0.061 | 51 | 49 |

in six of the ten trials, something not expected by chance. This result occurs because with the first random shock one of the parties is very likely to gain an electoral and a partisan advantage, which then translates into the substantial likelihood that further movements are likely to shift the electorate further in the direction of the position of the majority party, maintaining or enhancing its advantage. By contrast, with fixed preferences, the same sequences of random platform components produced results with very little deviation from an equal distribution of election wins between the parties. (In six of the ten simulations with fixed preferences, the dominant party won less than 55 percent of the elections, and no party won as many as 60 elections.) This provides further evidence that the general case, where preferences evolve along with party positions, yields substantially different properties than the special case with fixed preferences.

The outcome observed here, where an initial random shock to a party's platform is likely to give that party a competitive advantage, suggests one additional simulation and a need for a new approach to modeling party behavior. The additional simulation incorporates the earlier proposition about changes in party utility functions in response to election outcomes in the model with stochastic platforms. This is done in the next section.

### 4.4.4 *Stochastic Platforms and Adaptive Party Utility*

The inclusion of adaptive party utilities with stochastic platforms is quite straightforward. The same random number seeds, and hence the same sequence of random elements, used in the previous simulations are used here. They will not generate the same sequence of party platforms, however, because now the utility attached to ideology relative to the probability of winning an election shifts by −0.03 with each electoral loss and by +0.03 with each win. The threshold for voters to alter their preferences in response to changes in party positions changes accordingly, never getting below 0.2 but increasing by 0.03 for the losing party after each loss.

The expectation here is that the alteration of the losing party's utility after successive losses should make the whole process more evenly competitive and dampen the shifts in voter preferences. The losing party will take more aggressive actions to recapture partisans and votes, which will restrict the ability of the majority party to continue to move the voters further in its ideological direction. There

**Table 4.3**
Simulations with Random Platforms and Adaptive Party Utilities

| Seed | $\bar{X}$ | min $\bar{X}$ | max $\bar{X}$ | $N_R$ | $N_L$ |
|---|---|---|---|---|---|
| 225 | −0.106 | −0.19 | 0.00 | 49 | 51 |
| 19 | −0.082 | −0.09 | 0.06 | 49 | 51 |
| 945 | 0.027 | −0.06 | 0.05 | 50 | 50 |
| 127 | 0.087 | −0.05 | 0.09 | 52 | 48 |
| 177 | 0.150 | −0.20 | 0.21 | 51 | 49 |
| 585 | 0.177 | −0.13 | 0.20 | 50 | 50 |
| 983 | 0.007 | −0.20 | 0.02 | 50 | 50 |
| 705 | 0.037 | −0.04 | 0.05 | 50 | 50 |
| 93 | 0.103 | −0.00 | 0.29 | 51 | 49 |
| 215 | 0.043 | −0.18 | 0.04 | 50 | 50 |

will be cycles, but they will be much harder to discern because of the random element in each platform.

Table 4.3 shows the mean preference after 100 iterations, the minimum and the maximum value for this mean over those iterations, and the number of elections won by each party. The dampening effects of including adaptive utilities is very evident in these results. The range for mean preferences was from −0.2 to +0.3, with the mean preference at the end of 100 iterations generally not too far from zero. Also, the elections remained very competitive, with neither party able to win more than 52 of the 100 elections, and in half the simulations the outcomes were evenly divided.

### 4.4.5 *Strategic Party Behavior*

The last set of simulations allows the parties to act strategically in their choice of platforms. The term *strategic*, as used here, refers to actions by the parties that sacrifice utility in the current period in hopes of obtaining a competitive advantage in subsequent periods. The case of strategic behavior is shown in figure 4.4. In this case, $R$ adopts a platform that is less ideological than its equilibrium for one period, sacrificing some utility for that period, and then returns to its utility maximizing platform. In the process it attracts partisans, who then shift their preferences along with the party in the subsequent periods.

The far more interesting question is whether there are incentives for either party to act in such a strategic manner, and if so when and with what consequences. One possibility is that a strategic action

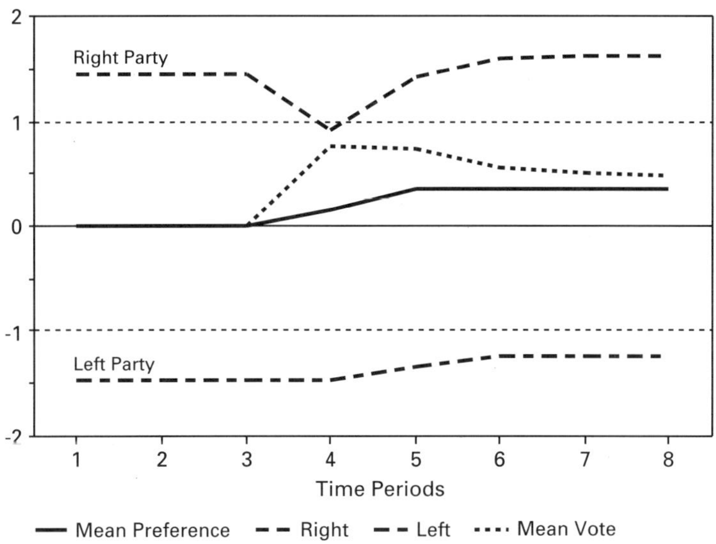


**Figure 4.4**
Two-Party Electoral Competition, Strategic Behavior by Right Party

by one party could be countered by the opposing party with no net advantage to either. In the simulation shown in figure 4.4, if party *L* adopted a platform 0.5 closer to the mean on the period after party *R* did, and *R* returned to a sincere platform, there would be no long-term effect on mean preferences and the system would return to its previous equilibrium. Alternatively, any party that can implement a series of strategic moves might be able to establish a permanent advantage. For example, *R* might anticipate *L*'s response and make a second strategic move in order to maintain its advantage. If *R* could continue to anticipate and counter *L*'s reactions, it might maintain its initial advantage.

The difficult part of adding this strategic behavior to the model is that it requires that each party determine the dynamic path of the entire system for several periods into the future, including the positions of the other party and their joint effects on the voters' mean preferences. The solution adopted here is a brute force one. A sequence of three platforms is first assumed for *L*. A subroutine then simulates the full electoral system for three periods for all possible sequences of platforms for *R* in the range 0.9545 to 1.8295. Increments of 0.025 are used in the search. It is then assumed that *R* adopts the sequence that produces the maximum utility after the third period. (This criterion is selected as it is the closest measure to the party's long-run welfare. This method discounts the utility losses incurred by the strategic behavior in the first two periods.) The simulation is then rerun with the roles reversed. $R$ is assigned the platforms just determined to be optimal, and $L$ is allowed to search over all possible platform sequences for its best strategy. This process is repeated until a stable set of platforms or a cycle of platforms is obtained. This process obviously assumes that each party knows what its competitor will do, and picks its maximizing strategy accordingly.

The first simulation uses the usual equilibrium as the starting point and treats each party as a fully strategic player. An equilibrium is reached in five iterations and consists of the platforms, $R_t = \{0.9545; 0.9545; 1.2795\}$ and $L_t = \{-0.9545; -0.9545; -1.2795\}$. The clear implication is that with both parties acting strategically and anticipating the competitor's strategy, neither one gains an advantage, and in terms of utility, both end up worse off than if both had acted sincerely throughout.

These results change dramatically if one of the parties is able to make a strategic move without a simultaneous response by the other. This simulation is done by letting $R$ adopt an initial platform of 0.9545 and then choose three successive platforms on the assumption that $L$'s position is constant. In the second iteration, $L$ can choose its best platforms, conditional on $R$'s initial move and subsequent positions. In the third iteration, $R$ chooses its three moves conditional on the results of the initial move to 0.9545 and $L$'s platforms. $L$ then picks its sequence of platforms, conditioned on $R$'s new positions, and so on. In this case, no equilibrium is reached. Rather, a small cycle exists among two different sequences for each party. Denote the two sequences for $R$ as $S_{R_1} = \{0.9545; 1.3795; 0.9545; 1.4545\}$ and $S_{R_2} = \{0.9545; 0.9545; 0.9545; 1.4795\}$ and the two for $L$ as $S_{L_1} = \{-1.1295; -0.9545; -1.0795\}$ and $S_{L_2} = \{-0.9545; -0.9545; -1.1545\}$. The cycle is then: if $R = S_{R_1}$ then $L$'s best strategy is $S_{L_2}$. If $R$ knows that $L$ will adopt $S_{L_2}$, then $R = S_{R_2}$. If $L$ believes that $R$ will choose $S_{R_2}$, it will choose $S_{L_1}$, and then $R$'s optimal strategy is back to $S_{R_1}$.

If we examine all four pairs of strategies, the long-run outcomes are fairly similar.[6] Table 4.4 shows for each strategy pair, the long-run equilibrium party positions and the means of the preference and vote evaluation distributions. The values for the two means are

**Table 4.4**
Strategic Outcomes

| Strategy Pair | $R$ | $L$ | $\bar{X}$ Step 4 | $\bar{X}$ Equil | $\bar{V}$ Step 4 | $\bar{V}$ Equil |
|---|---|---|---|---|---|---|
| $S_{R_1}, S_{L_1}$ | −1.33 | 1.57 | 0.22 | 0.23 | 0.15 | 0.31 |
| $S_{R_1}, S_{L_2}$ | −1.39 | 1.52 | 0.12 | 0.12 | −0.01 | 0.16 |
| $S_{R_2}, S_{L_1}$ | −1.36 | 1.55 | 0.18 | 0.18 | 0.05 | 0.24 |
| $S_{R_2}, S_{L_2}$ | −1.33 | 1.57 | 0.22 | 0.22 | 0.20 | 0.30 |

shown after the last strategically chosen position (labeled step 4) and at the long-run equilibrium. For $\bar{X}$ there is virtually no difference between these two points, while $\bar{V}$ continues to move in $R$'s favor. This is a consequence of the values for $B_1$ and $B_2$ in the model, which dampened the rate of adjustment of partisanship and vote evaluations to changes in party positions.

The significant result here is that even if parties can accurately anticipate their competitor's platforms, there is a significant advantage for any party that can act strategically while its competitor does not. Even under the most favorable matching of subsequent strategies, $L$ is at a substantial disadvantage if $R$ can act strategically in one period and $L$ does not. The obvious conclusion is that each party must act strategically at each election, as demonstrated in the first set of comparisons. If they do, then the strategic behavior and results shown in table 4.4 can be prevented.

## 4.5 Concluding Comments: Political Implications

The model presented here builds on early rational choice models of elections to integrate results from research on party elites and studies of preference evolution among the mass public. This extended model, though, is relatively simple and its major difference with the conventional spatial models is the parameter $B_3$. In fact, the traditional model is simply a special case of the model developed here, with $B_3 = 0$. The addition of $B_3$ is a radical departure from the rational choice model and permits individual preferences to evolve in response to information provided by changes in party platforms, as suggested by work in mass behavior. This addition yields new outcomes and views of electoral processes that can enrich our perspective on this central feature of all democracies.

The results obtained when $\gamma > 0$ replicate what others have found and proved analytically. With fixed values for $\gamma$ and with fixed individual preferences, this electoral system has a stable equilibrium. The only difference with the early spatial model is that the parties' platforms do not converge to the mean (or median). The more highly the activists value their party's platform, the further apart the parties' equilibrium positions become. The simulations reported here only considered symmetric parties where each has the same utility for winning and for their platform and where the ideal points have the same absolute value. Nonsymmetric cases also had a stable equilibrium, but the party whose ideological preference was furthest from the mean, or that valued its platform more, adopted a position further from the mean, making it a permanent minority party.

The behavior of party leaders in determining how much they value the party platform, as measured by $\gamma$, has significant implications for the electoral process when they are confronted with the possibility of being the permanent minority party. In one set of simulations leaders respond to this circumstance by adjusting their utility for having a platform they preferred relative to winning. The less successful the party is at winning elections, the more they come to value winning relative to their platform. The reverse held for the winning party. When both parties follow this behavior it rapidly introduces regular electoral cycles—a pattern regularly observed in U. S. national elections. The consequences of these utility adjustments are less pronounced when individual preferences are fixed, as party positions and electoral outcomes are relatively stable and outcomes stay in a fairly narrow range. When preferences evolve in response to changes in party positions, the actions of party leaders changing their utility for winning changes the properties of the electoral system substantially. These actions prevent one party from becoming permanently dominant and greatly restrict the ability of that party to shift the mean preference any significant distance from its original value. The systemic consequences of having adaptive utilities in the situation with evolving preferences are dramatically seen in tables 4.2 and 4.3.

The consequences of leaders' behavior becomes much more profound when individual preferences evolve simultaneously with party positions, that is, when $B_3 > 0$. Here the positions adopted by the parties in response to any disturbance in the form of a shift in individuals' preferences or in one party's platform have a significant bearing on the eventual equilibrium outcomes—a path-dependent system. This property has a wide range of important implications for the electoral process. As demonstrated in the section on strategic behavior, this property means that a party that adopts an overly ideological platform in one election risks the serious long-term consequences of having the opposing party dominate the electorate and possibly shift mass preferences in the direction of that party's ideology. For example, the Goldwater candidacy in 1968 and the McGovern platform in 1972 offered the Democrats and Republicans, respectively, substantial opportunities both to win that year's election and to exert a significant influence on the longer-term preferences and decisions of the electorate. As just commented, the response of the losing party to alter its utility to give less weight to ideology is critical in determining how serious are its long-term losses.

The presence of endogenous preferences also offers parties the possibility to deliberately adopt a sequence of platforms designed to shift aggregate preferences in the long run. If a party can gain an advantage in mass partisanship, either through some strategically selected platform or some exogenous event that promotes that party, it can use that advantage to influence the electorate's preferences. This, in turn, enables that party to gain a sizable electoral advantage and to adopt platforms closer to its own ideological preference. The leaders of a party handed a partisanship advantage, say, if the opposing party adopts a more extreme ideological platform, face an interesting choice. One option is to use this advantage to build a large electoral advantage by remaining close to the mean preference. A second option is to satisfy their own preferences by also adopting a more ideological platform and maintaining a smaller electoral advantage. A third option, which entails a multiperiod utility calculation, is to use the partisan advantage to shift voter preferences through a carefully crafted series of platforms. Adding this consideration to the model adds considerably more complexity than just appending another term to the party utility function. It requires an intertemporal component to the party utility function whereby a party can trade off certain losses in the short run for the possibility of getting shifts in preferences in the long run. Regardless of the scenario, the implications of the model are that the actions by party leaders become very influential in the long-term outcomes of the electoral process and in whatever equilibrium is eventually reached.

The possibility that parties may try to influence voter preferences has normative implications as well as behavioral ones. Most normative work in economics and political science comparing institutions is based on how well the outcomes predicted for different institutional forms reflect the distribution of individual preferences. The benchmark of how outcomes track with individual preferences is a problematic criterion for comparing institutions when those preferences are responding to the structure and behavior of the institutions themselves. One might go even further and include in the evaluation a measure of how well institutions help individuals learn their preferences, not just how they aggregate some given set of preferences. (See Gerber and Jackson (1993) for an elaboration of this argument.)

The chapter began by describing this model as a dog chasing its tail, as there are no fixed variables that anchor the model and from which one can predict likely outcomes. Integrating the different literatures on elections and parties produces a structure where the actions of mass and elite individuals are highly interdependent. The distribution of individual preferences constrains the actions of party leaders, who ultimately place a value on being elected and who then must compete for votes. Yet the long-run outcomes are also dependent upon the actions taken by party activists in setting platforms as they compete for votes and possibly try to influence voter preferences. The simulations demonstrate that the model will reach a stable equilibrium following any exogenous shock but that the location of this equilibrium is partly dependent upon the sequence of actions taken during the equilibrating process. This path dependency makes the study of political history and of the actions of party leaders at certain historical junctures important in understanding current political configurations. The implication here is that following significant shocks to the electoral system there will be a search for a new equilibrium. During this search the specific sequence of party platforms and the interactions between activists choosing platforms and the mass public will affect the terms of the subsequent equilibrium. Thus, in order to understand and to model current political structures one must also model this historical process, making history a very real part of contemporary analysis. (See Jackson (1996b) for a discussion of the empirical problems one may encounter in such an effort.) This is a daunting challenge, but one that economic historians seem to enjoy. With persistence, a comparable group of political historians may join them.

## Notes

I want to thank Jeff Banks, Marcus Berliant, Ken Kollman, Skip Lupia, Stephen Pollock, and Carl Simon for their ideas and suggestions on the model, but absolve them from any errors, which are my own doing.

An earlier version of this chapter was read at the annual meeting of the American Political Science Association, August 29, 1997, Washington, D.C., and at the Michigan Seminar on Democratic Institutions, November 14, 1996. This research was supported National Science Foundation grant SBR-9511469.

1. Much of the work on individual attitudes reaches the decidedly negative conclusion that individuals' preferences, at least as measured by survey research, are dominated by the absence of attitudes and that survey responses for most people are best modeled as a sequence of random responses. For a summary of this work, see Kinder and Sears (1985). Some articles also suggest that much of the randomness can be attributed to unreliability in the survey method and that, absent these measurement errors, individuals have relatively coherent and stable policy preferences (Achen 1975; Erikson 1978; 1979; Jackson 1983; 1985). I do not address this debate here but deal only with the literature that observes preferences and that connects preferences to the actions of parties and party leaders.

2. One important simplification provided by the model is that all the equations are linear in their parameters, so that the model of the aggregate electorate is a simple summation of the individual equations, which allows modeling of the means of the individuals' preference, partisanship, and vote preference distributions. For a significant relaxation of this constraint, see Jackson (1999).

3. For the sake of avoiding monotony, the terms *party position* and *party platform* are used synonymously.

4. To make the analytical work simple, $B_{3_t} = f(\Delta R^2, \Delta L^2)$, with $\frac{\partial B_{3_t}}{\partial(\Delta(R/L)^2)} > 0$ and $\frac{\partial^2 B_{3_t}}{\partial(\Delta(R/L)^2)^2} < 0$. A more sophisticated version would include platform changes in previous periods, with declining weights, but this would not add to the substantive aspects of the model.

5. Jackson (1999) develops a model with these features and demonstrates that its basic properties are very similar to those presented here.

6. The long run assumes that each party returns to play its sincere strategy after the three strategic plays. There were too many programming and combinatorial problems to continue the strategic play.

## References

Achen, Christopher H. 1975. "Mass Political Attitudes and the Survey Response." *American Political Science Review* 69 (4): 1218–1231.

———. 1992. "Social Psychology, Demographic Variables, and Linear Regression: Breaking the Iron Triangle in Voting Research." *Political Behavior* 14 (3): 195–211.

Aldrich, John H. 1983. "A Downsian Spatial Model with Party Activism." *American Political Science Review* 77 (4): 974–990.

Alesina, Alberto. 1988. "Credibility and Policy Convergence in a Two-Party System with Rational Voters." *American Economic Review* 78 (4): 796–805.

Arthur, W. Brian, Y. M. Ermoliev, and Y. M. Kaniovski. 1987. "Path-Dependent Processes and the Emergence of Macro-Structure." *European Journal of Operational Research* 30: 294–303.

Calvert, Randall. 1985. "Robustness of the Multidimensional Voting Model: Candidate Motivations, Uncertainty, and Convergence." *American Journal of Political Science* 29 (1): 69–95.

Carmines, Edward G., and James A. Stimson. 1989. *Issue Evolution: Race and the Transformation of American Politics*. Princeton, NJ: Princeton University Press.

Cohen, Michael E., and Robert Axelrod. 1984. "Coping with Complexity: The Adaptive Value of Changing Utility." *American Economic Review* 74 (1): 30–42.

Coughlin, Peter J. 1990. "Majority Rule and Election Models." *Journal of Economic Surveys* 3: 157–188.

Cutler, Fred. 2002. "The Simplest Shortcut of All: Voter-Candidate Sociodemographic Similarity and Electoral Choice." *Journal of Politics* 64 (2): 466–490.

Cyert, Richard M., and Morris H. DeGroot. 1975. "Adaptive Utility." In *Adaptive Economic Models*, ed. R. H. Day and T. Groves. New York: Academic Press.

———. 1987. *Bayesian Analysis and Uncertainty in Economic Theory*. Totowa, NJ: Rowman and Littlefield.

Davis, Otto A., and Melvin J. Hinich. 1967. "Some Results Related to a Mathematical Model of Policy Formation in a Democratic Society." In *Mathematical Applications in Political Science*, Vol. 3, ed. J. Bernd. Charlottesville: University of Virginia Press.

———. 1968. "On the Power and Importance of the Mean Preference in a Mathematical Model of Democratic Choice." *Public Choice* 5: 59–72.

Davis, Otto A., Melvin J. Hinich, and Peter C. Ordeshook. 1970. "An Expository Development of a Mathematical Model of the Electoral Process." *American Political Science Review* 64 (3): 426–448.

Downs, Anthony. 1957. *An Economic Theory of Democracy*. New York: Harper and Row.

Enelow, James, and Melvin J. Hinich. 1984a. *The Spatial Theory of Voting*. New York: Cambridge University Press.

———. 1984b. "Probabilistic Voting and the Importance of Centrist Ideologies in Democratic Elections." *Journal of Politics* 46: 459–478.

———. 1989. "A General Probabilistic Spatial Theory of Elections." *Public Choice* 61: 101–113.

Erikson, Robert S. 1978. "Analyzing One Variable–Three Wave Panel Data: A Comparison of Two Models." *Political Methodology* 5: 151–161.

———. 1979. "The SRC Panel Data and Mass Political Attitudes: Change and Uncertainty." *British Journal of Political Science* 9: 89–114.

Erikson, Robert S., and David W. Romero. 1990. "Candidate Equilibrium and the Behavioral Model of the Vote." *American Political Science Review* 84: 1103–1126.

Fiorina, Morris. 1981. *Retrospective Voting in American National Elections*. New Haven, CT: Yale University Press.

Franklin, Charles H., and John E. Jackson. 1983. "The Dynamics of Party Identification." *American Political Science Review* 77 (4): 957–973.

Gerber, Elisabeth and John E. Jackson. 1993. "Endogenous Preferences and the Study of Institutions." *American Political Science Review* 87 (3): 639–656.

Jackson, John E. 1973. "Intensities, Preferences, and Electoral Politics." *Social Science Research* 2 (3): 231–246.

———. 1975. "Issues, Party Choices, and Presidential Votes." *American Journal of Political Science* 19 (2): 161–185.

———. 1983. "The Systematic Beliefs of the Mass Public: Estimating Policy Preferences Preferences with Survey Data." *Journal of Politics* 45 (4): 840–865.

———. 1985. "Preference Evolution among the Mass Public: 1956–1964." *Political Methodology* 11 (3–4): 221–248.

———. 1992. "Estimating Models with Variable Coefficients." *Political Analysis* 3: 27–49.

———. 1996a. "Electoral Competition with Endogenous Voter Preferences." Paper, Midwest Political Science Association Conference, Chicago.

———. 1996b. "Political Methodology: An Overview." In *New Handbook of Political Science*, ed. Robert Goodin and Hans-Dieter Klingemann, 717–748. Oxford: Oxford University Press.

———. 1999. "Electoral Competition with Endogenous Activists." Paper, American Political Science Association Conference, Atlanta.

Kessel, John. 1988. *Presidential Campaign Politics*. Chicago: Dorsey Press.

Kinder, Donald R., and David O. Sears. 1985. "Public Opinion and Political Action." In *The Handbook of Social Psychology II*, 3d. ed., ed. Gardner Lindzey and Elliot Aronson, 659–741. New York: Random House.

Kollman, Ken, John H. Miller, and Scott E. Page. 1992. "Adaptive Parties in Spatial Elections." *American Political Science Review* 86 (4): 929–937.

Kollman, Ken, John H. Miller, and Scott E. Page. 1998. "Political Parties and Electoral Landscapes." *British Journal of Political Science* 28: 139–158.

Lindbeck, Assar, and Jörgen Weibull. 1993. "A Model of Political Equilibrium in a Representative Democracy." *Journal of Public Economics* 51: 195–209.

Lupia, Arthur. 1994. "Shortcuts versus Encyclopedias: Information and Voting Behavior in California Insurance Reform Elections." *American Political Science Review* 88: 63–76.

Lupia, Arthur, and Mathew D. McCubbins. 1998. *The Democratic Dilemma: Can Citizens Learn What They Need to Know?* New York: Cambridge University Press.

Markus, Gregory B., and Philip E. Converse. 1979. "A Dynamic Simultaneous Equation Model of Electoral Choice." *American Political Science Review* 73 (3): 1055–1070.

McCloskey, Herbert, Paul J. Hoffman, and Rosemary O'Hara. 1960. "Issue Conflict and Consensus among Party Leaders and Followers." *American Political Science Review* 54 (2): 406–427.

McKelvey, Richard. 1976. "Intransitivities in Multidimensional Voting Models and Some Implications for Agenda Control." *Journal of Economic Theory* 12: 472–482.

———. 1979. "General Conditions for Global Intransitivities in Formal Voting Models." *Econometrica* 47: 1086–1112.

Miller, Warren E., and M. Kent Jennings. 1986. *Parties in Transition*. New York: Russell Sage Foundation.

Morton, Rebecca B. 1993. "Incomplete Information and the Ideological Explanations of Platform Divergence." *American Political Science Review* 87 (2): 382–392.

Plott, Charles E. 1967. "A Notion of Equilibrium and Its Possibility under Majority Rule." *American Economic Review* 57: 787–806.

Schofield, Norman J. 1978. "Instability of Simple Dynamic Games." *Review of Economic Studies* 45: 575–594.

Wittman, Donald. 1983. "Candidate Motivation: A Synthesis of Alternative Theories." *American Political Science Review* 77 (1): 142–157.

Zaller, John. 1991. "Information, Values, and Opinion." *American Political Science Review* 85 (4): 1215–1237.

———. 1992. *The Nature and Origin of Mass Opinion*. Cambridge, UK: Cambridge University Press.

# 5 A Computational Model of Voter Sophistication, Ideology, and Candidate Position Taking

Scott de Marchi

## 5.1 Introduction

It has long been argued that many of the simplifying assumptions utilized by political theorists are akin to frictionless planes: they allow us to discover fundamental elements of causation without the distraction of details. In the area of voting behavior, theorists have variously relied upon the assumptions of Euclidean preferences, complete information on the part of both voters and candidates, and the existence of a median-in-all-directions.[1] If these assumptions resulted in models that were either predictive or descriptive of human behavior, they would be fully justified; sadly, our efforts to predict political decisions have not been successful. Instead, work is often directed toward post hoc explanations of National Election Study (NES) data, which amount to arguments over which particular voting model best fits the sample at hand. Given that one should be far more concerned with generalizations out of sample, this seems to be an odd approach for a subfield that prides itself upon technical accomplishment.

The baseline model in voting theory, as in most other areas of political science, is rational choice theory.[2] It is worth repeating that rational choice modeling has been widely accepted in large part because of analytic simplicity. Any model of human decision making must provide two working parts. First, one needs an instantiation for the problems that human beings confront. In rational choice, this instantiation is most often an extensive form game with explicit utility functions. Second, one needs a solution concept and an algorithm that "solves" a given problem; rational choice theory typically utilizes Nash equilibrium as the solution concept and backwards induction as the algorithm.

An enormous amount of research has focused upon whether people can actually frame problems correctly (Can we satisfy information requirements?) or apply the appropriate solution concept (Can we satisfy computational requirements?). It is abundantly clear that people fail at both aspects of decision making as defined by rational choice. Further, a fair reading of the cognitive psychology and artificial intelligence literatures suggests that rational choice is not even a good approximation of how human beings solve problems (Lupia, McCubbins, and Popkin 2000).

The problem is that it takes something to beat something, and building models that incorporate a more realistic set of assumptions about human cognition requires a different framework than is commonly employed in the social sciences. The goal of this chapter is to build a simple computational model of voter choice, but not so simple that it ignores the core results offered by the survey and experimental researchers in this field. These core results include such factors as voter sophistication, ideology, and the presence of incompletely informed candidates. By examining these effects in light of their impact upon electoral outcomes, it is my hope that we can limit the space of "possible" voting models, insofar as these empirical realities condition political behavior. This chapter thus adheres to a "brute force" kind of empiricism. Using the common spatial model as a basis for comparison, I measure the impact of the effects just mentioned on the ability of voters and candidates to arrive at near-optimal outcomes.

Despite the fact that the model presented here is simple, at least in terms of the number of moving parts, it is still complex enough such that a resort to computational modeling is necessary. Without the ability to include both voter and candidate behavior, one doesn't get very far, and it is precisely this kind of dynamic that computational models implement (that is, many agents who react in potentially co-adaptive ways). As such, this work builds upon two diverse literatures in American politics: political psychology and computational political economy.

## 5.2 A Counter-argument

It could instead be argued that the formal results I malign have indeed been useful, insofar as they establish boundaries on what we might expect to see in electoral outcomes. These formal results show that even if voter preferences obey simplifying assumptions, instability reigns (McKelvey 1976; Plott 1967). This instability takes two forms: no dominant platform exists, and incumbents are expected to lose to challengers. If one adopts more complex assumptions (e.g., bounded rationality or incomplete information), so the argument goes, we would expect even less stability in electoral outcomes.

The problem with this type of reasoning is that it extrapolates from complete information models to situations where incomplete information is ubiquitous across electoral agents. As Kollman, Miller, and Page (1992; 1998) and de Marchi (1999) have shown, when models explicitly account for incomplete information, electoral outcomes are *more* predictable and stable than one might expect.

In these models, incumbents often remain in office because of the challenger's inability to find a dominant platform, and voter sophistication is a key predictor of the amount of turnover as well as the quality of representation displayed by officeholders. Thus, the reality of incomplete information models is that they are qualitatively different than complete information models, and there really is no reason to expect otherwise.[3]

## 5.3 Overview

This chapter seeks to patch a hole in previous computational work on elections by examining how more realistic models of voter behavior affect the electoral regularities found by Kollman, Miller, and Page, and de Marchi. Given that the emphasis of this body of work was on candidate behavior, it is not surprising that very little effort was devoted to modeling voters accurately. It is, however, difficult to argue that incompletely informed candidates are an essential feature of electoral competition while at the same time ignoring the fact that voters are, if anything, less informed. Thus, the previous work, while suggestive, does not go far enough in testing whether the results are sensitive to the particular model of voter cognition that is utilized.

Given that there are a large number of algorithms that one might employ in modeling voter decision making, it seems reasonable to test the stability results of Kollman, Miller, and Page, and de Marchi using assumptions derived from the political psychology literature. To limit the scope of this project, I have chosen what seems to be two central results that have been thoroughly examined by political psychologists.

### 5.3.1 *Voter Sophistication*

Clearly, the level of interest and sophistication of an individual plays an enormous role in political choice. What is most interesting is that a variety of models have found that different levels of sophistication equate to qualitatively different mechanisms of decision making. The work of Carmines and Stimson (1980), Lodge and Hamill (1986), Zaller and Feldman (1992), and Zaller (1992) is central in defining the role of voter sophistication in determining political choices. The core of this literature holds the following:

- Two, or perhaps three, qualitatively different levels of sophistication exist in the electorate.
- Highly sophisticated voters have better integrated and more far-reaching preference structures, and are more prone to receive political information from their environment. They also display "attitude constraint," or an organized system of political opinions.[4]
- Voters of medium sophistication receive some signals from the political environment, and have some propensity to structure their preferences, but are not as consistent as the highest category.
- Voters with low sophistication do not structure preferences, receive relatively few signals from their political environment, and typically provide more volatile responses to issues (measured over time).[5]
- Voters respond to survey (or poll) questions in one of two ways: either they provide an ad hoc response that reflects their context at a given point in time, or they give a more considered response that is a better predictor of their true, underlying attitudes. Whether this behavior is driven by sophistication and intelligence (as Lodge and Hamill say) or by the amount of attention the voter dedicates to the task (as Zaller and Feldman say) is not clear, but it follows that this behavior would enormously complicate the ability of candidates to conduct polls and arrive at optimal platforms.

### 5.3.2 *Ideology*

An extension of the voter sophistication results has been developed for the elite level by Poole and Rosenthal (1991) and for the general electorate by Hinich and Munger (1994). The core of this research is that individuals choose in a space of lower dimensionality than one would expect given the size of the complete issue space at any given point in time. Consistency is not taken to be a global, deductively plausible set of constraints; rather, issues cluster into recognizable groups in one's memory.

For example, if I know your position on racial affirmative action, I can likely guess your feelings about women serving in combat roles. It also seems plausible that ideology acts in another important way. Given that candidates send signals to voters on a wide variety of issues, ideology allows incompletely informed voters to use these signals as a means of reducing the variance of their estimates of candidate location on the reduced ideological space.[6] With modest restrictions on the type of disturbance term involved with the reception of candidate signals, variance would decrease as a function of the number of issues a voter receives signals upon.

The basic plan guiding this work is very simple. If one includes both voter sophistication and ideology in a model of elections, are the stability results found by Kollman, Miller, and Page, and de Marchi still present? Stated another way, if *both* candidates and voters are incompletely informed, what type of electoral outcomes might one expect? As in previous computational work in this field, *stable* is taken to mean two things:

- Incumbents do not always lose to challengers; rather, incumbents have innate advantages because of greater resources or their "knowledge" of the electorate.
- Officeholders represent the policy preferences of their constituents (this is what is typically meant by a representative democracy) contingent upon the level of attention present in the electorate.

What we see is that the previous results are broadly supported, although voter sophistication seems to be more important in determining the level of responsiveness on the part of winning candidates for office.

## 5.4 The Model

The aim of this chapter is to test the resiliency of the computational results that predict stability in electoral outcomes under a more realistic set of voter dynamics. This section outlines the key assumptions of the computational model and, in particular, the instantiation I have chosen for the listed behavioral results. The goal is to determine how (if) more realistic models of voter cognition change the ability of incompletely informed parties to find successful or central platforms. At first glance, it seems the presence of poorly informed voters would hinder candidate polling efforts because of the innate response volatility in many members of the electorate.[7] Ideology, on the other hand, would aid candidates insofar as it would reduce not only the choice space but also the difficulty inherent in determining voter opinions.

The model assumptions are as follows.

*Assumption A1.* The issue space for these experiments is two-dimensional. Individual issues range from $-10$ to $+10$, and it is assumed that the prevailing ideology is equivalent to

$$(\text{Issue } 1) = -(\text{Issue } 2).$$

If one thinks of issue 1 as "Guns" and issue 2 as "Butter," with positive positions equivalent to spending more on that issue, the ideology becomes clearer, namely, someone who likes lots of guns would dislike butter. Finally, there are two candidates for office in all results presented here.

*Assumption A2.* Two groups of voters exist in this model.

The first group represents highly sophisticated voters, who account for $\alpha_1$ percent of the population. The question addressed by the parameter $\alpha_1$ is how much the level of sophisticated voters affects electoral outcomes.

- These voters utilize the prevailing ideology and thus have constrained issue positions.[8]
- They report their preferences without bias and with a small variance $\sim N\ (0, 1)$. Given this distribution for the error term, highly sophisticated voters report issue positions within one interval of their "true" position 68 percent of the time.[9]

The second group of voters displays less interest or aptitude in politics:

- They do not depend upon the prevailing ideology and thus have unconstrained issue positions (issue positions are derived from an independent, uniform distribution).
- They report their preferences without bias but with large variance $\sim N\ (0, \alpha_2)$. The key parameter here is $\alpha_2$, which represents the

amount of variance present in the responses of less sophisticated voters. One would expect that as $\alpha_2$ increases, candidates have a more and more difficult time finding "good" platforms. For example, if $\alpha_2 = 13$, less sophisticated voters report issue positions within one interval of their "true" attitude 22 percent of the time and within six intervals 90 percent of the time.

Voter preferences are represented by a policy vector **X** and a salience vector **S**.[10] Parties $\alpha$ and $\beta$ are represented by policy vectors $\mathbf{Y}_\alpha$ and $\mathbf{Y}_\beta$, where each issue has equal salience (to the party). Utility for voter $j$ given party $k$ across all issues $i \in N$ is given by

$$u_i(\mathbf{Y}_k) = -\sum_{i=1}^{n} s_{ij}(x_{ij} - y_{ik})^2.$$

*Assumption A3.* Parties lack complete information on the composition of the electorate and must instead take a number of polls during the course of the election. Parties have a limited budget available to poll the electorate, and after each turn, adjust their platforms to take advantage of the polling data. Specifically, parties choose an initial platform and poll in the neighborhood of this platform. They then utilize a hill-climbing algorithm to adapt party positions based upon the results of these polls. Incumbents, however, have the benefit of their adaptive experience from the previous election and are also allowed to adapt during their term. The exact measure of an incumbent's information advantage is a parameter in the model.

The justification for the incumbent's informational advantage is twofold. First, incumbents should have access to informational resources (experience, the ability to conduct polls, etc.) while in office that allows them to "tweak" or even alter their message for upcoming campaigns. Second, incumbents in federal elections typically are unchallenged in their party primary and thus avoid the game of sliding to the extreme to please primary voters and then sliding back to the middle for the general election—a game that can only be seen as consuming precious campaign resources.

## 5.5 Results

The computational experiments focused on three main questions. First, How much effect does response volatility have upon the quality of electoral outcomes? Second, Does the proportion of highly sophisticated voters in an electorate change electoral outcomes for the better, especially when less sophisticated voters are volatile? Last, Does ideology play a role in determining the quality of electoral outcomes?

In all the computational experiments presented here, the variable used as a proxy for the quality of the electoral outcome is the distance between the final candidate platform and the optimal distance possible.[11] Each candidate was allowed to iterate a hill-climbing procedure 50 times to achieve their final campaign platform.

### 5.5.1 *Less Sophisticated Voters and Response Instability*

The first question concerns the effect of parameter $\alpha_2$, the amount of variance present in less sophisticated voter responses, upon electoral outcomes. To answer this question, three categories of data were generated (see table 5.1).

The results of an ANOVA to test for the effect of $\alpha_2$ on electoral outcome are presented in table 5.2.

As is immediately apparent, $\alpha_2$ has a large effect on the ability of candidates to find an ideal platform. The overall curve (with more values) appears to be sigmoidal, which is not surprising given the assumptions of the model. The only violation of this general

**Table 5.1**
Variance in Voter Responses

| | | | |
|---|---|---|---|
| Cases used for less sophisticated voters (variance = $\alpha_2$) | $\sim N(0, 14)$ | $\sim N(0, 50)$ | $\sim N(0, 100)$ |
| Observations ($N$) | 200 | 200 | 200 |

**Table 5.2**
Effect of Response Variance on Electoral Outcome

| | | |
|---|---|---|
| | Number of observations: 600<br>Adj. $R2$: .02 | $F$ (2, 597): 6.51<br>Pr( ) > $F$: .0016 |
| Response Variance ($\alpha_2$) | Coefficient | $t$ statistic (Pr( ) > $\|t\|$) |
| $\alpha_2 = \sim 14$ | −9473.71 | −3.34 (.001) |
| $\alpha_2 = \sim 50$ | −8070.8 | −2.85 (.005) |
| $\alpha_2 = \sim 100$ | Baseline | Baseline |

tendency is the case where $\alpha_2$ is very small; candidates performed relatively poorly, but this is because a little noise is good for the hill-climbing procedure. Last, it should be noted that in the two "better" cases (where $\alpha_2 = 14$ and 50), candidates converged to within 25 percent of the optimal distance possible. The worst case, where $\alpha_2 = 100$, was difficult for the hill-climbing challengers, who were typically at double the optimal distance.

This result highlights the fact that once a certain variance in responses is reached, things fall apart rapidly. If less interested voters display significant variance in their responses over time, whether because of innate, cognitive factors or the impact of new events and information, it is very difficult for candidates to find "good" platforms. Limited resources prevent candidates from conducting complete canvassing of the electorate, and to some degree, this constraint is magnified by moving target in the simulation—the less interested voters.

### 5.5.2 *The Impact of Sophisticated Voters*

The second question concerns the importance of parameter $\alpha_1$, which measures the proportion of the electorate that is highly sophisticated. Data were generated using two different values for $\alpha_1$ and a fixed value of 100 for $\alpha_2$. The ANOVA results for this experiment are both disappointing and surprising. The differences between the two groups $\alpha_1 = 0.25$ and $\alpha_1 = 0.50$ are not significant ($F$ value $= 1.47$; $\Pr(\ ) > F = 0.23$). In fact, it is not until one increases the proportion of highly sophisticated voters, defined by $\alpha_1$, to greater than 0.66 that one finds significant differences between populations.[12]

The purpose of examining the influence of $\alpha_1$ (the percentage of highly sophisticated voters) in conjunction with $\alpha_2$ (the level of variance displayed by less sophisticated voters) is to determine which parameter matters more. That is, is it better to have a higher percentage of sophisticated voters in an electorate? Or, alternatively, does the level of volatility among the less sophisticated voters drive the model? Here, *better* is defined to mean an electorate that results in more central position taking by successful candidates. Centrality thus serves as a measure of party responsiveness and is defined in the same manner as in Kollman, Miller, and Page (1992): sum the utilities of all voters for the winning platform, and divide this by the sum of all voter utilities for the median platform.

Given the foregoing, two findings seem clear:

- When less sophisticated voters are extremely volatile, the presence of highly sophisticated voters does not aid candidates in arriving at a representative platform (until one gets to the extraordinary level of 0.66 or above for $\alpha_1$). The inclusion of mechanisms that allow less interested voters to acquire cues from information elites may help this problem (e.g., McKelvey and Ordeshook 1985b).[13]
- When less interested voters display less volatility (when $\alpha_2$ is not large), an increase in the number of sophisticated voters does aid candidates in finding competitive platforms, and electoral outcomes are both more stable and more representative. But given the proposed measure for centrality, it is better to have less response instability on the part of less sophisticated voters than a higher proportion of very sophisticated voters.

### 5.5.3 *Ideology, or Simply Response Stability?*

The final result concerns the effect of ideology upon electoral outcomes and the ability of candidates to find competitive platforms. To test the effect of ideology upon electoral outcomes, I generated two types of electorates. The first electorate modeled highly sophisticated voters who depended upon ideology, as detailed in assumption A1. The second electorate modeled highly sophisticated voters without ideology; the variance in their responses was very low, but they did *not* have constrained issue positions.

The results of the test to see if any difference emerges in candidate performance between these two electorate types are shown in table 5.3. As is clear, the presence of ideology was not significant, although the sign of the response is in the correct direction. Curiously, additional experiments show that ideology only achieves significance if two conditions hold:

**Table 5.3**
Effect of Electorate Types on Candidate Performance

| | Number of observations: 400<br>Adj. $R2$: .0001 | $F$: 1.05<br>Pr( ) > $F$: .31 |
|---|---|---|
| Class of Voters | Coefficient | $t$ statistic (Pr( ) > $\|t\|$) |
| Ideological | −986.43 | −1.03 (.31) |
| Nonideological | Baseline | Baseline |

• The proportion of highly sophisticated voters is greater than 0.5.

• The amount of variance displayed by less sophisticated voters is high ($\alpha_2 > 100$).

Thus, without additional assumptions that would model the ability of elites or highly sophisticated voters to send cues to other voters, ideology has no great effect upon electoral outcomes. One additional mitigating factor is that there is no cost to communication in these experiments. Obviously, if voters had *shared* constraints on issue positions, this would likely result in a larger role for ideology given that this kind of redundancy would greatly enhance the ability of candidates to send political cues.

## 5.6 A Complication and Further Work

First, the complication. Unlike those of other computational models currently in the political economy literature, the results detailed here depend crucially upon the exact search algorithm used by the candidates. Although I relied exclusively upon a hill-climbing algorithm to model candidate searches in the policy space, I also constructed matching experiments using a genetic algorithm for the candidates. Candidate efficiency not only varied from one search algorithm to another, but more important, results varied in a nonsystematic way. Despite my expectations that a genetic algorithm would outperform the hill-climbing algorithm, hill-climbing was more successful throughout the middle range of parameter values for $\alpha_2$. My best guess, based upon limited regression work and snapshots of the underlying topologies, is that underlying uniformity present in many of the electoral landscapes (caused by the presence of highly sophisticated voters) is better exploited by hill-climbing when significant noise is added because of high variance terms for the less sophisticated voters. The genetic algorithm did, however, perform better when highly sophisticated voters had constrained (ideological) issues, further muddying more general conclusions. More research is clearly needed to determine what the relationship is between particular sets of assumptions underlying the adaptive landscape and the relative success of different search algorithms. Note that this complication differs quite substantially from previous computational modeling in the domain of electoral politics (Kollman, Miller, and Page 1992; de Marchi 1999).

Despite this complication, it is encouraging that the first two results are fairly robust across a broad range of parameter choices. While the results presented here are clearly incomplete, the general thrust of these findings is that one can expect candidate convergence unless pathological amounts of volatility exist on the part of voters. Further, overall sophistication, as reflected by response stability, seems a more decisive component of electoral stability than the presence of constrained, highly sophisticated voters or the presence of ideology among sophisticated voters.

Further work in this area should aim at the more general question of providing a general measure of electoral complexity (that is, the difficulty of searching an adaptive landscape formed by actual voter preferences). Given the increasing number of results in computational political economy on this topic, such an empirical measure would allow our models to bridge the gap between abstract findings and more specific predictions about actual electorates. An empirical measure of electoral complexity would be particularly useful insofar as this seems to be the central determinant of the success or failure of incumbents as well as the more general effect of resources upon political success.

## Notes

The author acknowledges the helpful comments of Michael Bailey, Jennifer Harrod, Ken Kollman, Michael Munger, and Lyle Scruggs. All errors are mine.

1. See, for example, Calvert (1985), Enelow and Hinich (1983), and McKelvey and Ordeshook (1985a; 1985b).

2. Even models that purport to model "bounded" rationality do not, in large part, diverge from the core assumptions of spatial voting. For example, Hinich and Munger's (1994) work on ideology preserves complete information on the part of voters and preferences that meet the usual assumptions. Other models that amend spatial voting, such as directional theory (Rabinowitz and Macdonald 1989) and on-line tally models (Lodge and Hamill 1986), are qualitatively similar.

3. That dramatic changes in outcomes can be the result of changing information assumptions should be no surprise. Game theory is full of models that display this behavior; the most commonly cited is perhaps the Kreps and Wilson (1982) work on the chain store game.

4. This point and the next two closely follow the Receive-Accept-Sample (RAS) model detailed by Zaller (1992).

5. Given that highly sophisticated voters depend upon a qualitatively different choice mechanism (they use schema or ideology), it seems that one could safely collapse the bottom two groups into one.

6. Since issues are clustered, individual signals are redundant, thus allowing for better estimates of candidate location.

7. In essence, less sophisticated voters cannot be said to *report* single-peaked preferences!

8. These assumptions detailing highly sophisticated voters are much like those utilized by McKelvey and Ordeshook (1985b) except that instead of helping their fellow citizens reach a decision, they provide accurate information to polling candidates.

9. The distributions are actually truncated for both groups of voters at $\pm 10$.

10. For the results presented here, all issues are of equal salience.

11. Keep in mind that smaller distances are better, where distance is simple Euclidean distance between the candidate platform and the electorate. Also note that using 50 iterations was more than sufficient for candidates to "converge" (if indeed they were able to do so given the value of $\alpha_2$).

12. ANOVA results follow for a total of 500 observations in two cases: 400 generated using values of $\alpha_1$ between 0.25 and 0.50, and 100 using $\alpha_1 = 0.75$. As noted in the text, $\alpha_1 = 0.66$ is the inflection point, and differences between the populations increase monotonically as $\alpha_1$ increases. The value of 0.75 is chosen as an illustration.

| | Number of observations: 500<br>Adj. $R2$: .16 | $F$ (1, 498): 96.91<br>Pr( ) > $F$: .0000 |
|---|---|---|
| **% Sophisticated Voters ($\alpha_1$)** | **Coefficient** | ***t* statistic (Pr( ) > \|*t*\|)** |
| $\alpha_1$ between 0.25 and 0.5 | −45,252.7 | 9.84 (.000) |
| $\alpha_1 = 0.75$ | Baseline | Baseline |

13. Information exchange between voters is likely a difficult task to approach. While McKelvey and Ordeshook's (1985a; 1985b) work in this field is an important first step, the real problem is that competing information sources exist, and voters must still choose whom to listen to. The problem represented by the information costs of voting is thus pushed back one level and not really solved by models that rely upon a unitary, truthful fortuneteller (or interest group or set of elite voters or . . .).

## References

Bernhardt, M. Daniel, and Daniel E. Ingberman. 1985. "Candidate Reputations and the Incumbency Effect." *Journal of Public Economics* 27: 47–67.

Black, Duncan. 1958. *The Theory of Committees and Elections*. New York: Cambridge University Press. Reprinted 1987 by Kluwer Academic, Boston.

Calvert, Randall. 1985. "Robustness of the Multidimensional Voting Model: Candidate Motivations, Uncertainty, and Convergence." *American Journal of Political Science* 29: 69–95.

Carmines, Edward, and James Stimson. 1980. "The Two Faces of Issue Voting." *American Political Science Review* 74: 78–91.

Davis, Otto, Morris DeGroot, and Melvin Hinich. 1972. "Social Preference Orderings and Majority Rule." *Econometrica* 40: 147–157.

de Marchi, Scott. 1999. "Adaptive Models and Electoral Instability." *Journal of Theoretical Politics* 11 (3): 393–419.

Delli Carpini, Michael, and Scott Keeter. 1991. "Stability and Change in the U.S. Public's Knowledge of Politics." *Public Opinion Quarterly* 27: 133–141.

Downs, Anthony. 1957. *An Economic Theory of Democracy*. New York: Harper and Row.

Enelow, James, and Melvin Hinich. 1983. "On Plott's Pairwise Symmetry Condition for Majority Rule Equilibrium." *Public Choice* 40: 317–321.

———. 1984. *The Spatial Theory of Voting*. New York: Cambridge University Press.

Ferejohn, John. 1986. "Incumbent Performance and Electoral Control." *Public Choice* 50: 5–25.

———. 1993. "The Spatial Model and Elections." In *Information, Participation, and Choice*, ed. B. Grofman, 107–124. Ann Arbor: University of Michigan Press.

Fiorina, Morris. 1981. *Retrospective Voting in American National Elections*. New Haven, CT: Yale University Press.

Hinich, Melvin, and Michael Munger. 1994. *Ideology and the Theory of Political Choice*. Ann Arbor: University of Michigan Press.

Holland, John. 1975. *Adaptation in Natural and Artificial Systems*. Ann Arbor: University of Michigan Press.

Holland, John, and John Miller. 1991. "Artificial Adaptive Agents in Economic Theory." *American Economic Review* (*Papers and Proceedings*) 81: 365–370.

Kauffman, Stuart. 1993. *The Origins of Order*. New York: Oxford University Press.

Kollman, Ken, John Miller, and Scott Page. 1992. "Adaptive Parties in Spatial Elections." *American Political Science Review* 86: 929–938.

———. 1998. "Political Parties and Electoral Landscapes." *British Journal of Political Science* 28: 139–158.

Kramer, Gerald. 1973. "On a Class of Equilibrium Conditions for Majority Rule." *Econometrica* 41: 285–297.

Kreps, David, and Robert Wilson. 1982. "Reputation and Imperfect Information." *Journal of Economic Theory* 27: 253–279.

Lodge, Milton, and Ruth Hamill. 1986. "A Partisan Schema for Political Information Processing." *American Political Science Review* 80: 505–519.

Lupia, Arthur, Matthew McCubbins, and Samuel Popkin, eds. 2000. *Elements of Reason*. Cambridge: Cambridge University Press.

McKelvey, Richard. 1976. "General Conditions for Global Intransitivities in Formal Voting Models." *Econometrica* 47: 1085–1111.

McKelvey, Richard, and Peter Ordeshook. 1985a. "Sequential Elections with Limited Information." *American Journal of Political Science* 29: 480–512.

———. 1985b. "Elections with Limited Information: A Fulfilled Expectations Model Using Contemporaneous Data as Information Sources." *Journal of Economic Theory* 36: 55–85.

Mueller, Dennis. 1989. *Public Choice II*. New York: Cambridge University Press.

Page, Benjamin. 1977. "Elections and Social Choice: The State of the Evidence." *American Journal of Political Science* 21: 639–668.

Plott, Charles. 1967. "A Notion of Equilibrium and Its Possibility under Majority Rule." *American Economic Review* 57: 787–806.

Poole, Keith, and Howard Rosenthal. 1991. "Patterns of Congressional Voting." *American Journal of Political Science* 35: 228–278.

Rabinowitz, George, and Stuart Macdonald. 1989. "A Directional Theory of Issue Voting." *American Political Science Review* 83: 93–121.

Schelling, Thomas. 1978. *Micromotives and Macrobehavior*. New York: Norton.

Schofield, Norman. 1984. "Social Equilibrium and Cycles on Compact Sets." *Journal of Economic Theory* 33: 59–71.

Stokes, Donald. 1963. "Spatial Models of Party Competition." *American Political Science Review* 57: 368–377.

Zaller, John. 1992. *The Nature and Origins of Mass Opinion*. New York: Cambridge University Press.

Zaller, John, and Stanley Feldman. 1992. "A Simple Theory of the Survey Response: Answering Questions versus Revealing Preferences." *American Journal of Political Science* 36: 579–616.

# 6 The Other Side of the Coin: A Computational Analysis of Publicly Financed Campaigns

Michael Bailey

## 6.1 Introduction

Many students of politics are concerned that legislators overrepresent wealthy interest groups in order to raise campaign funds. Academics cite models in which election-seeking candidates align their preferences with moneyed interests in order to secure campaign contributions (Stigler 1971; Magee, Brock, and Young 1989; Baron 1994; Lohmann 1993). Policy analysts present commonsense claims that the money would not be passing hands if nothing were being bought. Journalists present anecdotes of unseemly relations between contributors and politicians (Rauch 1994). One result of this concern is increasing support for reforms that will "get the money out of politics."

However, the many people who focus on the pernicious effects of the *raising* of campaign funds tend to overlook the effects of the *spending* of these funds. This chapter argues that the other side of the coin, as it were, merits more theoretical attention. Using a formal model and computational methods, it shows that campaign spending can have a positive effect on the representation of diffuse interests—the long-suffering victims of the campaign finance system, in the conventional account.

The key to the model here is voter information. In many interest group dominance models, voter information levels are not only low (a reasonable assumption) but fixed at that low level (an unreasonable assumption). These interest group models elevate a stylized fact about voter ignorance that holds in equilibrium into a core assumption about the political process. In contrast, voters in the model in this chapter can become informed, inducing candidates to compete based on the appeal of their policies and the information they provide to voters.

Although some claims emerging from the model can be proven analytically, the most interesting aspects cannot be examined with conventional proofs. This chapter therefore uses computational methods to identify optimal policy and campaign choices by candidates across a series of political environments (Kollman, Miller, and Page 1995; Judd 1998).

Of particular interest is the effect of campaign spending on relatively uninformed and uninterested diffuse interests. These interests benefit from higher levels of campaign spending. The reason is similar to the mechanisms of diffuse representation discussed in Denzau and Munger (1986) and Arnold (1990): campaign resources enable candidates to mobilize diffuse interests. This causes all candidates to preemptively weigh the preferences of these interests more heavily in order to prevent an opponent from mobilizing them.

Observed spending patterns, however, may provide little evidence of such a dynamic. The action is "off the equilibrium path" (Weingast 1996), meaning that the effect of campaign funds binds before they are allocated. Once a candidate preempts mobilization of diffuse voters, the other candidate will have fewer incentives to mobilize them. Hence, the campaign resources can have their effect even if they are spent on nondiffuse voting blocs.

The computational analysis also indicates that the allocation of resources across the candidates is extremely important. When one candidate has very low levels of resources, an opponent with significant resources is virtually unconstrained. However, as the underfunded candidate gets more resources, the constraints bind quickly on the better-funded candidate, strengthening the link between candidate choices and constituency preferences.

The goal of this chapter is to identify a major lacuna in standard models and to point out what these models lose because of it. It does not purport, however, to tell the whole story of campaign finance. Most important, it does not endogenize the fund-*raising* aspects so central to critiques of the current system. The conclusion discusses the effect of merging this aspect of campaign finance with the effects presented here.

## 6.2 Campaigns and Voting

Scholars have identified four mechanisms for campaign expenditures to affect voter choices. The most common, and probably the least satisfactory, is that campaign expenditures are "a type of advertising, in which spending for a candidate increases the probability that the candidate wins the office he or she is seeking" (Snyder 1989, 637; Magee, Brock, and Young 1989, 53). This mechanism may be intuitive but at its core requires voters to be irrational (Fiorina and Noll 1979; Austen-Smith 1990; Morton and Cameron 1992). It means that voters respond favorably to campaign spending no matter what the issue positions of the candidates are.

It is not surprising that candidates in models with such voters serve only special interests, for the voters are completely oblivious to the policies represented by politicians. Magee, Brock, and Young (1989) even find "reasonable" conditions in which interest groups and candidates get caught in an ever-increasing escalating arms race of campaign contributions such that the entire economy disappears into a "black hole" of interest group service.

Baron's (1994) hybrid version of this approach partly addresses this problem. In his model, districts are divided into fixed proportions of uninformed and informed voters. Campaign spending buys the votes of uninformed voters, while informed voters are assumed to be perfectly informed and to vote rationally. However, the basic problem persists because part of the electorate continues to be not only uninformed but unalterably so. In addition, a central aspect of campaigns—the strategic conversion of uninformed voters to informed voters—is missing.

In a second approach, candidates spend money to affect the salience to voters of different issues (Fann and Mete 1998). For example, a candidate whose position on crime is more popular will flood the airwaves with crime commercials in order to lead people to place more weight on the crime issue. This approach also hinges on nonrational behavior by voters. In standard utility-maximizing models of individual choice, individuals have fixed preferences and make choices to maximize their utilities. If utility depends on multiple factors, the weights placed on these factors is fixed, as they are simply an element of preferences. Allowing candidates to change saliences, therefore, is equivalent to allowing them to change voter preferences.

Translating this into electoral politics, one can see that the model would hinge on voters' acting in a way inconsistent with this conventional view of rationality. A candidate whose policies were out of touch with those preferred by voters could win an election based on one issue. For example—to provide an extreme example—if voter saliences were simply a function of advertising, Barry Goldwater in 1964 could have, with enough money, won the election by changing voter utility functions such that voters cared more about how Johnson maltreated his pet beagle than about what the candidates would do to prevent nuclear war. In rational choices perspectives, such spending would resolve uncertainty about some aspects of Johnson's personality but would not lead voters to base their decisions only on these qualities.

A third approach proposes that campaign spending signals candidate quality (Prat 1997; Gerber 1996). In these models, political insiders—including political action committees and other sources of funding—observe candidate quality while poorly informed voters do not. Contributors avoid wasting money on low-quality candidates who will probably lose, so they only contribute to high-quality types. Spending by a candidate thereby can serve as a credible signal to uninformed voters of candidate quality.

These models maintain voter rationality but need further development. First, voters can really only infer "electability" instead of more relevant qualities such as ideological placement, honesty, and diligence. In fact, large amounts of campaign contributions may indicate poor quality in the sense that the candidates have been bought off by special interests. In addition, tractability concerns have prevented scholars from endogenizing policy positions, thereby excluding a crucial element of political interaction.

A fourth proposal is that candidates use campaign spending to affect voter information levels. Austen-Smith (1987) assumes that candidates spend resources to reduce uncertainty of all voters. With risk-averse voters, then, any spending to decrease uncertainty is valuable to voters and, by extension, to candidates. Hinich and Munger (1994) allow money *either* to reduce or increase uncertainty. The effect is the same as when money is simply assumed to increase the probability of winning, but here there is an explicit and defensible mechanism.

An important issue for this literature is whether campaign spending is constrained to increase information or can also decrease information. If the latter, politicians will presumably be more responsive to contributors if they can spend the money convincing voters that they are not responsive to contributors. An answer to this issue can be found in Banks (1990). He shows that if voters are rational, campaign spending can only reduce uncertainty, not increase it. In his model, voters try to infer the true policy positions of candidates from campaign announcements. Once elected, candidates (now legislators) face an exogenously determined cost of implementing a policy different than their announced positions. In equilibrium, if defection costs are low, voters gain no information from candidate announcements. As costs increase, however, candidates separate and send informative signals.

One can conclude that there is no misinformation equilibrium. Either information is credible and reduces the uncertainty of voters, or it is not credible and is ignored by voters. This result is consistent with empirical findings by Partin (1996), Coleman and Manna (2000), and others that campaign spending increases voter information. Note also that ads that the spending buys need not be directly informative. Significant research demonstrates the importance of heuristics in allowing complex information to be transmitted in simple media (Popkin 1991; Lupia and McCubbins 1998).

Hence, the informational perspective offers an attractive alternative that maintains voter rationality while presenting a specific mechanism for campaign spending to affect voting. However, existing informational perspectives have one problematic constraint. They assume that candidates spend money to reduce or increase the uncertainty of *all* voters, even those that dislike or like them very much. There is no allocation of information-changing resources across voting blocs. In fact, we know that information targeting and mobilization efforts are central tasks of campaigns (Faucheux 1999). Therefore, the next section takes the informational framework and adds an ability for candidates to target information.

## 6.3 The Model

The model is developed in the context of probabilistic voting theory (see Coughlin 1992; Enelow and Hinich 1989). Voters' choices are a stochastic function of the utility differences between candidates. As the utility difference gets larger, the probability voters vote for the candidate offering the higher utility increases. These models differ from deterministic models in which voters vote for the more attractive candidate with certainty, even if the difference between candidates is minuscule (see Downs 1957; Davis and Hinich 1966; McKelvey 1976).[1]

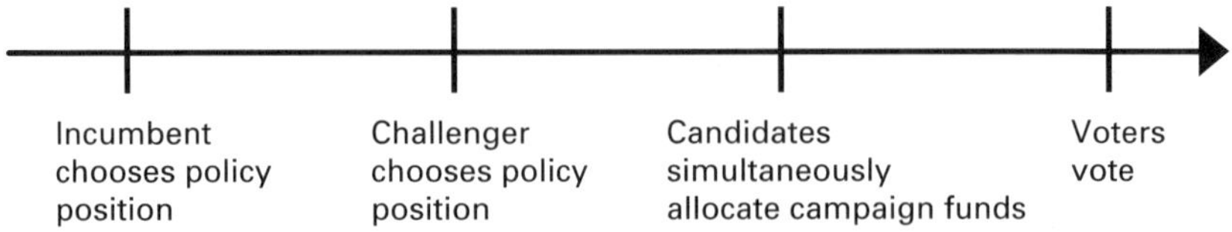


**Figure 6.1**
Game Sequence

There are two candidates and a fixed number of voters. The sequence of moves is depicted in figure 6.1. The incumbent moves first by selecting a policy position. In the analytical results that follow, this position can be multidimensional. In the computational results, I solve only for one dimension (see Bailey (2002) for multiple dimensional computational analysis). The policy dimensions can be considered predictive ideological dimensions (Hinich and Munger 1994). Next, the challenger observes the incumbent's policy position and selects his or her policy position. Then there is a campaign in which candidates simultaneously choose $N$ dimensional allocations of resources $(R^I, R^C)$ toward providing information to $N$ voting blocs. After the campaign, an election with stochastic voting is held. The candidate with the most votes is elected and payoffs are made.

The sequential nature of choice here approximates true ordering, as incumbents generally have to go on record before their opponents. It also guarantees an equilibrium. If the choice were simultaneous, an equilibrium would exist only for sufficiently high uncertainty. Moving second does not ensure a challenger victory, however, as incumbency advantage can be incorporated via a valence term or via a fundraising advantage.

Voters have spatial utility such that the utility of candidate $k$ is

$$u_i(\mathbf{x}^k) = -\sum_{m=1}^{M} \gamma_{im}(x_{im} - x_m^k)^2, \tag{6.1}$$

where $u_i$ is voter $i$'s utility, $\mathbf{x}^k$ is an $m$-dimensional vector of positions for candidate $k$, $\gamma_{im}$ is voter $i$'s intensity of preferences on issue $m$, and $x_{im}$ is the ideal point of voter $i$ on dimension $m$. The intensity parameter captures the fact that all voters do not value all issues equally; some care about abortion, others care about sugar beet subsidies.

Voters vote probabilistically because of uncertainty they have about positions of candidates and individual idiosyncracies. We characterize their voting so that the probability that a voter votes for the challenger is increasing in the utility difference to the voter between the challenger and the incumbent. Formally, the probability that $i$ votes for the challenger is

$$P(i \text{ votes for challenger})$$
$$= P\left(\varepsilon_i < -\sum_{m=1}^{M} \gamma_{im}(x_{im} - x_m^C)^2 + \sum_{m=1}^{M} \gamma_{im}(x_{im} - x_m^I)^2\right)$$
$$= \Phi\left(\frac{-(\mathbf{x}_i - \mathbf{x}^C)'\Gamma_i(\mathbf{x}_i - \mathbf{x}^C) + (\mathbf{x}_i - \mathbf{x}^I)'\Gamma_i(\mathbf{x}_i - \mathbf{x}^I)}{\sigma_i}\right), \tag{6.2}$$

where $\varepsilon_i$ is an independent, identically distributed normal random shock with mean zero and variance $\sigma_i^2$, $\Gamma_i$ is an $m \times m$ matrix with $\gamma_{im}$ on the diagonal and zeros elsewhere, and $\Phi$ is the standard normal cumulative density function. The random shock captures the sense that without full knowledge of the decision making of all voters, there appear to be random components in their voting processes, even if they are deterministic (Coughlin 1992, 21; Calvert 1986, 14). The error can be composed of normal errors associated with each dimension. The sum of such errors is a mean zero normal random variable with a variance equaling the sum of the individual variances. It is possible to rescale $\gamma_i$ by dividing by $\sigma_i$. Because $\sigma_i$ is of conceptual interest, however, we use the form in (6.2).

The standard deviation, $\sigma_i$, is a measure of information. When information is high, the standard deviation is low and voters tend to vote for the candidate who truly offers them the higher utility. When information is low, the standard deviation is high and voters' choices are less predictable. The level of $\sigma_i$ is determined by an exogenous level of initial uncertainty, $k_i$, and the total amount of resources allocated toward informing the bloc, $R_i = R_i^C + R_i^I$. The model uses a specific convex functional form: $\sigma_i = k_i/(1 + R_i)$.

The candidates seek to maximize the number of votes they receive. The objective functions of candidates are expressed in terms of $N$ voting blocs, each of which is composed of $n_i$ homogeneous voters (see Enelow and Hinich 1984, 83; Cameron and Enelow 1992, 119). This is not a restrictive assumption about voter clustering; in a district composed entirely of unique voters, each voter will constitute a separate voting bloc.

The nonrandom difference in utilities between the two candidates for an individual in voting bloc $i$ is $d_i = -(\mathbf{x}_i - \mathbf{x}^C)'\Gamma_i(\mathbf{x}_i - \mathbf{x}^C) + (\mathbf{x}_i - \mathbf{x}^I)'\Gamma_i(\mathbf{x}_i - \mathbf{x}^I)$. In a world with no uncertainty, $d_i > 0$ would indicate that voter $i$ prefers the challenger and $d_i < 0$ that voter $i$ prefers the incumbent. With uncertainty, random shocks can lead to voters' preferring candidates who offer lower nonrandom utility.

The expected votes of the two candidates are

$$E(V^C) = \sum_{i=1}^{N} n_i \Phi\left(\frac{d_i(1+R_i^*)}{k_i}\right)$$

$$E(V^I) = \sum_{i=1}^{N} n_i \left(1 - \Phi\left(\frac{d_i(1+R_i^*)}{k_i}\right)\right),$$

where $R_i^*$ is the optimal spending by candidates on group $i$. This optimal spending depends on $x^I$, $x^C$, $R^I$ and $R^C$.

## 6.4 Analytical Analysis of the Model

The game is solved using backward induction. At each stage, the candidates maximize their utility given the choices already made.

### *Stage 4: The Election*

Voters vote according to the voting equation defined earlier.

### *Stage 3: The Campaign*

In the campaign stage, candidates allocate their campaign resources. They decide how much to spend on each bloc by maximizing expected votes subject to a resource constraint. The first step in understanding this process is understanding to whom the candidates allocate resources. (Proofs of all propositions are in the appendix.)

***Definition 1*** A voting bloc is favorable to the spatially closer candidate. Voting blocs with $d_i > 0$ are favorable to the challenger; voting blocs with $d_i < 0$ are favorable to the incumbent.

***Proposition 1*** Candidates expend resources informing only favorable voting blocs.

The logic is straightforward: if the nonrandom utility derived from a candidate is higher than the nonrandom utility derived from the opponent, then that candidate desires as little randomness as possible. On the other hand, if nonrandom elements incline a voter to vote

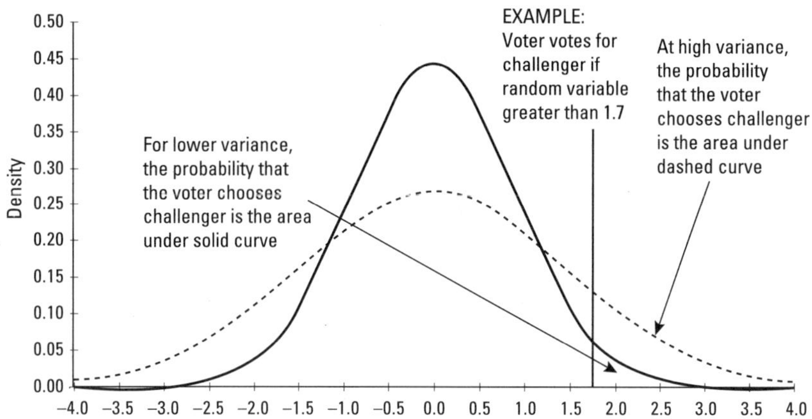


**Figure 6.2**
Targeting Voting Blocs

for an opponent, the candidate will want as much randomness as possible. Figure 6.2 provides an example. Suppose a voter votes for the incumbent if the realization of her random variable is less than 1.7 and votes for the challenger otherwise. Such a voter is favorable to the incumbent. The incumbent wants to minimize the area under the probability distribution to the right of 1.7 and will therefore want to reduce the variance of the distribution. The challenger, on the other hand, prefers a larger area under the probability distribution to the right of 1.7 and will therefore not be willing to reduce uncertainty. This property is consistent with conventional campaign wisdom. Typical is the statement of consultant Don Powell, "There is no reason to waste valuable time and resources on mailings or further voter contact with people who do not support your candidate or issues" (Powell 1995, 36).

Constrained maximization techniques permit specifying the spending levels of the candidates as functions of initial uncertainty parameter ($k_i$), group size ($n_i$), attachment to candidates ($d_i$), and shadow price ($\lambda$).

***Proposition 2*** Optimal campaign spending is

$$\text{Challenger: } R_i^{C*} = \begin{cases} \dfrac{k_i}{d_i}\sqrt{\left(2\log\left(\dfrac{d_i n_i}{\lambda^C\sqrt{2\pi}k_i}\right)\right)} - 1 & \text{if } d_i > \dfrac{\lambda^C\sqrt{2\pi}k_i}{n_i} \\ 0 & \text{if } d_i \leq \dfrac{\lambda^C\sqrt{2\pi}k_i}{n_i} \end{cases}$$

$$\text{Incumbent: } R_i^{I*} = \begin{cases} \dfrac{k_i}{d_i}\sqrt{\left(2\log\left(\dfrac{d_i n_i}{-\lambda^I\sqrt{2\pi}k_i}\right)\right)} - 1 & \text{if } d_i < \dfrac{-\lambda^I\sqrt{2\pi}k_i}{n_i} \\ 0 & \text{if } d_i \geq \dfrac{-\lambda^I\sqrt{2\pi}k_i}{n_i}. \end{cases}$$

These results are difficult to interpret directly. Therefore proposition 3 specifies the effect different parameters have on campaign spending. The first element states simply that the bigger the group, the more money candidates spend on informing it.

***Proposition 3*** For blocs targeted with nonzero spending, the effect on $R_i^*$ of

$n_i$ is $>0$

$$k_i \text{ is } \begin{cases} >0 & \text{if } d_i^2(1+R_i^*)^2 > k_i^2 \\ <0 & \text{otherwise} \end{cases}$$

$$d_i, \qquad i \in F^C \text{ is } \begin{cases} >0 & \text{if } d_i^2(1+R_i^*)^2 < k_i^2 \\ <0 & \text{otherwise} \end{cases}$$

$$d_i, \qquad i \in F^I \text{ is } \begin{cases} >0 & \text{if } d_i^2(1+R_i^*)^2 > k_i^2 \\ <0 & \text{otherwise.} \end{cases}$$

Other effects are conditional. The second element of proposition 3 indicates that the effect of initial uncertainty on campaign spending depends on the location of the candidates (which enters in $d_i$), the amount of spending on the group, $R_i^*$, and exogenous uncertainty, $k_i$. When spending is high and a group is very favorable to a candidate, increasing uncertainty of the group increases spending. If the candidate has little money or the group is not very favorable to the candidate, increasing uncertainty decreases spending. In other words, uncertain groups have money spent on them only if their preferred candidate locates close to them and has a lot of money.

The third and fourth elements state that spending no longer increases once a group is sufficiently favorable to a candidate or sufficient resources are already being spent on the group. That is, as long as $d_i$ and $R_i^*$ are low, moving toward a group causes the candidate to spend more on the group, but once $d_i$ or $R_i^*$ gets high enough, the advantage of the candidate over his or her opposition becomes so large that he or she need not spend more on the group as his or her position gets closer to the group's ideal position.[2]

### *Stage 2: The Challenger's Policy Choice*

In stage 2 of the game, the challenger chooses an optimal policy position in light of the incumbent's position and the expected campaign. That is, for any $x^I$, the challenger calculates how the campaign will unfold for each possible $x^C$ and selects the $x^C$ that maximizes expected challenger vote share. This entails choosing $X^C$ to maximize

$$E(V^C) = \sum_{i=1}^{N} n_i \Phi\left(\frac{d_i(1 + R_i^*)}{k_i}\right), \tag{6.3}$$

where $x^C$ enters directly in $d_i$ and indirectly through its impact on optimal campaign spending ($R_i^*$). The effect of the challenger's policy choice on $R_i^*$ has two aspects. First, $x^C$ determines which groups are favorable to the challenger, affecting the sets of groups targeted with information by the challenger. Second, given a set of favorable voting blocs, $x^C$ affects campaign spending through $d_i$ in proposition 2.

The maximization process for the challenger therefore proceeds in three steps:

1. Given $x^I$, define ranges over which each possible set of groups will be favorable.
2. Find the $x^C$ that maximizes expected vote within each range.
3. Select the $x^C$ that yields the highest expected vote across ranges.

### *Stage 1: The Incumbent's Policy Choice*

The incumbent goes through a similar process as the challenger, but with an additional twist. For each possible policy position, the incumbent calculates how the challenger would optimally respond and how, given the challenger's optimal response, the campaign would unfold. The incumbent chooses the policy that maximizes his or her expected vote share, which can be expressed as

$$E(V^I) = \sum_{i=1}^{N} n_i \left(1 - \Phi\left(\frac{d_i^*(1 + R_i^*)}{k_i}\right)\right), \tag{6.4}$$

where $d_i^*$ and $R_i^*$ are functions of $x^{C*}$ and $x^I$. Hence, the incumbent's optimal policy depends not only on the direct effect of his or her policy position on voters but also on the indirect effects on the challenger's optimal policy and on both candidates' campaigns.

Deriving an analytical solution to this game is not possible. There are many sources of complexity. One is that the objective functions are not concave (or quasi-concave); for example, $E(V^C)$ has two peaks for the one-dimensional case. There are two alternatives: simplify the game or solve it computationally. Because further simplification would eliminate fundamental elements of politics, this chapter takes the computational approach.

## 6.5 Computational Analysis

The computational analysis seeks to shed light on the effect of campaign spending on the representation. In particular, it is designed to determine how resource allocations affect diffuse interests. That is, what is the effect of changing levels of campaign funds on the distance between the optimal positions chosen by candidates and the preferred policy of diffuse interests? Diffuse interests are those interests that are relatively uninformed, uninterested, and large. The conventional view is that there are strong political biases against such interests, biases caused in part by money in the political system.

In the computational analysis, policy is unidimensional and each district has three voting blocs. Although multiple configurations were examined, results are presented for the two representative cases displayed in table 6.1. The results for other configurations were qualitatively similar. In district I, the diffuse bloc is an extreme group; in district II it is in the middle. In district I, the "special interest" bloc is bloc 3; in district II, both blocs 1 and 3 are "special interests." The median policy preference in district I is 0.2; the average in district I is 0.36. In district II, the median is 0.4 and the average is 0.56.

The game is solved via a grid search.[3] For each $x^C$ and $x^I$, it proceeds in two steps. First, it determines the coalitions implied by

**Table 6.1**
Representative Districts

| | | District I | | | District II | | |
|---|---|---|---|---|---|---|---|
| Variable | Parameter | Bloc 1 | Bloc 2 | Bloc 3 | Bloc 1 | Bloc 2 | Bloc 3 |
| Group size | $n$ | 600 | 200 | 200 | 200 | 600 | 200 |
| Ideal point | $x$ | 0.2 | 0.4 | 0.8 | 0.2 | 0.4 | 0.8 |
| Intensity | $\gamma$ | 0.6 | 1.0 | 2.0 | 2.0 | 0.6 | 2.0 |
| Uncertainty | $\sigma_0$ | 2.0 | 1.0 | 0.5 | 0.5 | 2.0 | 0.5 |

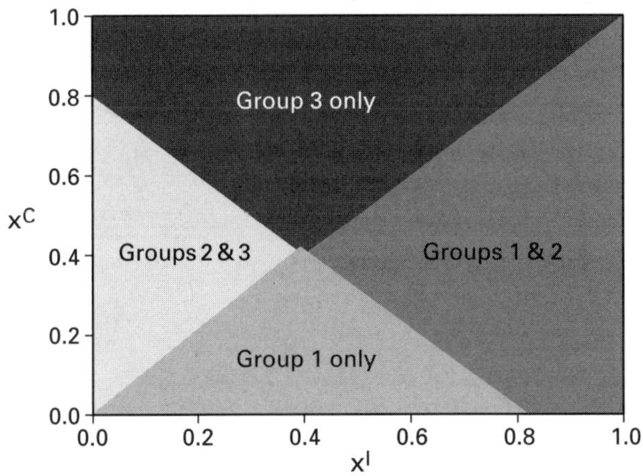


**Figure 6.3**
Challenger Coalitions as a Function of Candidate Positions

the positions of the candidates. Figure 6.3 displays the coalitions as a function of the policy choices of the candidates. Groups 1 and 2 are favorable to the challenger, for example, when the challenger's position is below the incumbent's position, but high enough to induce group 2 to favor the challenger over the incumbent (the right-hand piece of the figure). Second, given the coalition, it solves for the optimal allocation of campaign spending. This calculation is presented in the appendix for the three-bloc case. For more voting blocs, calculation of optimal campaign spending requires an iterative constrained maximization algorithm.

The $x^C$ yielding the highest expected vote for the challenger for a given $x^I$ is the optimal choice of the challenger. The $x^I$ that yields the highest expected vote for the incumbent given the optimal $x^C$ chosen by the challenger is the optimal incumbent policy. The optimal policy choices need not be unique.

To examine the effect of spending publicly provided campaign funds, the analysis seeks the effect of no funds, equal funds, and unequal funds on the optimal policy choices by candidates.

### 6.5.1 *No Spending by Either Candidate*

When neither candidate has any resources, the campaign stage is moot. The equilibrium is determined solely by the policy choice stages. In this situation, the equilibrium in district I is for both

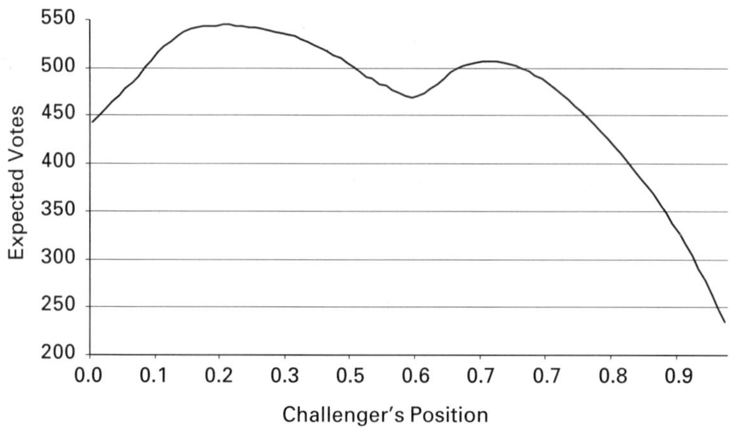


**Figure 6.4**
Challenger's Vote Share When Incumbent Remains at No-Spending Equilibrium

candidates to locate at 0.64, a position relatively close to the interests of the small, intense, and well-informed group on the right (see table 6.1). It is far from the median or average policy preference; bloc 1 and 2 voters are not very responsive to issue changes because of their high uncertainty. This means that a move left by either candidate loses more bloc 3 voters (who are very responsive to policy changes) than it increases bloc 1 or 2 voters (who are unresponsive because of low levels of information and an inability of politicians to mobilize them). In district II, the equilibrium is at 0.49, as the intensity and outlying preferences of bloc 3 pull the optimal policy to the right of the median.

### 6.5.2 *Equal Spending by Candidates*

Things change as the candidates gain resources. Consider the case when both candidates in district I have 20 units of campaign resources. Suppose for a moment that the incumbent locates at the nonspending equilibrium position of 0.64. How would the challenger respond? In this case, the challenger has the incentive to locate at a position that appeals to the two less informed voting blocs and provide information to them in the campaign so that these voters will choose the challenger. Figure 6.4 shows the expected vote of the challenger as a function of $x^C$. The peak on the left corresponds to locating left and mobilizing blocs 1 and 2; the lower peak

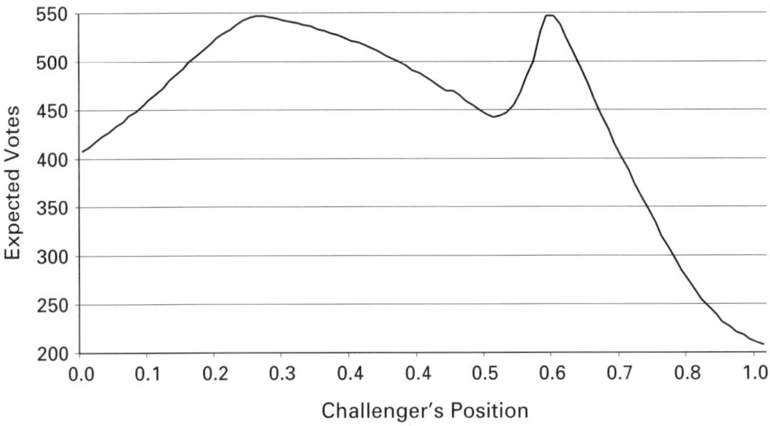


**Figure 6.5**
Challenger's Vote Share When Incumbent Optimizes

on the right corresponds to locating on the right and mobilizing bloc 3. The challenger prefers the left peak, 0.22. At it, he or she receives an expected vote share of 63.5 percent.

Of course, a rational incumbent anticipates both the policy and campaign response of the challenger. In particular, the incumbent moves to the left to attenuate the challenger's ability to mobilize voters on the left. In equilibrium, he or she will move far enough to the left to make the challenger indifferent between challenging on the left or the right. In this case, the optimal choice for the incumbent is 0.53.

The spending patterns provide few clues to these fundamental dynamics. In the case being discussed, the challenger spends all his resources on bloc 1 if he opts for the low strategy and spends all his resources on bloc 3 if he chooses the high strategy. The incumbent spends his money on whichever extreme bloc is in his coalition. But, regardless of whom the money gets spent on, the effect kicks in before the money is spent, meaning that one should not look to understand the effect of money by focusing on whom it is spent.

Figure 6.5 displays the expected vote share of the challenger given the optimal choice by the incumbent. If the challenger locates at the right peak, 0.56, she will target the intense bloc on the right and receive an expected vote share of 54.8 percent, almost 10 percent less than when the incumbent locates at the nonspending equilibrium. If

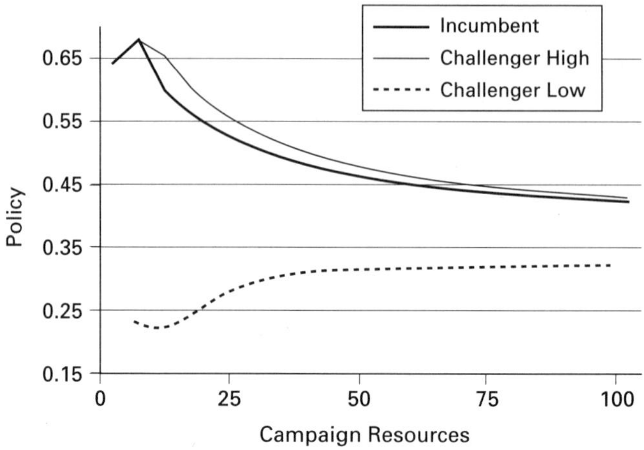


**Figure 6.6**
Optimal Positions as a Function of Campaign Resources for District I

the challenger locates on the left at 0.27 and mobilizes blocs 1 and 2, she will receive the same expected share of the vote.

Although the challenger is advantaged in these models by moving second, we can model incumbency advantage in two ways. First, it can be a valence advantage that gives a utility bump to the incumbent for all possible policy positions of the incumbent (see Erikson and Romero 1990). This has the effect of shifting the curve in figure 6.5, for example, down such that even an optimizing challenger has less than a 50 percent chance of winning. Second, incumbents may have resources advantages, a topic addressed in the next section.

Figure 6.6 shows the optimal candidate positions for varying levels of equal candidate resources in district I. Because the incumbent always moves far enough left to make the challenger indifferent between a challenge on the left or the right, the incumbent's optimal choice is usually in the middle of the two optimal choices of the challenger. At very low levels of resources, however, both candidates move right to please the well-informed bloc on the right. As resources increase, the incumbent unambiguously moves left. The challenger's "high" position moves left as well, while her "low" position moves right. For district II, there is a similar pattern, although now policy moves closer to the diffuse group in the middle.

The clear result here is that as resources increase, expected policy moves toward the diffuse group. In district I, this means that the

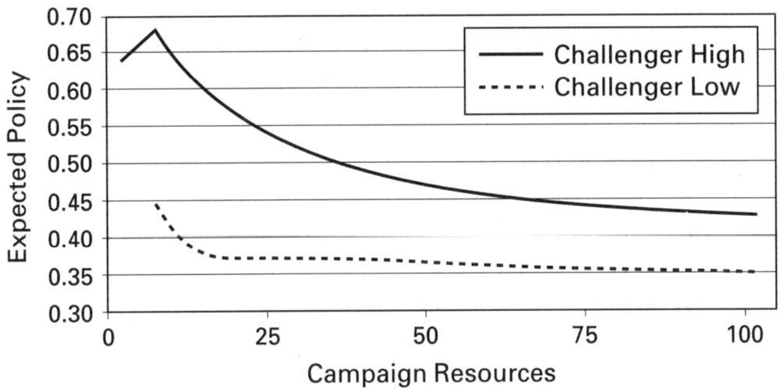


**Figure 6.7**
Expected Policy Campaign as a Function of Campaign Resources for District I

expected outcome moves lower as the level of resources available to the candidates increases.[4] This is depicted in figure 6.7. For district II, expected policy moves closer to 0.4, the preferred policy of the diffuse group. As resources increase indefinitely, the optimal policy converges to the policy preferred by the district's median voter.

### 6.5.3 *Incumbent Funding Advantage*

The results are quite different when one candidate has a resource advantage. For convenience, focus on the situation in which the incumbent has an advantage. Consider first the case in which the challenger in district I has no campaign resources. This means that he cannot mobilize any voters once policy positions have been chosen. Hence, if the incumbent chooses a policy far to the right, the challenger cannot mobilize the groups on the left; similarly, if the incumbent chooses a policy far to the left, the challenger cannot mobilize voters on the right. Given these constraints, the challenger is best off making policy-based mobilization by the incumbent ineffective by mimicking the incumbent. Only when the incumbent truly strays from reasonably attractive policies, will the challenger find it in his interest to locate at a point different than the incumbent.

Figure 6.8 displays the ranges of policies that are optimal for the incumbent in these situations as a function of the incumbent's level of resources. For all the policies in the shaded area, the challenger is best off imitating the incumbent. Clearly, as the disparity gets larger, the incumbent has a broader range of policies that he can optimally choose. When the incumbent has 40 units of campaign funding and

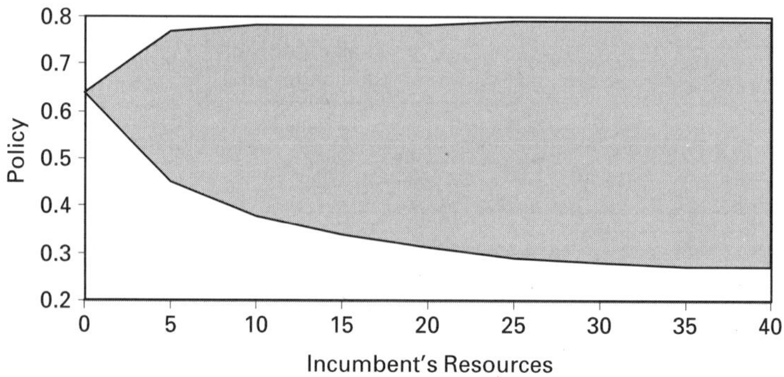


**Figure 6.8**
Optimal Incumbent Positions When Challenger Has No Money

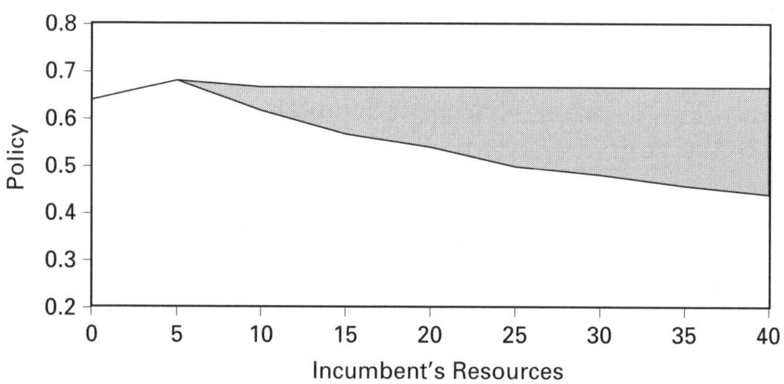


**Figure 6.9**
Optimal Incumbent Positions When Challenger Has Some Money

the challenger has none, the incumbent can locate virtually anywhere between the extreme parties, a troublesome finding for those who wish to see a close link between representative policy positions and voter preferences. District II has a similar pattern (not shown).

Challenger resources mitigate this broad latitude on the part of the incumbent. For example, if the challenger has five units of campaign resources, the latitude of the incumbent narrows considerably. Figure 6.9 demonstrates that for all levels of the incumbent's resources, the range has become considerably smaller. As the challenger's resources increase, the range of latitude for the incumbent continues to shrink. Again, similar results hold for district II.

In summary, campaign spending can fundamentally affect the representative relation and can do so in a manner that is difficult to observe directly. When there is no money available, candidates lean more heavily to well-informed (presumably elite) voters than is socially optimal. As the campaign funds increase—if they do so equally—both candidates become more responsive. If there is a bias in campaign funds toward the incumbent, however, money enables the incumbent to pay less attention to what the voters want.

## 6.6 Conclusion

This chapter argues that the effects of spending campaign money merit as much attention as the effects of raising campaign money. This conclusion summarizes the argument and sketches some future directions in thinking about campaign finance and representation.

The argument is simple: campaign *spending* tends to increase the representation of diffuse interests. The reason is that campaign resources give candidates the potential ability to inform voters. This causes candidates to weigh the preferences of diffuse interests more heavily in order to prevent opponents from mobilizing these relatively uninformed voters.

These effects can be subtle, however. Increasing the challenger's funds may not mean that the challenger uses them to mobilize diffuse interests. In fact, the challenger may use them to mobilize special interests. The equilibrium outcome, however, is that more money tends to move the incumbent and the expected outcome more toward diffuse interests than if there were less money. In addition, the analysis shows that the representative link between candidates and voters requires that both candidates have some resources. Otherwise, the advantaged candidate will be able optimally to locate anywhere across a broad range of policies. Put starkly, resource disparities weaken the representative link between constituencies and representatives.

The broader point is that it is vital to analyze the effect of *spending* in order to understand the effect of money on politics. However, the model does not completely characterize the campaign finance system. The fund-raising aspect of the system is taken as exogenous, much as existing work simplifies away the effect of campaign spending.

Future work should bring together both the raising and spending sides of the campaign finance story (see Bailey 2002). Clearly, if interest groups give money in order to advance their goals, this could partially or fully offset the positive effects of campaign spending by making money available only to those candidates who promote the policies preferred by interest groups. However, such offsets likely depend on the extent that fund-raising can occur on issues of little interest to voters. If candidates can raise money on issues that voters do not care about, this money will discipline candidates on issues that voters do care about because of the dynamics discussed here. When fund-raising occurs only on an issue voters care about and only one side has money, the positive effects discussed here may be limited or reversed.

Computational approaches are most intriguing for such extensions because endogenizing the behavior of campaign contributors adds complexity to an already complex model. Two different computational approaches may prove up to the task. First, one could use computational methods to solve for optimal behavior for all players in a model in which campaign contributions are endogenous and policy space is multidimensional (Bailey 2002). Second, one could work with an adaptive agent framework in which agents have limited information and limited search abilities (Kollman, Miller, and Page 1995; 1997). For example, de Marchi (1998) has looked at the ability of interest groups to provide information with such a model. This work could also extend the models to cover other important aspects of the political system. For example, candidates in the current model are not bound to one side of the ideological spectrum or another. Adding primaries and parties—perhaps in an adaptive agent framework such as Adams (1998)—may change the dynamics between campaign finance and representation in an interesting manner.

Even by emphasizing only one side (albeit an ignored side) of the debate, this chapter offers some ideas for current debates. Most important, the findings suggest that the debate should not be a narrow conversation about getting money out of politics. A better focus is on getting money into the process in the least damaging, most beneficial manner possible. That is, the debate should be about how to provide the benefits discussed here at the lowest cost to the public. For example, this chapter shows that public gain (in terms of representation of diffuse interests) is greatest when the disadvantaged side gets more resources. This implies that reforms should help viable candidates with little money raise at least enough money to keep the better-financed candidate honest. Whatever the findings, however, such work should turn the discussions from broad-brushed critiques of the role of money in politics to a more refined attempts to fund the democratic process in the most effective manner.

## Appendix

### *Note on Computation*

The results have been calculated in Visual Basic. Related work has been conducted in Matlab as well. For one-dimensional models (as reported here) the most efficient approach is a grid search. The steps are as follows:

1. Initialize district parameters and level of funding.
2. Select a start value for $x^I$.
3. For each $x^C$ in a specified range, calculate expected vote shares. This involves determining which coalition results are based on $x^I$ and $x^C$ and, given the coalition, calculating the allocation of campaign funds.
4. For each $x^I$, find the optimal $x^C$ for the challenger.
5. Find the optimal $x^I$ for the incumbent given the challenger's optimal behavior.

For more complicated versions of the game, a Nelder-Mead search algorithm is most appropriate. Visual Basic code and an Microsoft Excel interface is available from the author. Special thanks are due to Don Bailey for his work on this code. In addition, a separate program conducts a robustness search. In this, one can enter any number of districts and solve for the optimal policy position across them.

*Proof of Proposition 1* The effect of $R_i$ on $E(V^C) = \sum_{i=1}^{N} n_i\Phi(d_i(1+R_i)/k_i)$ is $n_i\phi(d_i(1+R_i)/k_i)(d_i/k_i)$, which is the same sign as $d_i$. Hence for $d_i < 0$ decreasing $R_i$ is always better and $E(V^C \mid R_i = 0) > E(V^C \mid R_i > 0)$. The effect of $R_i$ on $E(V^I) = \sum_{i=1}^{N} n_i(1 - \Phi(d_i(1+R_i)/k_i))$ is $-n_i\phi(d_i(1+R_i)/k_i)(d_i/k_i)$, which is the opposite sign as $d_i$. Hence for $d_i > 0$ decreasing $R_i$ is always better and $E(V^I \mid R_i = 0) > E(V^I \mid R_i > 0)$.

*Proof of Proposition 2* Proposition 1 implies that the challenger sets spending levels by maximizing the following Lagrangian:

$$\mathscr{L}^C = \sum^{i\in F^C} n_i\Phi\left(\frac{d_i(1+R_i)}{k_i}\right) + \lambda^C\left(R^C - \sum^{i\in F^C} R_i\right), \tag{6.5}$$

where $i \in F^C$ if $d_i > 0$. Letting $N_C =$ the number of groups favorable to the challenger, there will be $N_C + 1$ first-order conditions:

$$\frac{\partial \mathscr{L}^C}{\partial R_i} = 0 \Rightarrow n_i \phi\left(\frac{d_i(1+R_i)}{k_i}\right)\frac{d_i}{k_i} = \lambda^C \quad \text{for} \quad \forall i \in F^C$$

$$\frac{\partial \mathscr{L}}{\partial \lambda^C} = 0 \Rightarrow R^C = \sum^{i \in F^C} R_i.$$

Rewrite the first-order conditions as

$$n_i \phi\left(\frac{d_i(1+R_i)}{k_i}\right)\frac{d_i}{k_i} = \lambda^C, \quad i \in F^C$$

$$n_i \frac{1}{\sqrt{2\pi}} e^{-d_i^2(1+R_i)^2/(2k_i^2)} \frac{d_i}{k_i} = \lambda^C, \quad i \in F^C$$

$$\frac{-d_i^2(1+R_i)^2}{2k_i^2} = \log\left(\frac{\lambda^C \sqrt{2\pi} k_i}{d_i n_i}\right)$$

$$R_i = \frac{k_i}{d_i}\sqrt{\left(2 \log\left(\frac{d_i n_i}{\lambda^C \sqrt{2\pi} k_i}\right)\right)} - 1, \quad i \in F^C \quad \text{and} \quad d_i n_i > \lambda^C \sqrt{2\pi} k_i.$$

The condition $i \in F^C$ is superfluous as $i \notin F^C \Rightarrow d_i < 0 \Rightarrow d_i n_i > \lambda^C \sqrt{2\pi} k_i$. The calculations are similar for the incumbent. The $N_I + 1$ first-order conditions for the incumbent are

$$\frac{\partial \mathscr{L}^I}{\partial R_i} = 0 \Rightarrow -n_i \phi\left(\frac{d_i(1+R_i)}{k_i}\right)\frac{d_i}{k_i} = \lambda^I \quad \text{for} \quad \forall i \in F^I.$$

The resource constraint is the same. With $d_i < 0$ for $i \in F^I$, calculations yield

$$R_i = \frac{k_i}{d_i}\sqrt{\left(2 \log\left(\frac{d_i n_i}{-\lambda^I \sqrt{2\pi} k_i}\right)\right)} - 1, \quad i \in F^I \quad \text{and} \quad d_i n_i < -\lambda^I \sqrt{2\pi} k_i.$$

To determine that the equations characterize a maximum, the Hessians need to be negative definite. This is the case if the first $N_C$ leading principal minor alternate in sign, beginning with a negative sign (see Simon and Blume 1994, 391). The Hessians will be a bordered matrix, consisting of a diagonal second derivative matrix bordered by 1′s and with a zero in the corner (see the matrix in equation (6.6) for an example). The diagonal elements for the challenger will be

$$\frac{\partial^2 L}{(\partial R_i)^2} = \frac{-n_i d_i^3 (1 + R_i)}{k_i^3} \phi\left(\frac{d_i(1 + R_i)}{k_i}\right),$$

which will always be negative, ensuring that the leading principal minors will alternate in sign. The diagonal elements for the incumbent will be

$$\frac{\partial^2 L}{(\partial R_i)^2} = \frac{n_i d_i^3 (1 + R_i)}{k_i^3} \phi\left(\frac{d_i(1 + R_i)}{k_i}\right),$$

which will also always be negative because $d_i < 0$ for groups favorable to the incumbent.

*Proof of Proposition 3* To check for the effect of any exogenous variable on optimal spending, totally differentiate with respect to the endogenous variables and the exogenous variable of interest (labeled $Q$). Because the cross-partials for any two $R_i$'s are zero and the cross-partial for any $R_i$ and $\lambda$ is always 1, the Hessian (the matrix that needs to be inverted) consists of a diagonal matrix bordered by 1's, with a zero in the lower right-hand corner. The diagonal elements are the second derivatives which, by the second-order conditions, are negative.

$$\begin{bmatrix} \frac{\partial R_1}{\partial Q} \\ \vdots \\ \frac{\partial R_n}{\partial Q} \\ \frac{\partial \lambda}{\partial Q} \end{bmatrix} = -\begin{bmatrix} \frac{\partial^2 L}{(\partial R_1)^2} & 0 & \cdots & 1 \\ 0 & \frac{\partial^2 L}{(\partial R_2)^2} & \cdots & 1 \\ \vdots & \vdots & \vdots & \vdots \\ 1 & 1 & \cdots & 0 \end{bmatrix}^{-1} \begin{bmatrix} \frac{\partial^2 L}{\partial R_1 \partial Q} \\ \frac{\partial^2 L}{\partial R_2 \partial Q} \\ \vdots \\ \frac{\partial^2 L}{\partial \lambda \partial Q} \end{bmatrix}. \quad (6.6)$$

By Gauss-Jordan matrix inversion, this corresponds to

$$\begin{bmatrix} \frac{\partial R_1}{\partial Q} \\ \frac{\partial R_2}{\partial Q} \\ \frac{\partial R_3}{\partial Q} \\ \frac{\partial \lambda}{\partial Q} \end{bmatrix} = \frac{-1}{\Sigma} \begin{bmatrix} \Sigma \Pi_{-j} & -\Pi_{-ji} & \cdots & \Pi_{-j} \\ -\Pi_{-ji} & \Sigma \Pi_{-j} & \cdots & \Pi_{-j} \\ \vdots & \vdots & \vdots & \vdots \\ \Pi_{-i} & \Pi_{-i} & \cdots & \Pi \end{bmatrix} \begin{bmatrix} \frac{\partial^2 L}{\partial R_1 \, dQ} \\ \frac{\partial^2 L}{\partial R_2 \, dQ} \\ \frac{\partial^2 L}{\partial R_3 \, dQ} \\ \frac{\partial^2 L}{\partial \lambda \, dQ} \end{bmatrix},$$

where $j$ is row number, $i$ is column number, $\sum$ (alone) is the sum of all possible $(N_C - 1)$ length combinations, $\sum\prod_{-j}$ is the sum of all $(N_C - 2)$ length combinations without the $j$th second derivative, $\prod_{-ji}$ is product of all elements but $i$th and $j$th second derivatives, $\prod_{-j}$ is the product of all elements but the $j$th second derivative, and $\prod$ (alone) is the product of all second derivatives.

For the case where $N_C = 3$, let $a, b$, and $c$ be the second derivatives with respect to $R_1, R_2$, and $R_3$, respectively (the diagonal elements of the inverted matrix in equation (6.6). Then

$$\begin{bmatrix} \dfrac{\partial R_1}{\partial Q} \\ \dfrac{\partial R_2}{\partial Q} \\ \dfrac{\partial R_3}{\partial Q} \\ \dfrac{\partial \lambda}{\partial Q} \end{bmatrix} = \frac{-1}{bc + ac + ab} \begin{bmatrix} c+b & -c & -b & bc \\ -c & a+c & -a & ac \\ -b & -a & a+b & ab \\ bc & ac & ab & abc \end{bmatrix} \begin{bmatrix} \dfrac{\partial^2 L}{\partial R_1 \partial Q} \\ \dfrac{\partial^2 L}{\partial R_2 \partial Q} \\ \dfrac{\partial^2 L}{\partial R_3 \partial Q} \\ \dfrac{\partial^2 L}{\partial \lambda \partial Q} \end{bmatrix}. \tag{6.7}$$

Cross-partials are zero for all $R_j$, where $j \neq i$. The effect for $R_1$ simplifies to

$$\frac{\partial R_1}{\partial Q} = \frac{-(c+b)}{bc + ac + ab} \frac{\partial^2 L}{\partial R_i \partial Q}. \tag{6.8}$$

Because the first fraction is always positive, the effect of the exogenous variables on optimal spending will be the same sign as the cross-partial. For groups favorable to the challenger, these cross-partials are

$$\frac{\partial^2 L^C}{\partial R_i \partial n_i} = \phi\left(\frac{d_i(1 + R_i^*)}{k_i}\right) \frac{d_i}{k_i}$$

$$\frac{\partial^2 L^C}{\partial R_i \partial k_i} = \phi\left(\frac{d_i(1 + R_i^*)}{k_i}\right) \frac{d_i n_i}{k_i^4} (d_i^2 (1 + R_i^*)^2 - k_i^2)$$

$$\frac{\partial^2 L^C}{\partial R_i \partial d_i} = \phi\left(\frac{d_i(1 + R_i^*)}{k_i}\right) \frac{n_i}{k_i^3} (k_i^2 - d_i^2 (1 + R_i^*)^2).$$

For groups favorable to the incumbent ($d_i < 0$), these cross-partials are simply the negative of the preceding. The implications in the proposition follow directly from these equations.

### *Calculating Optimal Allocation of Campaign Spending*

If blocs 1 and 2 are favorable, the first-order conditions (when dealing with either the incumbent or the challenger) imply

$$n_i\phi\left(\frac{d_i(1+R_i)}{k_i}\right)\frac{d_i}{k_i} = n_j\phi\left(\frac{d_j(1+R^C-R_i)}{k_j}\right)\frac{d_j}{k_j}$$

$$\frac{\phi\left(\dfrac{d_i(1+R_i)}{k_i}\right)}{\phi\left(\dfrac{d_j(1+R^C-R_i)}{k_j}\right)} = \frac{k_i n_j d_j}{k_j n_i d_i}$$

$$e^{0.5(d_i^2(1+R_i)^2/k_i^2 - d_j^2(1+R^C-R_i)^2/k_j^2)} = \frac{k_i n_j d_j}{k_j n_i d_i}$$

$$\frac{d_i^2(1+R_i)^2}{k_i^2} - \frac{d_j^2(1+R^C-R_i)^2}{k_j^2} = -2\log\left(\frac{k_i n_j d_j}{k_j n_i d_i}\right)$$

$$R_i^2\left(\frac{d_i^2}{k_i^2}-\frac{d_j^2}{k_j^2}\right) + R_i\left(2\frac{d_i^2}{k_i^2}+2\frac{d_j^2}{k_j^2}(1+R^C)\right) + \frac{d_i^2}{k_i^2}-\frac{d_j^2}{k_j^2} - 2R^C\frac{d_j^2}{k_j^2} - \frac{d_j^2}{k_j^2}R^{C2}$$
$$+2\log\left(\frac{k_i n_j d_j}{k_j n_i d_i}\right) = 0.$$

Solve for optimal spending using the quadratic formula.

## Notes

I am grateful to Brandice Canes-Wrone, Rui de Figueiredo, Brian Gaines, Judy Goldstein, Jean-Pierre Langlois, James Lavin, Pat Lynch, Andrea Prat, Doug Rivers, Rich Timpone, Barry Weingast, and participants at the Computational Political Economy Conference, University of Michigan, October 1998, for their many helpful comments. I also thank Don Bailey for his work on the Visual Basic code used here. Remaining errors are my responsibility.

1. Probabilistic voting models are also attractive because they bridge theoretical and empirical analyses (see Burden 1997). When theoretical models are tested empirically, analysts provide for error. Introducing error into many deterministic models, however, often causes the results to change.

2. The effects of $x^C$ and $x^I$ on $R_i^*$ are more complicated (see the appendix).

3. The main analysis was conducted in Visual Basic (see the appendix).

4. The expected outcome is $P(\text{incumbent wins})x^I + P(\text{challenger wins})x^C$, where the probability of winning is calculated using a normal approximation for a binomial distribution.

## References

Adams, Greg. 1998. "Beyond Control: A Model of Parties as Complex Adaptive Systems." Paper, Computational Political Economy Conference, University of Michigan.

Arnold, R. Douglas. 1990. *The Logic of Congressional Action.* New Haven, CT: Yale University Press.

Austen-Smith, David. 1987. "Interest Groups, Campaign Contributions, and Probabilistic Voting." *Public Choice* 54: 123–139.

———. 1990. "Rational Consumers and Irrational Voters: A Review Essay on Black Hole Tariffs and Endogenous Policy Theory." *Economics and Politics* 3: 73–92.

Bailey, Michael. 2002. "Can Representation Be Fair When Campaign Contributions Come Mostly from Business? An Exploration in Multiple Dimensions." Unpublished manuscript, Georgetown University.

Banks, Jeffrey. 1990. "A Model of Electoral Competition with Incomplete Information." *Journal of Economic Theory* 50: 309–325.

Baron, David. 1994. "Electoral Competition with Informed and Uninformed Voters." *American Political Science Review* 88: 33–47.

Burden, Barry. 1997. "Deterministic and Probabilistic Voting Models." *American Journal of Political Science.* 41 (4): 1150–1169.

Calvert, Randall. 1986. *Models of Imperfect Information in Politics.* New York: Harwood Academic Publishers.

Cameron, Charles, and James Enelow. 1992. "Asymmetric Policy Effects, Campaign Contributions, and the Spatial Theory of Elections." *Mathematical and Computer Modeling* 16 (8/9): 117–132.

Coleman, John, and Paul Manna. 2000. "Congressional Campaign Spending and the Quality of Democracy." *Journal of Politics* 62 (3): 757–789.

Coughlin, Peter. 1992. *Probabilistic Voting Theory.* New York: Cambridge University Press.

Davis, Otto, and Melvin Hinich. 1966. "A Mathematical Model of Policy Formation in a Democratic Society." In *Mathematical Applications in Political Science,* Vol 2, ed. J. L. Bernd. Dallas, TX: Southern Methodist University Press.

de Marchi, Scott. 1998. Interest Groups as Information Providers. Unpublished manuscript, Washington University, St. Louis, Missouri.

Denzau, Arthur, and Michael Munger. 1986. "Legislators and Interest Groups: How Unorganized Interests Get Represented." *American Political Science Review* 80: 89–106.

Downs, Anthony. 1957. *An Economic Theory of Democracy.* New York: Harper and Row.

Enelow, James, and Melvin Hinich. 1984. *The Spatial Theory of Voting.* New York: Cambridge University Press.

———. 1989. "A General Probabilistic Spatial Theory of Elections." *Public Choice* 61: 101–113.

Erikson, Robert S., and David Romero. 1990. "Candidate Equilibrium and the Behavioral Model of the Vote." *American Political Science Review* 84: 1103–1126.

Fann, Guang-Jong, and Mihriye Mete. 1998. "Assessing the Optimal Strategies of Allocating Campaign Resources Based on a Probabilistic Model." Paper, Midwest Political Science Association Conference.

Faucheux, Ron. 1999. "Hitting the Bull's Eye: How to Use Targeting and Database Management to Win Votes and Save Money in Local and District Campaigns." *Campaigns and Elections* 20 (6): 20–26.

Fiorina, Morris, and Roger Noll. 1979. "Majority Rule Models and Legislative Elections." *Journal of Politics* 41: 1081–1104.

Gerber, Alan. 1996. "Rational Voters, Candidate Spending, and Incomplete Information: A Theoretical Analysis with Implications for Campaign Finance Reform." Unpublished manuscript, Yale University.

Hinich, Melvin. 1977. "Equilibrium in Spatial Voting: The Median Voter Is an Artifact." *Journal of Economic Theory* 16: 208–219.

Hinich, Melvin, and Michael Munger. 1994. *Ideology and the Theory of Political Choice.* Ann Arbor: University of Michigan Press.

Judd, Kenneth. 1998. *Numerical Methods in Economics.* Cambridge, MA: MIT Press.

Kollman, Ken, John H. Miller and Scott E. Page. 1995. "Computational Political Economy." Unpublished manuscript, University of Michigan.

———. 1997. "Political Institutions and Sorting in a Tiebout Model." *American Economic Review* 87 (5): 977–992.

Lohmann, Susanne. 1993. "A Signaling Model of Informative and Manipulative Political Action." *The American Political Science Review* 87 (2): 319–333.

Lupia, Arthur, and Matt McCubbins. 1998. *The Democratic Dilemma.* New York: Cambridge University Press.

Magee, Stephen, William Brock, and Leslie Young. 1989. *Black Hole Tariffs and Endogenous Policy Theory.* New York: Cambridge University Press.

McKelvey, Richard. 1976. "Intransitivities in Multidimensional Voting Models and Some Implications for Agenda Control." *Journal of Economic Theory* 12: 472–482.

Morton, Rebecca, and Charles Cameron. 1992. "Elections and the Theory of Campaign Contributions: A Survey and Critical Analysis." *Economics and Politics* 4: 79–108.

Partin, Randall. 1996. "Campaign Intensity and Voter Information: A Look at Gubernatorial Contests." Paper, American Political Science Association Conference, San Francisco.

Popkin, Samuel. 1991. *The Reasoning Voter: Communication and Persuasion in Presidential Campaigns.* Chicago: University of Chicago Press.

Powell, Don. 1995. "Linking Phones and Mail for Maximum Efficiency." *Campaigns and Elections* (April): 36.

Prat, Andrea. 1999. "Campaign Advertising and Welfare." Unpublished manuscript, London School of Economics.

Rauch, Jonathan. 1994. *Demosclerosis: the Silent Killer of American Government.* New York: Random House.

Snyder, James. 1989. "Election Goals and the Allocation of Campaign Resources." *Econometrica* 57 (3): 637–660.

Stigler, George. 1971. "The Theory of Economic Regulation." *Bell Journal of Economics and Management Science* 2: 3–21.

Weingast, Barry. 1996. "Off-the-Path Behavior: A Game-Theoretic Approach to Counterfactuals and Its Implications for Political Analysis." In *Counterfactual Thought Experiments in World Politics*, ed. Philip Tetlock and Aaron Belkin. Princeton: Princeton University Press.

# 7 Political Institutions and Sorting in a Tiebout Model

Ken Kollman, John H. Miller, and Scott E. Page

Political or economic institutions are often evaluated by their ability to structure microlevel incentives to be in agreement with macrolevel goals (Schelling 1978). In many important situations, microlevel incentives are consistent with multiple equilibria (Axelrod and Bennett 1993; DeVany 1994), and one role of institutions may be to steer agents in the direction of configurations of highest aggregate utility, or at least bias outcomes toward better configurations. Here we compare the performance of three common political institutions in a model of Tiebout competition. We examine the ability of alternative political institutions to induce better sorting of citizens among competing local jurisdictions, where better sorting means higher aggregate utility among citizens. While our focus is on Tiebout models, the underlying process we analyze—the decentralized sorting of interacting individuals—is of much broader interest, playing a role in labor markets, industrial location, and coalition formation.

In a Tiebout model, local jurisdictions compete for citizens by offering bundles of public goods. Citizens then sort themselves among jurisdictions according to their preferences. Charles M. Tiebout's (1956) original hypothesis challenged Paul Samuelson's (1954) conjecture that public goods could not be allocated efficiently. The Tiebout hypothesis has since been extended to include additional propositions. Prominent among them is that competition, as a result of enforcing efficiency, renders local politics unimportant: a jurisdiction able to attract and retain citizens cannot waste resources (Hoyt 1990). This argument does not, however, preclude the possibility that political institutions may differ in their ability to sort citizens according to preferences. In fact, we find that important differences do exist among institutions.

To analyze institutional differences, we construct a computational Tiebout model. Using the model we directly investigate the dynamics of agent sorting in the context of institutional arrangements that model existing political structures. The focus on dynamics (as opposed to final equilibrium states) and the use of institutions that resemble those actually employed (versus a fictional, profit-maximizing entrepreneur) distinguish our work from prior research on the Tiebout hypothesis. The computational approach complements existing efforts by enabling us to study questions that are currently unassailable if we require closed-form, equilibrium solutions. We use computation as a way to guide and test our intuitions as to how these more complex systems operate.

We find that significant differences arise in the performance of different political institutions. In the model, each political jurisdiction confronts a finite number of issues, which may be considered as either local policies or public projects. Citizens have linearly separable preferences over these issues, and they choose to locate in the jurisdiction offering the most attractive set of policies on the issues. Jurisdictions decide policies using one of three possible types of political institutions: democratic referenda, direct competition, or proportional representation. Like standard Tiebout models, we find that, regardless of the political institution employed, aggregate utility increases with the number of jurisdictions. However, quite unexpectedly, we also find that institutions that perform relatively poorly in the presence of a single jurisdiction perform relatively well under multiple jurisdictions. In fact, institutions characterized by higher degrees of "political instability" appear to induce better sorting when multiple jurisdictions are present.

We offer an explanation for this phenomenon based on insights from the literature on nonlinear search algorithms, specifically models of simulated annealing. The analysis suggests that in order for political instability to improve outcomes in a multiple-jurisdiction environment, the degree of instability must be positively correlated with the heterogeneity of citizens' preferences. Such a correlation allows the system to break out of inferior configurations and eventually stabilize on superior ones.

The potential benefit of policy instability on aggregate welfare is suggested by the following simple example. Consider a situation in which two towns must choose between either allowing alcohol sales or being dry. There are three citizens in each town, two of whom favor having alcohol over being dry. Under majority rule on the issue, both towns allow alcohol, and no citizen wants to move. Clearly majority rule prevents the symmetry from ever being broken in the two towns. However, suppose that one of the towns happens to become dry. When this occurs, citizens immediately re-sort, resulting in one town of four citizens that allows alcohol and one of two citizens that does not. The policy instability has broken the initial symmetry and leads to the creation of an equilibrium configuration of the citizens with a higher level of aggregate welfare.

Economic processes are often governed by the decentralized sorting of agents, such as buyers seeking sellers, workers looking for employers, firms finding locations, and individuals forming coalitions. The existence of multiple equilibria under decentralized sorting suggests that the dynamics implied by alternative institutional arrangements may influence the final configuration of agents. We find that certain institutions create conditions under which the sorting of agents naturally tends towards those equilibria with superior configurations.

## 7.1 The Tiebout Hypothesis

This section briefly summarizes research concerning Tiebout's model and indicates how our work departs from previous research. Tiebout's (1956) hypothesis is that local public goods might be efficiently allocated if agents can freely choose among alternative jurisdictions actively seeking citizens. The Tiebout hypothesis has been investigated in depth both theoretically and empirically.

The theoretical literature has uncovered some problems with Tiebout's argument, and many theorists have clarified and extended Tiebout's original model. Truman F. Bewley (1981) showed through a series of examples that regardless of whether the costs of local public goods are independent of, or proportional to, the size of the local population, there exist economies with equilibria that are not Pareto optimal. In other words, the pure Tiebout hypothesis does not hold. The existence of examples with suboptimal equilibria is not sufficient to dispose of Tiebout's theory. More troubling is Bewley's result that the Tiebout hypothesis can be expected to hold only when the number of jurisdictions is at least as large as the number of citizens—a rather unlikely situation. By relaxing some of Bewley's assumptions, efficient equilibria can be generated more easily. One approach employs $\varepsilon$-equilibrium as a proxy for moving costs (see Wooders 1994 for an overview). Other work (for example, Konishi 1996) has generated equilibrium properties by assuming particular preferences or a single political institution. There are also models in which public goods suffer from differential crowding (Berglas 1976; Conley and Wooders 1997), and models with divisible land (Rose-Ackerman 1979). We depart here from the existing theoretical research by comparing the performance of different political institutions in a Tiebout setting.

The empirical literature on Tiebout (see Dowding et al. 1994 for a recent survey) has focused on a variety of questions, including whether competition among jurisdictions leads to efficiency, the impact of bundles of local public goods on jurisdictional choice, and the role of political institutions in public goods provision. Empirical findings concerning the first question are inconclusive and appear to depend upon whether the local jurisdictions are single or multipurpose (Zax 1989).[1] The analysis of how bundles of public goods enter into jurisdictional choice fall into macro- and microlevel studies. In a number of cases using aggregate data, fiscal differences among jurisdictions have been shown to have a significant effect on migration (Reschovsky 1979).[2] These studies find that fiscal factors play a larger role in pushing people out of jurisdictions than in pulling people into new jurisdictions, which is not surprising given the asymmetric information (Fox et al. 1989). Other studies rely on microlevel survey data to examine the link between public services and goods, and jurisdictional choice. The findings in these studies are less conclusive, although school quality and tax rates appear as significant in several studies (Sharp 1984; Percy and Hawkins 1992; Percy 1993). Finally, welfare policies across states in the United States do seem to influence migration patterns of the poor (Peterson and Rom 1989). The question of how political institutions influence public goods provision is perhaps the most relevant to our analysis. Unfortunately, with the notable exception of Thomas Romer and Howard Rosenthal's (1979) work on school spending referenda, this area has not been as widely investigated. Romer and Rosenthal find that the reversion level (what the policy will be if the referendum fails) influences the outcomes of referenda.

Our model departs from previous approaches in several important respects. First, with a few exceptions, our primary interest in comparing the performance of political institutions has been largely neglected in the Tiebout literature. A typical Tiebout model takes the political institution, usually majority rule, as constant. Here we vary institutions and measure performance, an approach more consistent with the literature on mechanism design. Second, aside from an example used to demonstrate the annealing phenomenon, we do not explicitly compare equilibria. This decision stems partly from a desire to avoid oversimplifying an already stark model by making the restrictive assumptions necessary to guarantee the existence of equilibria. It is also consistent with our emphasis on the dynamic nature of agent migration, political responsiveness, and the production of public goods. People may continue relocating in response to changing policies, while local policies shift, in turn, to changes in constituencies. The system of policy choices by governments and jurisdictional choices by citizens can be viewed as a complex adaptive system in which movements and policies are determined by the preferences of citizens and the existing political institutions. Some institutions may create systems which settle quickly into equilibrium while others may never equilibrate. Finally, our assumptions of how jurisdictions make decisions differ from much of the previous literature. Rather than model political parties as fully informed and optimizing, we rely on an adaptive party model in which parties gather information by taking polls, and decide on platforms by using simple search heuristics (Holland and Miller 1991; Kollman et al. 1992).

## 7.2 The Model

We construct a simple version of a Tiebout world. Agents (citizens) seek their favorite location from among a fixed set of jurisdictions each of which offers a particular platform of local public goods and policies. Each jurisdiction's platform is then determined by a political institution that aggregates the preferences of the agents currently residing in the jurisdiction. Once new platforms are determined, agents are allowed to move, and the above process is iterated. Agents do not take into account the effects of their own movements on future policies.

We assume a set of $N_a$ agents, each of whom must reside in one of $N_j$ possible jurisdictions. Within any jurisdiction, the local government is obliged to decide positions on a set of $N_i$ local public issues.[3]

All jurisdictions must take positions on each of the $N_i$ issues. For simplicity we assume that all such positions are binary. Examples of such issues include the presence (or absence) of a public good (say, a community swimming pool) or policy (like smoking in public buildings).[4] Let $p_{ji} \in \{Yes,\ No\}$ give the position of jurisdiction $j$ on issue $i$, and let a platform, $\mathbf{P}_j \in \{Yes,\ No\}^{N_i}$, denote the vector of decisions across all $N_i$ issues in jurisdiction $j$. Finally, define a configuration as a mapping of agents to jurisdictions.

Agents have linearly separable preferences on the issues and their per unit value for each issue lies in the interval $[-400/N_i, 400/N_i]$ distributed uniformly. Let $v_{ai}$ give agent $a$'s utility for issue $i$. If the project is undertaken, then the agent obtains a utility of $v_{ai}$, and if the project is not undertaken, then the agent obtains no utility. Thus, agent $a$'s utility from $\mathbf{P}_j$ is given by

$$u_a(\mathbf{P}_j) = \sum_{i=1}^{N_i} v_{ai} \cdot \delta(p_{ji}),$$

where $\delta(Yes) = 1$ and $\delta(No) = 0$. A straightforward calculation verifies that the expected value to an agent of an arbitrary platform equals zero, and the expected value of her optimal platform equals 100.

### 7.2.1 *Political Institutions*

We compare three political institutions: democratic referenda, direct competition, and proportional representation.[5] The simplified versions of these institutions used in the model attempt to capture the relevant features of each institution without overly complicating the analysis.

#### 7.2.1.1 Democratic Referenda

We model democratic referenda as simple majority rule on each issue.[6] Our assumption that there are no external effects between projects implies that sincere voting is a dominant strategy for all agents within a given election. The outcome of democratic referenda is the median platform, $\mathbf{P}_j^m$, for the jurisdiction, where $p_{ji}^m = Yes$ if the number of agents in $j$ with $v_{ai} > 0$ exceeds the number of agents in $j$ with $v_{ai} < 0$; otherwise $p_{ji}^m = No$. The median platform maximizes aggregate utility *in* jurisdiction $j$ if and only if on every issue the mean and median agent values have identical signs. Generally speaking, democratic referenda adopt platforms of relatively high aggregate utility given a group of agents.

Democratic referenda are relatively stable, since the implied platform is unique and individual agents migrating into or out of a jurisdiction rarely change the platform. Suppose that a single agent moving into a jurisdiction prefers *Yes* on issue one. The only way that she can change the decision on this issue is if she is pivotal; that is, if prior to her moving, an equal number of agents had positive and negative values on the issue.

#### 7.2.1.2 Direct Competition

We model direct competition as winner-take-all plurality voting among parties advocating different platforms. Under direct competition, each agent votes for the party proposing the platform that yields her the highest utility, and the winning party wholly implements its platform in the jurisdiction.

Direct competition may not be as stable as democratic referenda. Even with the linearly separable preferences considered here, policy predictions under direct competition cannot be guaranteed to produce unique solutions without severe restrictions on preferences (Plott 1967)—cycling is endemic to plurality rule. Given the potential for cycling, various alternative solutions have been proposed, including the top-cycle set (McKelvey 1976), the uncovered set (McKelvey 1986), and the minmax set (Kramer 1977). Unfortunately, even these solutions often imply disparate platforms or fail to narrow the potential set of platforms.[7] The absence of a unique equilibrium in direct competition for large classes of preferences has led some to call into question the effectiveness of democratic decision making (Riker 1982). For our purposes, predicting an exact platform is less important than knowing the bounds on the set from which platforms will be chosen. Here we rely on an adaptive party model in which parties with incomplete information choose platforms using simple search heuristics. The platforms that emerge in the adaptive model often correspond to the equilibria generated by the mathematical solutions. Evidence from our experiments suggests that when a single platform is predicted using mathematical techniques, the adaptive parties tend to find it within a few elections, while in situations where the formal predictions are set valued, the adaptive parties tend to advocate platforms from within or near the proposed solution set.

#### 7.2.1.3 Proportional Representation

Under proportional representation each agent votes for a single party, and each party receives a number of seats in a decision-making body proportional to its popular vote. In our model, we assume no distortion between the percentage of the vote that a party receives and the percentage of seats it obtains in the legislature. In the model, once each party is allocated seats, the final decision on each issue is the weighted (by popular vote) sum of each party's platform position on each issue. In essence, each party sincerely votes in a series of referenda across the issues. For example, if a party advocating the platform (*Yes*, *No*, *Yes*) receives 18 percent of the popular vote, then that party would vote *Yes*, *No*, and *Yes* on the first, second, and third issues respectively, and these three votes would each be assigned a weight of 0.18. The final decision on each issue equals *Yes* if the total weight of all parties in the jurisdiction advocating *Yes* exceeds 0.5 and *No* otherwise.[8] We assume that agents vote sincerely, although we discuss the issue of strategic voting at the end of the chapter.[9]

Although we did not report it here, we also experimented with a version of proportional representation that relied on a Borda-like weighting scheme. In this version, an agent was allowed to allocate $m - 1$ votes to her favorite party, $m - 2$ to her next favorite, and so on, where $m$ is equal to the number of parties on the ballot. The number of seats used in the final weighting was then set to the proportion of votes received by each party. We found that such a system often leads to superior outcomes, most likely because of its ability to convey intensity of preferences among the electorate. Nonetheless, given the relative lack of real-world examples of such a system (Australia and Ireland do rely somewhat on related systems), and our desire to simplify the presentation, we do not report the results.

Under direct competition and proportional representation there is the potential for more than two parties. Note that proportional representation and direct competition lead to identical outcomes when there are only two parties in the system, since under proportional representation the party with the majority of votes will be able to impose its entire platform. As the number of parties increases above two, the platform used in a jurisdiction may differ between the two institutions if no party receives more than half the vote, since platforms other than the winning party's will affect the final policy decisions under proportional representation. In our model, we assume that the number of parties is given exogenously. While party formation is of theoretical and practical importance, we leave the analysis of this process to future research.

### 7.2.2 *Adaptive Parties*

As discussed, mathematical models of party behavior may not adequately restrict the set of potential platforms. To overcome this problem, we use a model developed by Kollman et al. (1992) in which parties adapt platforms using search heuristics applied to polling information. In this model, parties adaptively search for new platforms in an attempt to increase the number of votes they receive in an election. We can use the model to explore the influence of the platform selection process on the final equilibrium state achieved by the system.

Parties in our model are incrementally adaptive and incompletely informed. This contrasts with standard rational choice approaches in which parties are either completely informed optimizers (with knowledge of each voter's utility function) or act as Bayesians. In reality, practical considerations impose restrictions on a party's computational ability, the amount and type of information it has access to, and on the maximum allowable policy change it can make in any one election. For example, parties rely on imperfect and imprecise polling data to gather information about voters' preferences and must restrict platform changes from year to year to maintain both credibility and a coherent organization.

From our perspective, no single model of party behavior is likely to be accurate. Computational modeling grants us the flexibility to consider various types of behavior and to learn which findings are particular to the assumptions and which are generic. We initially used three alternative adaptive algorithms: random search, hill-climbing, and genetic algorithms. In all of these methods parties attempt to improve the number of votes their platforms receive by adaptively generating new platforms. In random search, a party first generates a set of random new platforms constrained to be close to its current platform, and then adopts the best one. In hill-climbing (discussed in further detail later), a party generates a new random platform near its current platform, and keeps the better of the two (of course, this may imply that its current platform remains unchanged). This procedure is then iterated for a fixed number of steps. Finally, genetic algorithms (Holland 1975) generate new platforms from a biased (by performance) set of old platforms via some simple platform formation operators (Kollman et al. 1992). Our findings suggest that few implications depend significantly on the heuristic used by parties, provided the parties are neither omniscient nor dim-witted. Thus, in the experiments presented here we only report the results from hill-climbing.

Our actual hill-climbing procedure works as follows. A randomly generated current platform is given to each party prior to any elections. When a party is given a chance to adapt, it first generates a new platform by randomly perturbing its current platform on up to three issues. Thus, the new platform is constrained to lie in a neighborhood of the current one. If the new platform yields a higher vote total, it becomes the party's current platform; otherwise the current platform remains unchanged. This search process continues for eight iterations. Hill-climbing always bases its search on the current best-known platform.[10] After the eighth iteration, another party is given a similar chance to adapt. After each party adapts, we return to the first party and begin a new cycle of adaptation. In the work reported here, five such cycles are allowed. At the end of these five cycles, an election is held in which each party proposes its current platform.

## 7.3 The Computational Model

In this section, we describe findings from computational experiments on Tiebout competition. Computational findings can be particular to the parameter values selected, so we have endeavored to test many sets of parameter values, and the results reported here appear to be robust to reasonable variations. For these experiments, we used 1,000 agents (citizens) and 11 binary issues.

### *7.3.1 Sequence of Events*

The computational model begins by randomly creating preferences for each agent, and then randomly assigning each agent to a jurisdiction. Next, a series of ten Tiebout cycles is initiated. In each cycle, agents are first allowed to relocate. Following standard Tiebout models we assume that an agent moves to the jurisdiction providing her the highest utility.[11] The next step in the cycle is to allow each jurisdiction to alter its platform. Under democratic referenda, each jurisdiction adopts the median position on each issue. With direct competition and proportional representation, parties alternate adapting their platforms via the hill-climbing algorithm.

We find that the configuration of agents and party platforms in our model typically settle down by the end of ten Tiebout cycles. Democratic referenda almost always settle into an equilibrium within about four cycles. The other institutions often achieve a steady state by the end of ten cycles, and even when this is not the case, they rarely show any significant increases in aggregate utility after this time.

The primary focus of the analysis is on the per capita utility of the citizens at the end of the tenth Tiebout cycle. Recall that each agent has an expected payoff of zero from a random platform and 100 from an ideal one. The standard errors reported in the tables are the standard errors of the estimate within a given cell.

### 7.3.2 *Single-Jurisdiction Findings*

The findings for a single-jurisdiction model are given in table 7.1. Regardless of the institution, the final platforms provide significantly more utility than randomly generated platforms. Democratic referenda provide the highest aggregate utility, followed by two-party direct competition (and two-party proportional representation[12]), and seven- and three-party proportional representation. Democratic referenda result in median platforms, which, given our assumptions on the distribution of preferences, provide nearly maximal utility in a single jurisdiction. Under adaptive parties, the dynamics depend on the number of parties in the system. With only two parties, regions of the platform space that produce relatively high aggregate

**Table 7.1**
Single Jurisdiction: Per Capita Utility after Ten Elections (200 Trials)

| Institution | Per Capita Utility | (s.e. of the mean) |
|---|---|---|
| Democratic referenda | 2.69 | (0.12) |
| Direct competition (2 parties) | 1.45 | (0.13) |
| Direct competition (3 parties) | 0.67 | (0.13) |
| Direct competition (7 parties) | 0.33 | (0.13) |
| Proportional representation (3 parties) | 1.33 | (0.13) |
| Proportional representation (7 parties) | 1.36 | (0.13) |

utility are quickly located by both parties. Once found, the parties tend to wander within these regions, often alternating which party carries the majority. Thus, we find relatively good performance under two-party institutions, with some diminution over democratic referenda due to the search process.

With more than two parties the dynamics are more complex. In these systems, parties initially tend toward a high utility region of the platform space, but once this occurs, single-party transients away from this region are common—if the other parties are closely clustered, then a single party may find increasing support if it moves away from the cluster and toward more extreme voters. The presence of transients and the likelihood that such extreme platforms will win increases with the number of parties in the system. Under direct competition this has a detrimental effect on aggregate utility, since the winning party implements its entire platform (this explains the low values observed under three- and seven-party direct competition). Under proportional representation, however, the platform implemented by a jurisdiction usually does not belong to a single party but rather is decided by weighted majority rule. This weighting process mitigates the impact of extreme parties. Note that as the number of parties increases under proportional representation, each agent is able to pick a party that advocates a platform near her own utility-maximizing platform, and thus proportional representation will begin to approximate democratic referenda.

### *7.3.3 Multiple Jurisdictions*

With multiple jurisdictions agents can begin to sort according to their preferences. As long as jurisdictions are responsive to constituencies, aggregate utility should be nondecreasing in the number of jurisdictions, and will likely increase as multiple jurisdictions are better able to sort agents by preferences. Table 7.2 presents findings from models with three, seven, and eleven jurisdictions.[13] For all institutions considered, per capita utility increases with the number of jurisdictions. The addition of even a few jurisdictions allows a dramatic increase in utility. While the increase in utility was expected, what was not anticipated was that the *performance of the various political institutions completely reverses.* Democratic referenda, which were best in the one-jurisdiction model, are now worst, while proportional representation now performs best. With seven or more

**Table 7.2**
Multiple Jurisdictions: Per Capita Utility after Ten Elections (200 Trials)

| Institution | 3 Jurisdictions | (s.e. of the mean) | 7 Jurisdictions | (s.e. of the mean) | 11 Jurisdictions | (s.e. of the mean) |
|---|---|---|---|---|---|---|
| Democratic referenda | 34.39 | (0.15) | 48.29 | (0.13) | 55.46 | (0.12) |
| Direct competition (2 parties) | 34.15 | (0.14) | 49.90 | (0.13) | 57.03 | (0.13) |
| Proportional representation (3 parties) | 35.56 | (0.11) | 51.80 | (0.12) | 58.93 | (0.12) |

jurisdictions, three-party proportional representation is significantly better than two-party direct competition, which is significantly better than democratic referenda.

A full explanation of this performance reversal is left for the next section. Intuitively, the reversal is linked to the effectiveness of different institutions in sorting agents across jurisdictions. An institution like democratic referenda leads to very stable platforms and little sorting among the agents, while the instability of the platforms induced by proportional representation is such that low utility configurations of agents are easily disrupted. If platform instability is directly related to agent heterogeneity, then the system will naturally lead to configurations of high aggregate utility—configurations of agents that have relatively low aggregate utility are associated with high agent heterogeneity, and therefore are likely to lead to unstable platforms, which in turn cause agent migration. Eventually, as agents become better sorted, platform stability ensues, migration ceases, and equilibrium is achieved.

## 7.4 The Power of Political Instability

In this section, we discuss how political instability may permit greater sorting of citizens and therefore be beneficial in a model of Tiebout competition. The argument hinges on the relationship between the level of political instability within jurisdictions and the degree of heterogeneity of preferences at each jurisdiction. At present we do not have analytic proofs for many of the these ideas. What follows is an informal explanation of our results, supported by evidence derived from the model. While mathematically derived results

**Table 7.3**
Agent Preferences

| Agent | Issue 1 | Issue 2 | Issue 3 |
|---|---|---|---|
| 1 | +1 | +1 | +1 |
| 2 | +1 | −1 | +0.5 |
| 3 | +1 | +0.5 | −1 |
| 4 | +1 | −1 | −1 |
| 5 | +1 | −1 | −1 |
| 6 | −1 | −0.5 | −1 |
| 7 | −1 | +0.5 | −1 |
| 8 | −1 | +0.5 | −1 |

may be possible, such results may be difficult to obtain even in a much simplified model. We believe, however, that the lack of sufficient mathematical tools should not preclude analysis. In fact, results from our computational analysis should provide insights into how more formal proofs might proceed.

### 7.4.1 *An Example*

At the beginning of the chapter, we presented an example concerning alcohol policies in two small towns. Recall that policy instability in the system breaks the symmetry of an inferior equilibrium and results in an improved sorting of agents. Here we provide a more precise example that shows how two-party direct competition may be preferred to democratic referenda in a multiple-jurisdiction model.

In table 7.3 we list the utility values for each of eight agents across three issues. Let a Tiebout equilibrium with respect to an institution exist when in each jurisdiction the current platform is consistent with the political institution and no agent wants to relocate (where consistency implies that the institution could have generated the observed platform given the agents in the jurisdiction). To simplify the discussion, we assume that for two-party direct competition any platform within the top-cycle set is consistent.[14] Note that under this assumption, a platform in a jurisdiction may be overturned for two reasons: either it is defeated by another platform in the top-cycle set, or agent migration alters underlying voter preferences in the jurisdiction to such a degree that a new top-cycle set emerges.

First, consider a jurisdiction containing the first three agents. If the institution is democratic referenda, then the platform will be (*Yes*,

*Yes*, *Yes*), and the aggregate utility will be 4.0. In this jurisdiction, the platforms (*Yes*, *Yes*, *Yes*), (*Yes*, *Yes*, *No*), (*Yes*, *No*, *Yes*), and (*Yes*, *No*, *No*) are all members of the top-cycle set. The aggregate utilities from these platforms are 4.0, 3.5, 3.5, and 3.0, respectively. If we assume that the platform resulting from two-party direct competition is randomly chosen from this set, then democratic referenda are preferred to direct competition on utility grounds.

Now, suppose we add a second jurisdiction that contains agents 4–8. In this jurisdiction, democratic referenda will lead to (*No*, *No*, *No*). It is easy to show that no agent wants to relocate between the two jurisdictions under democratic referenda, and therefore this configuration is a Tiebout equilibrium with respect to this institution. A simple calculation shows that the aggregate utility in this equilibrium equals 4.0.

However, this equilibrium is not necessarily stable under two-party direct competition. In two-party direct competition the platform (*Yes*, *Yes*, *Yes*) can be defeated by (*Yes*, *No*, *No*) in the first jurisdiction. Note that this new platform lowers the aggregate utility of the first group from 4.0 to 3.0. Under the new platform, agents 4 and 5 will now move from the second jurisdiction into the first, and (*Yes*, *No*, *No*) becomes the only member of the new top-cycle set in this jurisdiction. Without agents 4 and 5, (*No*, *Yes*, *No*) becomes the only member of the second jurisdiction's top-cycle set. It is straightforward to show that this new configuration of agents is a Tiebout equilibrium with respect to two-party direct competition (as well as democratic referenda). More important, the aggregate utility of this new configuration equals 5.5.

This example demonstrates how with multiple jurisdictions, the lack of a unique outcome from direct competition may induce sorting and increase aggregate utility. Like the example in the introduction of this chapter, this increase in utility requires a temporary decrease of utility in a given jurisdiction in order to induce agent migration. However, the migration eventually leads to a higher aggregate utility for the overall system.

### 7.4.2 *Insights from Simulated Annealing*

To provide intuition for our computational results and the examples presented, we apply insights from the literature on simulated annealing, a nonlinear optimization algorithm. Simulated annealing is a sequential search algorithm applied to a real-valued function, $f$.

In simulated annealing, a neighborhood structure on the domain is first created. Each point, $x$, in $f$'s domain belongs to a neighborhood, $N(x)$, which contains at least one point different from $x$. Similar to hill-climbing, at each step simulated annealing randomly chooses a new point in the neighborhood of the status quo point and makes that new point the status quo if it has a higher value under $f$. Where simulated annealing differs from hill-climbing is that it may also move to new points that have lower values. This occurs with a probability that depends on the difference in the function values, $\Delta(x, \hat{x}) = f(x) - f(\hat{x})$, and a temperature, $T(t)$, which is a decreasing function of the time spent searching, $t$. Formally, if $x$ is the status quo point and $\hat{x}$ is a randomly chosen neighboring point of lower value, the probability of accepting this new point as the status quo is

$$p(x, \hat{x}, t) = e^{-\Delta(x,\hat{x})/T(t)}.$$

Note that inferior points are more likely to be accepted when the temperature is high or the value of the inferior point is close to the status quo. If the difference in function values, $\Delta(x, \hat{x})$, is large relative to the temperature, $T(t)$, then the probability of acceptance is low. The temperature can be interpreted as the degree of leniency: high temperatures allow for almost any new point to be accepted, while low ones allow for a new point to be accepted only if the loss in value is small. The temperature decreases to zero according to an annealing schedule. As the temperature nears zero, only increasing moves are accepted, and search converges to a local optimum with respect to the neighborhood structure.

A substantial body of theory exists to explain the performance of simulated annealing. Bruce Hajek (1988) has shown that given any function there exists an annealing schedule such that the simulated annealing procedure converges to the global optimum.[15] To some extent these results are misleading, as the proofs, whether relying on Markov chain theory or real analysis, require that every point in the domain be evaluated. This obviously begs the question of why simulated annealing should be preferred over exhaustive search. In practice, even though simulated annealing often fails to locate the global optimum, it has been shown to be very effective at locating good solutions with relatively few searches.

A promising line of inquiry into the performance of simulated annealing analyzes the structure of the function's local optima. Consider search via a hill-climbing algorithm. Given a neighborhood structure, each local optimum has a basin of attraction defined by all those points that are located "down the hill" from the optimum. The larger a local optimum's basin of attraction, the more likely search ends at that optimum. Simulated annealing performs better on those functions with positive correlations between the values of local optima and the sizes of their associated basin of attraction. On such functions, local optima with relatively low values, and therefore small basins of attraction, are more likely to be rendered unstable by the noise from the annealing schedule. In effect, the mistakes due to the temperature smooth over the lesser-valued optima, and eventually, the high-valued optima—with large basins of attraction—become inescapable as the temperature tends to zero. In such spaces, simulated annealing performs "as if" it can recognize whether a local optimum's value was relatively high or low, escaping lower-valued optima in favor of higher-valued ones (Page 1996).

In relating these insights to the performance of political institutions in a Tiebout model, we find strong, though not exact, connections. Consider a set of platforms across all jurisdictions, and the corresponding configuration of agents each attracts, as a point in the domain of the aggregate utility function. A neighborhood of such a point could consist of all platforms (along with their corresponding reconfiguration of agents) that are located within a fixed distance (according to some metric) of the given set of platforms.

For explanatory purposes, we restrict the discussion to two political institutions: democratic referenda and two-party direct competition. Previously we have shown that democratic referenda yield a unique platform in each jurisdiction and that direct competition offers less stability since it may alternate platforms from among those available in the top-cycle set. We can interpret this instability as making mistakes, in the sense that the platforms chosen by direct competition typically have lower utility than the median platforms generated by democratic referenda. As was demonstrated, these mistakes can be fortuitous in the long run, as they allow the system to break out of old equilibrium and to form new configurations of agents that promote the creation of new, utility-improving equilibria.

Of course, the presence of instability by itself is insufficient to lead to higher equilibria since it will disrupt, as well as find, good equilibria. Therefore, to account for the increase in performance we observe in our model, the instability must be systematically tied to the aggregate utility of the various equilibria.

We propose that, like simulated annealing, institutions that make more mistakes in relatively low-valued configurations will enable the system to act "as if" it recognizes the potential value of a local optimum and to escape inferior equilibria. Two characteristics of our model generate this fortuitous bias in error making. First, aggregate utility for a configuration of agents is positively correlated with the homogeneity of preferences at each jurisdiction. Second, the instability of direct competition is linked to the heterogeneity of preferences in a jurisdiction.[16] Combining these two effects, if agents in a configuration are not very homogeneous at each jurisdiction, aggregate utility will be low, and direct competition will generate new platforms which render the existing configuration unstable. If, however, the agents in a configuration are homogeneous at each jurisdiction, aggregate utility will be high and platforms will be stable. Thus, Tiebout equilibria with respect to direct competition are biased towards those platforms and agent configurations with higher aggregate utility.

To test these ideas, we turn to our computational model. If instability in the better performing institutions induces superior sorting, then we should observe significantly more relocations of agents under the better institutions. Table 7.4 shows the average number of agent relocations observed during each ten-cycle trial. As predicted, the performance of a given institution is closely tied to the number of relocations observed. Comparing tables 7.4 and 7.2, relocations correlate positively with aggregate utility in multiple jurisdictions.

**Table 7.4**
Average Number of Agent Relocations per Trial (50 Trials)

| Institution | 3 Jurisdictions | (s.e. of the mean) | 7 Jurisdictions | (s.e. of the mean) | 11 Jurisdictions | (s.e. of the mean) |
|---|---|---|---|---|---|---|
| Democratic referenda | 864.16 | (17.24) | 863.2 | (10.41) | 887.3 | (5.26) |
| Direct competition (2 parties) | 915.68 | (14.67) | 1162.5 | (8.63) | 1293.7 | (7.13) |
| Proportional representation (3 parties) | 1277.60 | (34.41) | 1371.06 | (25.75) | 1420.28 | (21.74) |

A more direct test of the sorting abilities of each institution is to measure the variance of the agent preferences within each jurisdiction or of the platforms across all jurisdictions. The former measurement indicates that democratic referenda result in the most preference variance, followed by two-party direct competition, and then three-party proportional representation. The results on platform variation are given in table 7.5. In this table we report the average percentage of issues on which the platforms from two different jurisdictions differ (thus, if the platforms differ on exactly three issues, their value is 3/11 or 28 percent). In all cases, proportional representation results in the most heterogeneous platforms across jurisdictions, followed by direct competition, and democratic referenda, respectively. These rankings correspond with the rankings of aggregate utility and the number of relocations. More relocations and greater platform heterogeneity imply better sorting and therefore higher aggregate utility. Note that average platform heterogeneity decreases as the number of jurisdictions increases—this must occur since as the number of jurisdictions increases, the maximal possible average heterogeneity must decrease (two platforms may differ across all issues, but it is impossible for three platforms to each differ across all positions from the other two). In general, as the number of jurisdictions increases the average heterogeneity decreases as the space of possible platforms becomes more crowded.

Much of our argument as to performance differences among institutions requires that platforms need to be less stable as agent preferences become more heterogeneous. We test whether this in fact

**Table 7.5**
Average Distance between Platforms (50 Trials)

| Institution | 3 Jurisdictions | (s.e. of the mean) | 7 Jurisdictions | (s.e. of the mean) | 11 Jurisdictions | (s.e. of the mean) |
|---|---|---|---|---|---|---|
| Democratic referenda | 61.58 | (0.84) | 51.64 | (0.32) | 50.76 | (0.23) |
| Direct competition (2 parties) | 65.21 | (0.41) | 53.96 | (0.23) | 52.26 | (0.13) |
| Proportional representation (3 parties) | 66.67 | (0.36) | 56.12 | (0.15) | 53.32 | (0.09) |

**Table 7.6**
Flips as a Function of Heterogeneity (50 Trials)

| $\theta$ | Democratic Referenda | Direct Competition (2 Parties) | Proportional Representation (3 Parties) |
|---|---|---|---|
| 0.50 | 0.00 (0.00) | 0.24 (0.15) | 0.69 (0.38) |
| 0.55 | 0.00 (0.00) | 0.21 (0.16) | 0.80 (0.33) |
| 0.60 | 0.00 (0.00) | 0.23 (0.24) | 0.80 (0.37) |
| 0.65 | 0.00 (0.00) | 0.26 (0.24) | 0.77 (0.40) |
| 0.70 | 0.00 (0.00) | 0.31 (0.37) | 0.88 (0.48) |
| 0.75 | 0.00 (0.00) | 0.38 (0.44) | 1.01 (0.53) |
| 0.80 | 0.00 (0.00) | 0.53 (0.49) | 1.26 (0.55) |
| 0.85 | 0.00 (0.00) | 0.68 (0.73) | 1.94 (0.69) |
| 0.90 | 0.00 (0.00) | 1.37 (1.11) | 2.84 (0.71) |
| 0.95 | 0.00 (0.00) | 2.65 (1.08) | 3.78 (0.62) |
| 1.00 | 0.00 (0.00) | 3.36 (1.12) | 4.02 (0.59) |

occurs by creating populations of agents with varying degrees of heterogeneity, and then measure the number of platform changes. To vary population heterogeneity, each agent's ideal point is made a convex combination of a base preference, common across all agents, and an individual preference:

$$(1 - \theta) \cdot base + \theta \cdot individual,$$

where the individual and base preference were drawn from the same preference distribution used in the original model. We refer to $\theta$ as the degree of heterogeneity.

The results of a one-jurisdiction model with 250 agents are given in table 7.6. The restriction to one jurisdiction guarantees that none of the changes in platforms are attributable to agent migration. We vary $\theta$ between 0.5 and 1.0. Values of $\theta$ below this range create agents whose preferences are too homogeneous: almost all have the same preferred platform. The findings are from 50 series of ten elections, and *flips* equals the average number of issues that change on the platform during each election.

Democratic referenda have no flips across all degrees of heterogeneity since the lack of agent migration implies the identical median platform during all time periods. For the other institutions we find, as expected, that the average number of flips increases with the degree of heterogeneity. These findings strongly support our hypothesis that as preferences in a jurisdiction become less homogeneous the propensity for platform instability increases.

An additional test to support our annealing hypothesis is whether the introduction of an annealing process could improve the performance of democratic referenda. We create annealing in this situation by randomly forcing agents to move to suboptimal jurisdictions during each Tiebout cycle. Over time, we lower the probability of suboptimal moves to create an annealing effect. For example, we set the initial probability of moving to a suboptimal jurisdiction at 5 percent and decrease this probability by 5 percent each period. When we do this, the average utility significantly increases in almost all cases. Even though the utility increases, it does not achieve the level attained under the other two institutions—perhaps reflecting the crudeness of this process relative to mechanisms that are more responsive to the local conditions in each jurisdiction. Nonetheless, this experiment indicates that direct annealing can improve the outcome of democratic referenda.

The computational evidence strongly supports our hypotheses that (1) annealing can improve aggregate utility in these systems by insuring better sorting of agents, and (2) that institutions vary in their ability to anneal the system. Although instability or noise may help break a system out of an inferior equilibrium, it does not, in and of itself, guarantee that better equilibria will be selected. For this to occur, the noise must be reduced as the system converges on superior outcomes. While in general this may require some global knowledge of the objective function or some exogenous control factor, here decentralized institutions can achieve this end by linking instability to the degree of heterogeneity present in the local jurisdiction. Of course, this property was not explicitly designed into the institutions used here, but arises serendipitously.

## 7.5 Discussion

We find that in a model of Tiebout competition with multiple jurisdictions, some political institutions perform better than others by inducing better agent sorting and thereby generating higher aggregate utility. Ironically, these same institutions often perform relatively poorly in a single-jurisdiction model. The reason for this performance reversal is that multiple jurisdictions create a system with multiple equilibria. A minor mistake, which is harmful in the single-jurisdiction model, may be beneficial in the multiple-jurisdiction model since it can dislodge the system from a relatively bad local optimum, and induce agents to re-sort themselves into a better configuration.

Mistakes alone are not sufficient for finding and maintaining superior equilibria. In the multiple-jurisdiction model, institutions that generate high aggregate utility are those that create less stable platforms only when agents have locally more heterogeneous preferences. Since aggregate utility decreases as agent heterogeneity increases, this systematic instability induces more agent migration in low-valued configurations, yet simultaneously allows the system to settle on high-valued ones. Such a process is consistent with the annealing argument presented in the previous section.

There are many simplifying assumptions in the current model. The parties lack policy preferences, voters are not strategic, and preferences are assumed to be linearly separable. If parties have policy preferences, then platforms may be even less representative than under the current model. Of course, even with less representative platforms, the relevant issue is whether the correlation of platform changes with the degree of heterogeneity of preferences is positive, and we see no reason why this would not be the case. The introduction of strategic voting may also influence the results. Clearly the existence of multiple equilibria and the complex dynamics in the model greatly complicate the task of voting strategically, and even with strategic voting there is no prima facie reason to suspect that the linkage between preference heterogeneity and policy instability will be lessened. In fact, this linkage may even increase for democratic referenda. If voters believe that they are in a configuration of low aggregate utility, they may be able to benefit by misrepresenting their preferences in order to force policy changes that spur relocations. Finally, experiments using nonlinear preferences generate similar results to those reported here.

The idea that decentralized mechanisms can be used to refine equilibrium outcomes toward those equilibria with higher aggregate payoff has important implications for mechanism design. Our results indicate that three conditions help in the effective design of such mechanisms. First, the decentralized mechanism must be able to acquire information about the state of aggregate payoff from local information. In our model, agent heterogeneity at any given jurisdiction is a good proxy for the quality of global sorting. Second, the mechanism must be able to disrupt global equilibria through local action. For example, a platform change at a single jurisdiction might cause sufficient migration to result in a cascade of platform changes at other jurisdictions. Finally, the decentralized mechanism must link the local information to local action in such a way that as the global system improves, local action is dampened. Given these three conditions, a decentralized mechanism can bias the outcome towards those configurations of higher aggregate payoff.

The notion that institutions can act as natural annealing mechanisms may be useful in understanding the dynamic behavior and performance characteristics of many other systems. Tiebout models are just one example of a broad class of phenomena that must "sort" agents among alternative configurations with multiple equilibria. Other examples include traders pairing off in markets, laborers finding jobs, firms choosing production sites or product attributes, and individuals forming organizations. Under decentralized sorting mechanisms, these systems may get trapped in suboptimal configurations. If, however, there are means by which these poor configurations can be annealed in an appropriate manner, then the global system can escape these traps and achieve superior outcomes.

## Notes

A portion of this work was funded by National Science Foundation Grants SBR 94-09602, SBR 94-11025, and SBR 94-10948. Page's work was funded by the MacArthur Foundation. The authors wish to thank Robert Axelrod, Jenna Bednar, Roger Lagunoff, and two anonymous referees for helpful comments.

1. Zax shows that the lowest levels of tax appears to be paid when there is high fragmentation among multipurpose jurisdictions, low fragmentation of single-purpose jurisdictions, and decentralized governments.

2. Richard J. Cebula (1974) shows that welfare payments had a significant effect on interstate migration in the United States from 1965 to 1970.

3. For convenience each agent, jurisdiction, and issue is given an integer label on $\{1,\ldots,N_k\}$, where $k = a$, $j$, and $i$, respectively.

4. Although real-valued issues are often used in Tiebout models (for example, jurisdictions differ in the amounts of public goods or tax rates they offer), using binary issues simplifies the modeling of the requisite political institutions. Experiments with real-valued versions of the model under direct competition and proportional representation indicate that our results appear robust to this change.

5. Democratic referenda are used by many cities and states in the United States to decide particular policy issues. National referenda were used by Norway and Great Britain to decide whether to enter the European Union, and Australia and several

smaller European countries (including Switzerland, Denmark, and Ireland) regularly employ this institution on a national basis. Direct competition (winner-take-all plurality voting) is used by most major cities and all states in the United States to elect executives (mayors and governors). Many countries, including Canada, South Africa, and the United Kingdom, also use direct competition to elect local and national leaders. Proportional representation is widely used by most of the world's democracies. Proportional systems vary greatly, but they all have the common feature of attempting to link legislative representation to proportionality of the popular vote.

6. In the case of a tie, we assume that the decision is *No*.

7. For example, one can generate situations in which the top-cycle set encompasses the entire platform space, while the uncovered set—a refinement of the top-cycle set—contains every platform except the median one.

8. These assumptions do not preclude a party that receives a small percentage of the vote from having substantial power.

9. In elections with more than two parties, a voter may have an incentive to act strategically. Suppose that a voter with ideal platform (*Yes*, *No*, *No*) is given a choice between the platforms (*No*, *No*, *No*) and (*Yes*, *Yes*, *Yes*), and given this choice she would pick (*No*, *No*, *No*). If the weighted vote on *Yes* for the first issue is close to 0.5 and significantly below 0.5 on the second and third issues, then the voter may gain by choosing the party advocating the (*Yes*, *Yes*, *Yes*) platform.

10. In contrast a random search first generates the set of new platforms (all based on the same current platform) and then selects the best one.

11. If two or more jurisdictions have identical payoffs, the agent stays in her current location if it is one of these jurisdictions or, if not, moves to the jurisdiction with the lowest "address" (each jurisdiction is given a unique address).

12. The values for two-party proportional representation are not shown in the tables, but they are indistinguishable from those for two-party direct competition.

13. To simplify the subsequent discussion, we will only focus on the institutions of democratic referenda, two-party direct competition, and three-party proportional representation. These institutions are representative of the broader set of institutions used in the single-jurisdiction analysis.

14. A platform belongs to the top-cycle set if it could be victorious over any other possible platform via some sequence of pairwise elections.

15. Similar results can be found in a special issue of *Algorithmica* (1991) dedicated to simulated annealing.

16. McKelvey (1986) has shown in a mathematical model that the size of the uncovered set decreases with the level of symmetry of preferences.

## References

*Algorithmica*. 1991. Ottawa, Canada: Springer-Verlag.

Axelrod, Robert, and P. Scott Bennett. 1993. "A Landscape Theory of Aggregation." *British Journal of Political Science* 23 (2): 211–233.

Berglas, Eitan. 1976. "Distribution of Tastes and Skills and the Provision of Local Public Goods." *Journal of Public Economics* 6 (4): 409–423.

Bewley, Truman F. 1981. "A Critique of Tiebout's Theory of Local Public Expenditures." *Econometrica* 49 (3): 713–740.

Cebula, Richard J. 1974. "Interstate Migration and the Tiebout Hypothesis: An Analysis According to Race, Sex and Age." *Journal of the American Statistical Association* 69 (348): 876–879.

Conley, John P. and Myrna Wooders. 1997. "Equivalence of the Core and Competitive Equilibrium in a Tiebout Economy with Crowding Types." *Journal of Urban Economics* 41: 421–440.

DeVany, Arthur. 1994. "Hard Cores, Soft Cores, and the Emergence of Self-Organized Coalitions." Working paper, University of California-Irvine.

Dowding, Keith, Peter John, and Stephen Biggs. 1994. "Tiebout: A Survey of the Empirical Literature." *Urban Studies* 31 (4–5): 767–797.

Durlauf, Steven N. 1991. "Multiple Equilibria and Persistence in Aggregate Fluctuations." *American Economic Review* (*Papers and Proceedings*) 81 (2): 70–74.

Fox, William F., Henry W. Herzog, Jr., and Alan M. Schlottmann. 1989. "Metropolitan Fiscal Structure and Migration." *Journal of Regional Science* 29 (4): 523–536.

Hajek, Bruce. 1988. "Cooling Schedules for Optimal Annealing." *Mathematics of Operations Research* 13 (4): 331–360.

Holland, John H. 1975. *Adaptation in Natural and Artificial Systems.* Ann Arbor, MI: University of Michigan Press.

Holland, John H., and John H. Miller. 1991. "Artificial Adaptive Agents and Economic Theory." *American Economic Review* (*Papers and Proceedings*) 81 (2): 365–371.

Hoyt, William H. 1990. "Local Government Inefficiency and the Tiebout Hypothesis: Does Competition among Municipalities Limit Local Government Inefficiency." *Southern Economic Journal* 57 (2): 481–496.

Kollman, Ken, John H. Miller, and Scott E. Page. 1992. "Adaptive Parties in Spatial Elections." *American Political Science Review* 86 (4): 929–937.

Konishi, Hideo. 1996. "Voting with Ballots and Feet: Existence of Equilibria in a Local Public Good Economy." *Journal of Economic Theory* 68 (2): 480–509.

Kramer, Gerald H. 1977. "A Dynamical Model of Political Equilibrium." *Journal of Economic Theory* 16 (2): 310–334.

McKelvey, Richard D. 1976. "Intransitivities in Multidimensional Voting Models and Some Implications for Agenda Control." *Journal of Economic Theory* 12 (3): 472–482.

———. 1986. "Covering, Dominance, and the Institution-Free Properties of Social Choice." *American Journal of Political Science* 30 (2): 283–314.

Page, Scott E. 1996. "Two Measures of Difficulty." *Economic Theory* 8 (2): 321–346.

Percy, Stephen L. 1993. "Revisiting Tiebout: Moving Rationales, Exiting Behavior, and Governmental Responses to Metropolitan Mobility." Paper, Midwest Political Science Association Conference, Chicago.

Percy, Stephen L., and Brett W. Hawkins. 1992. "Further Tests of Individual-Level Propositions from the Tiebout Model." *Journal of Politics* 54 (4): 1149–1157.

Peterson, Paul, and Mark Rom. 1989. "American Federalism, Welfare Policy, and Residential Choices." *American Political Science Review* 83 (3): 711–728.

Plott, Charles R. 1967. "A Notion of Equilibrium and Its Possibility under Majority Rule." *American Economic Review* 57 (4): 787–806.

Reschovsky, Andrew. 1979. "Residential Choice and the Local Public Sector: An Alternative Test of the Tiebout Hypothesis." *Journal of Urban Economics* 6 (4): 501–520.

Riker, William. 1982. *Liberalism against Populism.* San Francisco: Freeman.

Romer, Thomas, and Howard Rosenthal. 1979. "Bureaucrats versus Voters: On the Political Economy of Resource Allocation by Direct Democracy." *Quarterly Journal of Economics* 93 (4): 563–587.

Rose-Ackerman, Susan. 1979. "Market Models of Local Government: Exit, Voting, and the Land Market." *Journal of Urban Economics* 6 (2): 319–337.

Samuelson, Paul. 1954. "The Pure Theory of Public Expenditure." *Review of Economics and Statistics* 36 (3): 387–389.

Schelling, Thomas C. 1978. *Micromotives and macrobehavior.* New York: Norton.

Sharp, E. B. 1984. "Exit, Voice and Loyalty in the Context of Local Government Problems." *Western Political Quarterly* 37 (1): 67–83.

Tiebout, Charles M. 1956. "A Pure Theory of Local Expenditures." *Journal of Political Economy* 64 (3): 416–424.

Wooders, Myrna H. 1994. "Large Games and Economies with Effective Small Groups." In *Game-Theoretic Methods in General Equilibrium Analysis*, ed. J.-F. Mertens and S. Sorin. Boston: Kluwer.

Zax, Jeffrey S. 1989. "Is There a Leviathan in Your Neighborhood?" *American Economic Review* 79 (3): 560–567.

# 8 Recovering Behavioralism: Adaptively Rational Strategic Behavior with Endogenous Aspirations

Jonathan Bendor, Daniel Diermeier, and Michael Ting

## 8.1 Introduction

A quiet revolution is occurring in game theory: it is becoming more behaviorally oriented. Ideas of imperfect (non-Bayesian) learning, of myopic adaptation, even of satisficing—all these are now being incorporated into game-theoretic models (e.g., Fudenberg and Levine 1998; Young 1998). This trend is so pervasive that a term has been coined to name it: *behavioral game theory* (Camerer 1990).

This is, we believe, a very significant intellectual development. As the name suggests, this new field brings together two approaches: game theory, with its emphasis on the formal analysis of strategic interaction, and behavioral decision theory, with its emphasis on the cognitive constraints of real decision makers.

Behavioral game theory in economic applications has focused on two main issues. First, researchers have tried to provide behavioral foundations for Nash equilibria. Here the goal has been to identify the class of behavioral rules that in the limit converge to strategy profiles that constitute Nash equilibria. Second, many adaptive processes lead to a unique limiting distribution over strategy profiles. In many cases this can be interpreted as a selection among the Nash equilibria in a game.

This chapter has a different purpose. Our goal is to suggest a synthesis between previously competing research programs in political science: behavioralism and (neo-)institutionalism. That is, behavior in the model is based on two elements (which have a natural affinity for each other): reinforcement-oriented learning theory—agents become more disposed to try actions that work and less likely to try those that fail—and satisficing—agents code outcomes as satisfactory or unsatisfactory (Simon 1955). Regarding institutionalism, we use normal form games to capture strategic interdependence, but our players, instead of being fully rational and having common knowledge about the game form, adapt their behavior over time in response to their past payoffs. Thus in a sense we "recover behavioralism" by embedding some of its key notions—in particular, bounded rationality—in a (game-theoretic) institutionalist framework.

Contrary to widespread belief (Green and Shapiro 1994), institutionalism—even its rational choice variant—uses a variety of methodologies (Diermeier 1998). Perhaps the most prominent approaches are structure-induced equilibrium theory (Shepsle 1979) and noncooperative game theory (e.g., Myerson 1996). What is common to all versions of institutionalism is an emphasis on the structural details of interactions among political agents. A key element of the theoretical analysis is thus to vary institutional constraints and then assess whether the predicted behavior is consistent with empirical regularities.

A critical component of institutionalism is a behavioral postulate that in the interest of generality is independent of the particular institution under discussion. To be both theoretically and empirically useful in institutional analysis such a postulate must satisfy two requirements: it must imply an equilibrium concept that exists in many choice situations, and the equilibrium predictions must vary with institutional detail. Diermeier (1998) has argued that compared to other approaches noncooperative game theory (with best-response correspondence as its behavioral postulate and Nash equilibrium as its solution concept) provides the most promising method for institutionalist analysis. However, game theory has been criticized for its unrealistic rationality requirements and, because most games of interest to political scientists exhibit multiple equilibria, for its lack of predictive power as well.

In this chapter we investigate an alternative behavioral postulate that is more closely connected to psychological research. Its main disadvantage lies in the mathematical difficulties that it entails, which is why we resort to computational methods. More specifically, we examine a variety of $2 \times 2$ games of interest to political scientists, for instance, Chicken, Prisoner's Dilemma, and Stag Hunt (Snidal 1991). These games capture different kinds of cooperation and coordination problems.

Our simulations yield five main results. First, for any analyzed game the process converges to a unique limiting distribution. That is, for any of our $2 \times 2$ games a unique (probabilistic) solution exists that is independent of the system's initial states. Second, the model's predictions vary systematically with the incentives captured by the games' payoffs. Thus, our approach satisfies both postulates of institutionalism and adds the advantage of predicting a unique outcome. Third, while in some games the model's predictions are consistent with Nash equilibrium, in the more conflictual games like Chicken and Prisoner's Dilemma (PD) our model yields predictions that are not Nash. Indeed, in PD it predicts that under certain parametric conditions the players will wind up using a strictly dominated strategy (cooperating). Fourth, in some cases our model predicts a mixed solution, analogous to a Nash equilibrium in mixed strategies. That is, players do not settle down to any one action but randomize between them. However, in contrast to mixed strategy equilibria, where each agent's mixing probability depends only on changes in the *other* player's payoffs, in our model an actor's propensity to choose an action depends on changes in his *own* payoff. Fifth, propensities for an action are not necessarily monotonic in that action's payoffs. This nonmonotonicity is due to the mediating effect of aspirations.

## 8.2 The Verbal Theory, the Formal Model, and the Program

The theory's basic ideas are quite simple. It is assumed that an agent learns by trial-and-error. Thus, an action is tried; if it works, the agent becomes more disposed to try it again in the future. Following standard terminology, we call this positive feedback and say that the relevant action has been reinforced. If the action fails (negative feedback), an agent is less likely to try it in the future; thus the action has been inhibited.[1] There is considerable experimental evidence supporting these assumptions, when decision makers have binary choices and the payoffs are unambiguously successes or failures.[2]

However, because we want to embed agents who learn by trial-and-error in strategic situations, we must confront two facts that require a conceptual modification of the theory of reinforcement learning. First, in strategic situations there are generally more than two types of payoffs. Indeed, except for the knife-edge (unlikely) circumstance of complete indifference, even in $2 \times 2$ games there are generically four different outcomes.

Second, which of these outcomes the agents will code as successes and which as failures is not nearly as clear in naturally occurring strategic situations as it is in the laboratory. While it is reasonable to posit that getting money in an experiment is reinforcing and getting nothing is inhibiting, it is not obvious what decision makers in a Prisoner's Dilemma game will consider successes or failures. Is the payoff from mutual cooperation a success? Or is only the maximal payoff?

We address this problem in two steps. First, we assume that the actors satisfice: they have an aspiration level that partitions all payoffs into satisfactory (the associated action is reinforced) and unsatisfactory (the associated action is inhibited).[3] Thus classical reinforcement theory might be interpreted as having an implicit aspiration level—one outcome is "obviously" successful, the other not—whereas in our theory aspirations are (necessarily) made explicit.

Second, we endogenize aspirations by assuming that they adjust to experience, moving up in good times and down in bad (Cyert and March 1963). Thus it will be possible for mutual cooperation in Prisoner's Dilemma to be initially coded as unsatisfactory (by, say, agents with overly ambitious aspirations), but if aspirations adjust downward over time, the agents may become satisfied with the payoff produced by mutual cooperation.[4]

### 8.2.1 *The Model*

The model represents a specific type of adaptively rational behavior in any $2 \times 2$ game. We assume here that there are only two players, though both restrictions—two players and each agent's having two actions—can be relaxed. For convenience in this section we refer to the Row player's moves as *up* and *down*, and the Column player's moves as *left* and *right*. (In section 8.3, when describing the substantive games, which mostly depict mixed motive situations involving both cooperation and conflict, we change the terminology to *cooperate* and *defect*.)

The adaptive dynamic that drives behavior in this model combines two elements: reinforcement learning and dynamically endogenous aspirations. At time $t$, each player may be described by the pair $(a_{i,t}, p_{i,t})$, where $a_{i,t}$ is player $i$'s aspiration level, $p_{r,t}$ is Row player's propensity for playing *up*, and $p_{c,t}$ is Column player's propensity for playing *left*.[5] We assume that this state pair takes on values in a discrete space, which we fix at three decimal digits of precision. Thus, for example, the possible values of a propensity are $(0, .001, .002, \ldots, .999, 1)$.

At $t = 1$, each player begins with initial (user-specified) aspirations and propensities to make certain moves. At the beginning of each period each player's propensity is trembled independently with probability $\rho$. Each player's aspiration is then trembled independently with probability $\sigma$. For each state variable, if a tremble occurs, its value is increased or decreased to the next "step" (by .001, if feasible) with equal probability. Given the trembled vector of propensities, *intended* actions are determined for each player. These choices may also be trembled independently with probability $\varepsilon$, so that actors may occasionally do the opposite of what they had intended. That is, suppose that Column's intended action is *right*, and that the probability of a tremble is 1 in 100. Then with a chance of .01, she plays *left*. We introduce trembles in order to ensure that the model has empirical content. Without trembles, *any* outcome could be predicted, given suitable initial conditions (Bendor, Diermeier, and Ting 2002). For example, in a two-person Prisoner's Dilemma with a tremble-free environment, the outcome in which a player is continually suckered could be generated with suitable initial conditions; for instance, she would have to start with aspirations that are no higher than the sucker's payoff, and so on. By producing experimentation, trembles eliminate such possibilities and so restore empirical content to the model.[6]

Because of the symmetry in state trembles, if player $i$'s propensity at the beginning of period $t$ lies in the interval $(0, 1)$, then the chance that she actually plays *left* (or *up*) in period $t$ equals

$$p_{i,t} \cdot (1 - \varepsilon) + (1 - p_{i,t}) \cdot \varepsilon.$$

After the actual actions are realized, the outcome and payoffs are revealed. Each player then adjusts her propensities and aspirations as follows. We assume that these adjustments may exhibit inertia, that is, with some fixed probability $\eta$, all player states in $t + 1$ remain as they were in period $t$.[7] With probability $1 - \eta$, reinforcement learning takes place. If, for example, Row's actual action was $u$ and her payoff exceeds her aspiration, or her actual action was $d$ and her payoff is lower than her aspiration, then her propensity to choose $u$ in the next period rises. (Column's adjustment follows the same logic.) The equation is the classical Bush-Mosteller equation:

$$p_{i,t+1} = p_{i,t} + \alpha(1 - p_{i,t}), \tag{8.1}$$

where $\alpha \in (0, 1)$, is a parameter that represents the speed of learning or adaptation, given a successful outcome.

Similarly, if Row's actual action was $u$ and her payoff is lower than her aspiration, or her actual action was $d$ and her payoff exceeds her aspiration, then her propensity to choose *up* falls:

$$p_{i,t+1} = p_{i,t} - \beta \cdot p_{i,t}, \tag{8.2}$$

where $\beta \in (0, 1)$ represents the speed of learning in the face of failure. Notice that if $\alpha = \beta$, then for each player the consequences of either action's succeeding (exceeding aspirations) are the same as those of the other action's failing. Thus if $\alpha = \beta$, the propensity adjustments would be symmetric with respect to successes and failures.

Aspirations are endogenous and also adjust to experience. We follow Cyert and March (1963) by assuming that aspirations at $t + 1$ are a weighted average of current aspirations and payoffs:

$$a_{i,t+1} = \lambda \cdot a_{i,t} + (1 - \lambda)\pi_{i,t}, \tag{8.3}$$

where $\pi_{i,t}$ is player $i$'s payoff at period $t$ and $\lambda \in (0, 1)$.

Although aspirations adjust to experience, before a game starts agents must be endowed with an initial aspiration level that naturally cannot have been influenced by a player's payoffs. In principle, therefore, initial aspiration levels could be anything. However, we require that they not be too unrealistic, that is, that they not be too far away from the feasible payoffs of the game that the agents are about to play. Specifically, we assume that there must exist positive real numbers $x$ and $y$ such that the initial aspirations for player $i$ are in $[\underline{\pi}_i - x, \bar{\pi}_i + y]$, where $\underline{\pi}_i$ is player $i$'s minimum possible payoff and $\bar{\pi}_i$ the maximum.

Because aspirations are initially bounded and over time adjust to experience, eventually they will be confined to the set of feasible payoffs. That is, in a steady state the aspiration of each player must be a convex combination of the game's possible payoffs (e.g., for Column player $a_{c,t}$ belongs in the interval $[\underline{\pi}_c, \bar{\pi}_c]$ for $t$ sufficiently large).

A full cycle of learning is depicted in figure 8.1. As the figure suggests, the model is a Markov process: the probability of being in a particular state of the process tomorrow is completely determined by the process's current state and its dynamics, that is, its state-to-state transition probabilities. (Previously, we implicitly assumed that these transition probabilities are independent of the date $t$, so this

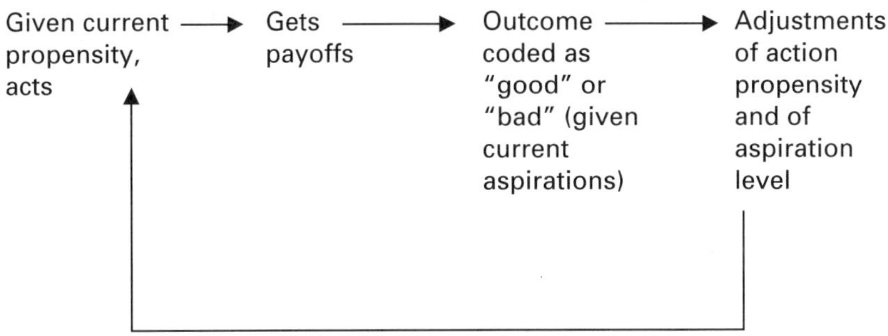


**Figure 8.1**
Basic Learning Cycle

is what is known as a stationary Markov process.) A state of this Markov process is a four-tuple, $(p_{r,t}, p_{c,t}, a_{r,t}, a_{c,t})$, composed of the players' propensities and aspirations. In principle each state variable could take on a continuum of values; in practice, since the model is implemented on a computer—a discrete machine that truncates numbers after a fixed number of decimal places—the state variables can take on only finitely many values.[8]

Thus, the implemented model is a discrete-time, finite-state Markov process with stationary transition probabilities. A great deal is known analytically about such stochastic processes, in particular, the conditions under which they have unique limiting distributions.[9] The relevant knowledge is summarized by the following result. Because it follows directly from a basic theorem on finite-state Markov processes with stationary transition probabilities (e.g., Kemeny and Snell 1960, 71), it is stated here without proof.

*Remark 1* The Markov process of the implemented model has a unique limiting distribution, and it must converge to that distribution from any set of initial propensities and aspirations.

This result provides an analytical foundation for our simulations.

This theory is close to—indeed was inspired by—a formulation of Bendor, Mookherjee, and Ray (1998; abbreviated as BMR). There are three key differences between BMR and the present work: two are substantive, and the other concerns the method of analysis. These differences are intertwined. First, BMR assume that aspirations are fixed throughout the interactions of a pair of players. (They do impose a consistency requirement, however: in the "steady state," expected payoffs must equal aspirations. So aspirations are endogenous in BMR, though statically rather than dynamically.) This was associated with a preference for a particular method of analysis: assuming fixed (though consistent) aspirations kept the model tractable, thus enabling BMR to derive *analytical* results. Finally, because they did not use computational methods, they were not forced to stipulate a specific form of adaptation, as would have been necessary in a simulation. Instead, they were able to work with a rather large class of learning rules, identified by general properties of adaptation. In this chapter we have made different choices and have accordingly wound up with a model with a combination of strengths and weaknesses that complements BMR's. First, for substantive reasons we chose to make aspirations adjust to experience. Second, we realized that the resulting model was indeed, as BMR had found out, analytically intractable. Hence we were forced to generate results via simulation rather than analytically. Finally, since the computer requires an exact specification of how agents adjust, in our computational model we had to provide this specification; we could not work at the same level of generality as BMR did. Thus in our case a substantive choice about theoretical assumptions essentially dictated a method of analysis, which in turn dictated other substantive choices.[10]

Because our work and BMR's are closely related, throughout this chapter we point out interesting connections between the two. Of particular interest are results—where they coincide and where they differ.

Another descendant of BMR that develops a model of aspiration-based learning is an article by Karandikar et al. (1998). In the standard ameboid process of scientific progress, Karandikar et al. take some steps forward and some back, relative to BMR. One step forward is that they dynamically endogenize aspirations by making them adjust to payoffs. The steps back are that they simplify the adaptive properties of agents by having them switch in a bang-bang satisficing manner between actions rather than continuously adjusting propensities to take different actions as in pychological reinforcement theory, and their model is applied to a much smaller class of games than is BMR's (essentially Prisoner's Dilemma and several related $2 \times 2$ games that exhibit cooperation or coordination problems). But these restrictions and simplifications do enable them to obtain a rather remarkable analytical result for their set of games: as the rate of aspiration adjustment goes to zero, in the long run both players must cooperate most of the time (Karandikar et al. 1998, 293).

In some respects one might view this chapter as an attempt to combine features of the BMR and the Karandikar work. Like the former, our model specifies continuously adjusting action propensities and can be applied to a very large class of $2 \times 2$ games (symmetry, for example, is unnecessary). Like the latter, our model makes aspirations dynamically endogenous. But as noted, we pay for this ambitious construction: unlike the other researchers, we are forced to use computation to obtain results.

### 8.2.2 *The Program*

Because of the serious tractability issues involved, we have written a program in ANSI C to simulate the described adaptively rational behavior. The program is compiled with the GNU C compiler and is compatible with most UNIX operating system configurations. We adopt the following terminology in describing our use of the program. A *period* is a one-shot play of the $2 \times 2$ game in question. A *simulation* is a sequence of periods, for a specific pair of players. Finally, a *run* is a collection of simulations (typically of 1,000 pairs of players).

When started, the program allows the user to set the following parameters before each run:

- Number of simulations
- Number of periods per simulation
- Payoff matrix
- Tremble and inertia probabilities, $\varepsilon$ and $\eta$
- Row's (Column's) probability of playing *up* (*left*) at $t = 0$ ($p_{i,0}$)
- Each player's aspiration level at $t = 0$ ($a_{i,0}$)
- Aspiration-updating parameter, $\lambda$

When a run begins, the program initializes a pseudo-random number generator with an integer representating the current time. This standard procedure effectively ensures that each run's parameter values are independent of those of other runs. The program then initializes a custom data structure that keeps track of state variables (propensities and aspirations, which may change over the course of a run) and statistics related to the history of play.

In each period, intended moves are determined and then trembled to produce actual moves in the manner described previously. For simplicity, in the subsequent analysis we constrain all tremble probabilities to be equal, so that $\varepsilon = \rho = \sigma$. After payoffs are revealed, the data structure is updated to reflect the changed propensities and aspirations, rounding appropriately to retain the discreteness of the state space. These variables revert to their original values for each new simulation.

The data structure associated with each run can be used to recover statistics at different levels of a run. To reduce run times, only those statistics that are requested by the user are collected. In particular, the user may opt to view or save to disk any of the following:

- The moves, payoffs, and adjusted propensities and aspirations after each period
- Average and cumulative propensities and aspirations for each simulation
- Average propensities and aspirations across simulations for certain periods
- A histogram of final-period propensity and aspiration levels across simulations

For the games investigated here, the histogram statistics proved to be the most useful. While the program does not generate graphics on its own, the output files it creates are easily read into other programs for further processing.

The program is able to generate large samples of game play very quickly. Typical systems should be capable of running over a million periods per minute, thus facilitating replication and increasing our confidence in the robustness of our results. (Because each run includes many simulations, with each simulation lasting for many periods, one can be confident that a run's summary statistics are a good approximation of the properties of the underlying unique limiting distribution.) We now use some of these statistics to examine the dynamics of adaptively rational behavior.

## 8.3 The Games

To demonstrate the model's versatility, we want to exercise it on a variety of $2 \times 2$ games that represent strategic problems of relevance to politics. An obvious dimension to focus on concerns possible tensions between what is individually desirable versus what is collectively optimal. These are sometimes called collective action problems or problems of cooperation. Snidal (1991) economically identifies six such games. These games are determined by three properties.[11] First, for simplicity, restrict attention to *symmetric* $2 \times 2$ games. Second, each player has a *strict* preference ordering over the four outcomes; indifference, a knife-edge condition, is ruled out. Note, before proceeding to the last property, that symmetry plus strict preferences together imply that the payoffs to one of the pairs of symmetric actions, say $(a, a)$, must Pareto-dominate the payoffs to the other symmetric action pair, say $(b, b)$. As Snidal points out, it makes sense to call the action that yields the higher symmetric payoff "cooperation" and the action that yields the lower symmetric payoff "noncooperation" or "defection." We do this henceforth, using the standard abbreviations of $C$ for cooperation and $D$ for defection. Third—and this is the main substantive assumption—we assume that it is better to "exploit" (to defect while one's partner cooperates) than to "be exploited" (cooperate while the partner defects).[12]

Together, these three properties yield Snidal's six "games of cooperation" (figure 8.2): Harmony, two versions of Stag Hunt, Coordination, Chicken, and Prisoner's Dilemma. Of these, Harmony exhibits the least conflict of interest—cooperating strictly dominates defecting and $(C, C)$ delivers the game's highest payoff—and Prisoner's Dilemma has the most conflict. In all these games there is something to cooperate about, in the sense that $(C, C)$ Pareto-dominates $(D, D)$, but achieving cooperation is presumably easy in Harmony while it is hard in Prisoner's Dilemma.

To this set of games we have added a seventh, Win-Lose, which as its name suggests is a game of complete conflict: if Row wins, then Column loses, and vice versa. Adding this game provides a still wider spectrum of possibilities: it enables us to exercise the model on games that range from near-perfect harmony to unremitting conflict. Win-Lose also provides a useful contrast to the others in that it has no Nash equilibrium in pure strategies, while all of Snidal's games do have pure equilibria.

The payoffs shown in figure 8.2 are our benchmark values. When discussing the simulations, we refer to these benchmark values unless otherwise indicated. Of course, the games themselves are defined by their ordinal properties, not by the specific payoff quantities shown in figure 8.2. These more general, defining properties of the games are shown in figure 8.3.

Low-Conflict Games

Harmony

| | C | D |
|---|---|---|
| C | 3,3 | 1,2 |
| D | 2,1 | 0,0 |

Stag Hunt I

| | C | D |
|---|---|---|
| C | 3,3 | 0,2 |
| D | 2,0 | 1,1 |

Stag Hunt II

| | C | D |
|---|---|---|
| C | 3,3 | 0,1 |
| D | 1,0 | 2,2 |

Higher-Conflict Games

Coordination

| | C | D |
|---|---|---|
| C | 1,1 | 2,3 |
| D | 3,2 | 0,0 |

Chicken

| | C | D |
|---|---|---|
| C | 2,2 | 1,3 |
| D | 3,1 | 0,0 |

Prisoner's Dilemma

| | C | D |
|---|---|---|
| C | 2,2 | 0,3 |
| D | 3,0 | 1,1 |

Game of Complete Conflict

Win-Lose

| | L | R |
|---|---|---|
| U | 1,0 | 0,1 |
| D | 0,1 | 1,0 |

**Figure 8.2**
Benchmark Values of the Payoffs

## 8.4 Results

For an introduction to the model's behavior, one could look at runs 8.1–8.7, the benchmark versions for each of the seven games (see the appendix).

### *8.4.1 Major Patterns and Their Logic*

#### 8.4.1.1 Ergodicity

We already know on analytical grounds (remark 1) that the process is ergodic: it has a unique limiting distribution, and it must converge

Low-Conflict Games

| Harmony | Stag Hunt I | Stag Hunt II |
|---|---|---|
| R > T > S > P | R > T > P > S | R > P > T > S |

Higher-Conflict Games

| Coordination | Chicken | Prisoner's Dilemma |
|---|---|---|
| T > S > R > P | T > R > S > P | T > R > P > S |

Game of Complete Conflict

Win-Lose

| | L | R |
|---|---|---|
| U | x,0 | 0,x |
| D | 0,x | x,0 |

Payoff to winning = x > 0
Payoff to losing = 0

| | C | D |
|---|---|---|
| C | R,R | S,T |
| D | T,S | P,P |

**Figure 8.3**
General Payoffs for the Seven Games
*Note:* For Snidal's six "games of cooperation" we use the standard notation: R is the payoff to mutual cooperation, P for mutual defection, T for exploiting, and S for being exploited.

to that distribution from any set of initial propensities and aspirations. (These properties are illustrated, for example, by runs 8.6 and 8.8. Although they begin with very different initial aspirations and propensities, by period 1,000 their overall distributions are quite similar.) However, for different parameter values (e.g., different payoffs), the system reaches different limiting distributions: if the vector of parameter values is $(a, b, c, \ldots)$, then the steady-state values of propensities and aspirations are one set of values, whereas if the vector is $(x, y, z, \ldots)$, then they are another. These two properties (existence of a unique solution and dependence on the parameters of interest) together constitute a large part of the model's empirical content and make the model suitable for analyzing the strategic incentives provided by political institutions.

It is important to understand the nature of this claim. We do *not* mean that the players' *behavior* necessarily settles down in the long run (e.g., to cooperation). This would happen only if their propensities settled down to the corresponding pure values (e.g., if all pairs of players reached a cooperation propensity of 1). This need not happen, even for arbitrarily rare trembles. Instead, what we mean is this. Take a large number of pairs of players (simulations)—in our runs, 1,000. Let these pairs play for a long time. Consider the state space, which is a four-dimensional (finite) grid of propensity values and aspiration values. Then, in the long run, the frequency distribution of these 2,000 players over this grid will settle down, as will the corresponding statistics (the average propensity to cooperate, and so forth). In the simple, "degenerate" cases, almost all players will be packed around a pure propensity (e.g., a cooperation propensity of 1), but there are also cases in which the frequency distribution of players over states is not degenerate. Note also that the notion of a limiting distribution does *not* imply that any particular pair settles down on one point of the state space grid. Given trembles, a pair may move around indefinitely, both in terms of behavior and of the underlying states (propensities and aspirations). What settles down is a large *population* of pairs.[13]

Given that the system is ergodic and the simulations are probably very close to their corresponding limiting distributions, we henceforth use a shorthand when describing results: for a given vector of parameter values, we say that the system is converging to a certain distribution of propensities (and corresponding aspirations).

#### 8.4.1.2 The Effect of Trembles

It is clear that given a set of propensities and aspirations today, the probability of realizing a particular outcome (and hence payoffs) today is continuous in the tremble probabilities. It therefore follows that the probability of getting positive or negative feedback changes continuously in the tremble probability. Hence the system's transition probabilities are also continuous in the tremble probabilities. In short, the system "behaves nicely" with respect to trembles: (sufficiently) small changes in their frequency produce small changes in the system. The logic of this argument is amply exemplified by the simulations. (Compare, for example, runs 8.6 and 8.9. The latter differs only in having a slightly lower tremble probability, and the resulting patterns are very close.)

This has the following important implication. Suppose we start out with our benchmark tremble probability of .01 and gradually reduce it toward zero, holding all other parameters constant. Then we get a *sequence* of (unique) limiting distributions and their associated statistics (e.g., the population's average propensity to cooperate). As the tremble probabilities get sufficiently small, by continuity further diminutions in these probabilities can have only negligible effects on the associated limiting distributions. In short, as the trembles go to zero, the limiting distributions themselves converge. What is lovely about this is the following. Although it is true that when the tremble probability is *exactly* zero, there are multiple steady-state distributions—for instance, with the appropriate initial propensities and aspirations, any pure outcome of the stage game is stable—for any strictly positive tremble probability, there is only one such distribution. Hence the sequence of (unique) limiting distributions must be converging, as trembles become very rare, to *one* of the (many) zero-tremble steady-state distributions, thereby increasing the model's empirical content.[14]

A fortunate side effect of this method is that the simulation patterns get clearer as trembles become less frequent. Since trembles are random shocks, this makes sense.

Given the points about ergodicity and the effect of trembles, the fundamental question regarding our model is quite simple: Toward what are the processes in the different games converging? The following sections narrow down the answer to this question.

#### 8.4.1.3 Degenerate or Nondegenerate Distributions

Logically, the system must converge either to a degenerate distribution or to a nondegenerate one. There are two types of degenerate distributions: either the whole population piles up on a "pure" (zero or 1) propensity or everyone reaches the same mixed propensity. None of our simulations yields the latter; all the degenerate distributions involve pure propensities. An argument from Bendor, Mookherjee, and Ray (1998) explains why. Suppose hypothetically we obtain for Prisoner's Dilemma a simulation in which everyone has a steady-state cooperation propensity of .5.[15] Then steady-state aspirations must equal the average of the four pure PD payoffs, i.e.,

$(T+R+P+S)/4$. Since everyone's propensity to cooperate is .5, all four outcomes can and will occur. But then sometimes payoffs exceed aspirations and sometimes fall below them, which in turn means that propensities must adjust. Hence they cannot stabilize at exactly .5, so the entire population cannot in the steady state have this propensity. It is easy to see that the argument generalizes to exclude any degenerate frequency distribution on a mixed propensity.

Accordingly, we can only find either degenerate frequency distributions on pure propensities or nondegenerate distributions over mixed propensities.

#### 8.4.1.4 Many Pure States Cannot Be Stable

Many pure states can be excluded on theoretical grounds. Let us call a stage game's lowest payoff $\underline{\pi}$ and its highest payoff $\bar{\pi}$. Given trembles and endogenous aspirations, we know that eventually aspirations must be in $(\underline{\pi}, \bar{\pi})$. Hence, in the steady state, getting the game's lowest payoff must be dissatisfying. So it follows immediately that no pure propensity state in which either player gets $\underline{\pi}$ can be stable.[16]

This wipes out two of the four pure outcomes in Stag Hunt I, Stag Hunt II, and Prisoner's Dilemma, all four pure outcomes in Win-Lose, and one pure outcome in Harmony, Coordination, and Chicken (see the benchmark runs 8.1–8.7).

#### 8.4.1.5 Inefficient Mixed Propensity States Tend to Be Unstable

The average payoff from a mixed propensity state is either Pareto-dominated by the payoffs from a pure outcome, or it isn't. If it is, the analysis by Bendor, Mookherji, and Ray (1998) shows that in their model with statically endogenous aspirations mixed states are unstable. In our simulations the same appears to hold for dynamically endogenous aspirations. Again, consider the example of a hypothetical stable mixed propensity state in Prisoner's Dilemma. Call the average payoff in this purportedly stable state $\tilde{v}$, and suppose that this is less than the cooperative payoff of $R$. Since $\tilde{v} < R$ and since aspirations must on average be close to $\tilde{v}$, mutual cooperation must be satisfying to most players. Hence, when both players in a particular pair cooperate (which will happen, since it's a mixed propensity state), their propensity to cooperate will tend to rise. Cooperation will tend to rise over time, thus increasing aspirations.

Hence, the original distribution of propensities and aspirations could not have been stable after all. And this is the pattern observed in the simulations: inefficient mixed propensity states tend to be unstable, and the less efficient they are, the less likely they are to be stable.[17] (Compare, for example, runs 8.2 and 8.10. Both are Stag Hunt I, but in run 8.10 mixed propensity states are extremely inefficient and very unstable as well.)

Accordingly, we have narrowed our search down to degenerate distributions on pure propensities (and so pure outcomes) and efficient, nondegenerate distributions over mixed propensities.

Next we discuss the specific results for each game. It is convenient to break the seven games down into three sets: the low-conflict games (Harmony, Stag Hunt I, and Stag Hunt II), the higher conflict games (Coordination, Chicken, and Prisoner's Dilemma), and that of complete conflict (Win-Lose).

#### 8.4.1.6 The Low-Conflict Games Are Simple

In the three low-conflict games the players get the game's maximal payoff by cooperating, so all mixed propensities are inefficient. For these games the process should converge to a pure outcome. And, since many pure states cannot be stable, no pure outcome delivering $\underline{\pi}$ to either player is stable. So we are down to three pure outcomes in Harmony and the two pure Nash outcomes in the Stag Hunt games.

In Harmony, intuition suggests that the $(C, D)$ and $(D, C)$ outcomes should not be stable. Suppose they were. Then each player's aspiration must be below $R$, since $R$ is that game's maximal payoff. If the defecting player trembled and cooperated, his payoff must then exceed his aspiration. Hence, his propensity to cooperate must rise, and so his propensity to defect cannot stabilize at 1. Thus neither $(C, D)$ nor $(D, C)$ can be a stable pure propensity state. This is what happens in the simulations: as the trembles fall toward zero, the population's long-run frequency distribution piles up on $(C, C)$. (Compare run 8.11, with its lower tremble, to run 8.1.) This appears to be the unique stable state of Harmony.

In the Stag Hunts, however, a Pareto-deficient outcome—the bad Nash equilibrium of the stage game—*can* be stable. The simulation results seem to turn on the relative magnitudes of $\underline{\pi}$ and $\bar{\pi}$, which in the Stag Hunts are $S$ and $R$, respectively. Suppose first that $S$, the payoff obtained when one hunts for big game by oneself, is very low compared to benchmark values of the other payoffs. Because hunting by oneself for big game is so disastrous, even small trembles ensure that aspirations stay quite low, below both $T$ and $P$. Because occasional disasters depress aspirations this much, defecting is always satisfying. In contrast, cooperating evokes positive feedback only when both people do it. Hence it is stochastically easy for pairs to drift toward mutual defection, and once they get there, it is positively reinforcing for both players. Thus their propensities to defect will drift up toward 1 (runs 8.10 and 8.12).

On the other hand, suppose that even though $S$ is quite bad, $R$ is very large (runs 8.13 and 8.14). Then aspirations will tend to be higher—joint hunting yields woolly mammoths and food for weeks—and will exceed the payoff to individualistic hunting. The latter cannot be reinforcing, and so the only stable distribution involves the pure propensity to cooperate.

#### 8.4.1.7 The Higher-Conflict Games Are Complicated

Since mixing can be efficient in Coordination, Chicken, and Prisoner's Dilemma, we cannot exclude mixed propensity states in these games. And in fact we do get such results for all three games. It is not hard to identify conditions that produce stable mixed propensity states, and the logic is clear. A simple condition that does this pertains to the value of the game's maximal payoff. (In all three of these games the maximal payoff is $T$, the payoff from exploiting a cooperative partner.) Suppose $T$ is extremely high, while the other payoffs have their benchmark values (runs 8.15–8.17). Then the aspirations of both players will be elevated enough so that the only payoff that provides positive feedback is $T$ itself. (Even occasional glimpses of paradise make one unhappy with anything else.) But both players cannot get $T$ at the same time. Hence in every outcome at least one player must be disgruntled with his payoff, and so they cannot settle down on a pure propensity state.

However, whenever mixing *is* inefficient, our prior reasoning suggests, the process will converge to a pure outcome in Coordination, Chicken, and Prisoner's Dilemma. For example, in PD a sufficient condition for (symmetric) mixing to be inefficient is the standard auxiliary PD property of $2R > T + S$. And so in most of the runs in which this condition held, the simulation converged to a pure outcome.

But in each of these high-conflict games, there is (still) more than one feasible pure outcome to which the process can converge. Can we narrow it down further?

In Coordination, $(D, D)$ is ruled out because it gives both players $\underline{\pi}$. But what about $(C, C)$, which, though its payoff exceeds $\underline{\pi}$, is neither Nash nor Pareto optimal? If it were stable, then the players' aspirations would have to be slightly below $R$ (for small trembles). But then if Row trembled and defected, she would get a higher payoff, since $(C, C)$ is not Nash. Hence her propensity to defect would rise. Meanwhile her partner would be happy to stay with $C$, since his payoffs also rise (and so exceed his aspirations) once Row trembles. So the way is paved for a single player to experiment and lead the pair away from the inefficient $(C, C)$. Consequently, if we let the simulations run long enough, all the pairs converge to one of the two Nash equilibria, when trembles are rare (run 8.18).[18]

All of the pure outcomes discussed thus far have been Nash. This is not true in Chicken or Prisoner's Dilemma. In Chicken, the $(C, C)$ outcome is not Nash, but it is Pareto optimal, unlike $(C, C)$ in Coordination. And this turns out to make a difference: $(C, C)$ *can* be stable in Chicken when the speed of propensity adjustment, $\alpha$, is sufficiently high. To see how, suppose that $T$, $S$, and $P$ take on their benchmark values but $R$ is not far below $T$ (run 8.19). Suppose a pair have been cooperating a long time so their aspirations are both close to $R$. Again, suppose that Row deviates by defecting. As in Coordination, $(C, C)$ is not Nash in Chicken, so Row's propensity to defect rises. But *unlike* Coordination, $(C, C)$ in Chicken is efficient, so Column is dissatisfied with the short end of the asymmetric Nash that he has gotten when Row experimented away from mutual cooperation. Thus while Row becomes more predisposed to defecting, and so moving toward $(D, C)$, Column becomes disenchanted with cooperating and starts to defect himself. This moves the pair into $(D, D)$, which neither likes. Thus, in an adaptive analogue to a punishment phase of a trigger strategy regime, the players learn to become more predisposed to cooperate again. And so the initial move down to $(D, C)$ doesn't stick.

On the other hand, run 8.20 decreases $R$ so that it is only slightly above $S$, holding everything else essentially the same as it was in the previous version. Then, as before, $(C, C)$ is still vulnerable to experimentation by one of the players, and in addition the $(C, C)$-induced aspiration level is sufficiently close to $S$ so that it is possible for the other (still cooperating) player to learn to become satisfied with it. Under these conditions the process converges to one of the two asymmetric Nash equilibria. Which one a particular pair winds up in involves path dependence, as was true of Coordination.

In Prisoner's Dilemma, when inefficiency rules out mixed propensity states as long-run outcomes, there are only the two symmetric pure outcomes—mutual cooperation and mutual defection—left to consider. These outcomes are Pareto-ranked, as are the equilibria in Stag Hunt, so it is not surprising that similar factors come into play.[19] For example, suppose $S$ is very low (run 8.21). Then aspirations will be depressed, and in particular will fall below $P$. Hence defecting will always be satisfying, while cooperating will sometimes disappoint. Therefore the process converges to mutual defection. If, however, $P$ is itself not much better than the (still-bad) $S$ (run 8.22), then aspirations will tend to fall between $P$ and $R$, so the process converges to mutual cooperation.[20]

#### 8.4.1.8 Complete Conflict Is Simple

Many pure states cannot be stable, and all pure outcomes are unstable in Win-Lose, so the process must converge to a mixed propensity state in this game (see the benchmark version of run 8.7). It bears some resemblance to the mixed Nash equilibrium of the stage game, but as we discuss in section 8.4.3, there are also some significant differences.

A summary of these main properties of the model is given in table 8.1. Table 8.2 summarizes what happens in each of the seven games.

### *8.4.2 Some General Observations and Conjectures*

Two observations are worth making about the convergence patterns in the games. First, whenever a stage game has pure Nash equilibria, we have found *some* quantitative variant on the payoffs of the game such that the process converges to each pure Nash. One might hazard a conjecture that this holds for all pure Nash equilibria for all strictly ordinal two-person games. There is an obvious reason why it might: experimentation away from Nash in such games immediately triggers negative feedback. To see this, suppose a pair has developed pure propensities to play a Nash equilibrium in a strictly ordinal game. Suppose then that Row trembles away from the Nash, while

**Table 8.1**
The Model's Basic Properties

| Property | Comments |
|---|---|
| Ergodicity | For any fixed set of parameter values, the process has a *unique* limiting distribution over propensities and aspirations. It must converge to this distribution from any starting point (i.e., from any set of initial propensities and aspirations). |
| Empirical content | No "folk theorem" problems. |
| Trembles | As trembles become arbitrarily small, the associated sequence of limiting distributions (of propensities and aspirations) converges to *one* of the zero-tremble steady-state distributions. |
| Degenerate distributions of propensities | Degenerate populational distributions over propensities are always over pure propensities |
| Some pure states can be eliminated a priori | No pure propensity state in which either player gets $\pi$ is stable. |
| Inefficient mixed propensity states tend to be unstable | |

**Table 8.2**
What Happens in the Different Games?

| | (a) Can the process converge to a mixed propensity state? | (b) Can the process converge to a pure propensity state? | (c) If answer to (b) is yes, to which one(s)? |
|---|---|---|---|
| Harmony | no | yes | (C,C) only |
| Stag Hunt I | no | yes | (D,D) if S is too low; otherwise, (C,C) |
| Stag Hunt II | no | yes | Same as stag hunt I |
| Coordination | yes (when T is sufficiently big) | yes | A bimodal distribution: 1/2 pop. → (C,D) 1/2 pop. → (D,C) |
| Chicken | yes (when T is sufficiently big) | yes | Everyone to (C,C) if R is sufficiently big; otherwise, bimodal: 1/2 pop. → (C,D) 1/2 pop. → (D,C) |
| Prisoner's Dilemma | yes (when T is sufficiently big) | yes | (D,D) if S is too low or P too big; (C,C) otherwise |
| Win-Lose | yes | no | — |

Column doesn't tremble. Since the game is strictly ordinal (no indifference) and the status quo ante was Nash, the outcome of this one-sided experimentation must be unsatisfactory to Row. And so Row's experimentation is inhibited. This reasoning is plausible, but it overreaches: it seems to imply that pure Nash in strictly ordinal two-person games should *always* be stable, yet the simulations strongly suggest that that is false (e.g., mutual defection in Prisoner's Dilemma is not always stable). This remains an open problem.

The second observation is that when the process converges to pure propensities, the outcome is always either Nash or Pareto optimal. For the games examined here, this is not a very powerful generalization: in most of the games at least half of the outcomes are either one or the other. But this pattern does suggest the following more interesting conjecture. For *any* two-person game, whenever the process converges to a pure propensity state, it is either a Nash equilibrium (of the *stage* game) or a Pareto optimal outcome.[21]

The reader may find this conjecture puzzling in one respect. Although our adaptive mechanism is thoroughly individualistic—it is similar to Nash analysis in this respect—we are claiming that any (pure) non-Nash convergence in symmetric games must be to a *collectively* optimal outcome. Why the leap from individualistic learning to Pareto optimality? The answer is twofold. First, we are not asserting that Pareto optimality is *sufficient* for convergence, only that (among the set of pure non-Nash outcomes) it is *necessary*. Second, then, why do we think it is necessary? Suppose the claim were false. Consider then an outcome—produced, say, by actions $(a, b)$—which is neither Nash nor efficient, yet the process has converged to it nonetheless. Since it is stable and aspirations are endogenous, the players must in the steady state have aspirations that are very close to, and no greater than, the payoffs delivered by outcome $(a, b)$. But since this outcome is inefficient, there must be at least one other outcome, produced, say, by actions $(e, f)$, wherein the payoffs to both players would be strictly greater than their current respective aspirations. Hence, outcome $(e, f)$ would be reinforcing for both players, so if tremble experimentation brought them to $(e, f)$, their propensities to play the corresponding actions would rise.[22] Moreover, since aspirations adjust to experience, while the players stayed in $(e, f)$ their aspirations would rise as well, eventually exceeding the payoffs of the putatively stable outcome of $(a, b)$. Then the latter would no longer satisfice. Hence, while the players could travel from

$(a, b)$ to $(e, f)$, the reverse path would eventually be blocked. Therefore a pure propensity state on the inefficient $(a, b)$ outcome can be destabilized.

Nevertheless, the claim that convergence to (pure) non-Nash must entail convergence to efficient outcomes still does not have enough individualistic content. This claim does not rule out, for example, convergence to one of the exploitative outcomes of $(C, D)$ or $(D, C)$ in Prisoner's Dilemma, for those outcomes are Pareto optimal. Yet converging to an exploitative outcome is implausible because one of the players must then get the game's minimal payoff, and $\underline{\pi}$ must fall below aspirations (given trembles). So the conjecture needs to be tightened up. We should be able to exclude *some* non-Nash efficient pure states. Based on our prior reasoning, we immediately rule out efficient states in which either player gets $\underline{\pi}$. But we think more can be said. Bendor, Mookherji, and Ray (1998) show that given static aspirations, convergence to any pure state must entail that each player gets at least her maxmin payoff, that is, her security level (so called because each player can secure at least that much by playing the appropriate action). Here we conjecture that this result extends to settings with dynamic aspirations. Again, reasoning by contradiction suggests why this should hold. Suppose that outcome $(e, f)$ is efficient but Row does not obtain her maxmin payoff there. Nevertheless, by assumption the process has converged to pure propensities on $(e, f)$. Then by the usual reasoning Row's steady-state aspiration must no greater than her payoff from $(e, f)$. Because, however, $e$ cannot be her maxmin action, there must be another action, call it $g$, that *is* her maxmin action and that accordingly guarantees her at least the maxmin payoff. Because Row is getting less than her maxmin in $(e, f)$, *any* deviation to $g$ would be reinforced. Hence, following any such experimentation her propensity to play $g$ must rise. Moreover, while this occurs her aspiration level must rise toward her maxmin payoff. Therefore it would eventually exceed her payoff from $(e, f)$. Consequently Row would eventually find $(e, f)$ to be dissatisfying. And so while Row could tremble experiment her way from $e$ to $g$, eventually she would not want to go back. (Wolfe's law: you can't go home again.) Hence a pure propensity state on $(e, f)$ cannot be stable if a player gets less than her maxmin payoff there.

If this reasoning is valid, it would mean that this adaptive process contains an important degree of individual rationality. Convergence to a pure propensity state must entail that in the long run both players get at least their security levels. Thus simple aspiration-based learning would (eventually) ensure at least that much in individualistic terms.

### *8.4.3 Some Nonobvious Consequences of Aspiration-Based Learning*

#### 8.4.3.1 Non-negligible Trembles, Misleading Feedback, and Endogenous Aspirations

It is all very well to analyze the limiting properties of adaptive systems (as trembles go to zero), but in the real world random shocks are often not negligible. Hence examining what happens when trembles are *not* vanishing is important. And when trembles are non-negligible—even a 1 percent chance, as in our benchmark setting—there are patterns of suboptimal behavior that require explaining.

Consider, for example, Harmony. Although players in this game do not have identical interests (if there is to be unilateral cooperation, each prefers the other to bear that burden), there is relatively little conflict here. Mutual cooperation yields the game's highest payoff, so there is no temptation to defect; further, $C$ strictly dominates $D$. So adaptively rational players should be able to learn to cooperate in Harmony.

The benchmark version (run 8.1) shows that this does happen, but quite imperfectly. Given a 1 percent chance of trembles, by period 1,000 only about 47 percent of the pairs have locked in on cooperation. (We use as a measure of locking in on a pure outcome if each player in a pair has a propensity of at least .95 on his corresponding action.) Why don't more do so? In order to answer this question we must understand how two key elements of the model interact: dynamically endogenous aspirations, and misleading feedback. These two elements combine to drive many results that are suboptimal, so it is worthwhile figuring out how they work in some detail.

Consider first dynamic aspirations. Suppose a pair of agents playing Harmony repeatedly have locked into the mutually cooperative outcome: each player's propensity of playing $C$ is in the $[.95, 1.0]$ interval. Because aspirations adjust to experience, each player's aspiration level will eventually be close to 3.0; because the mutually cooperative outcome is the game's highest payoff, their aspirations eventually must also be less than 3.0 (even if they were initially higher). Hence mutual cooperation is reinforcing, whereas the feedback from any other outcome inhibits the corresponding actions. Consider, then, what happens when Row makes the right move (cooperates), while Column does the wrong thing (defects), either because of a tremble or because his propensity to cooperate is not exactly at 1.0. Column gets a payoff of 2, so he realizes that he erred; hence his propensity to cooperate rises or stays at 1. But now *Row*'s feedback is misleading: although she did the right thing, she nevertheless gets a payoff (of 1) that is below her current aspiration level. Hence, she mistakenly reduces her propensity to cooperate. Finally, notice that all this can happen even if both agents had locked in fully on cooperation at the start of the period (both had cooperation propensities of 1.0), because trembles are always possible. Thus trembles make it impossible for a pair of players to stabilize forever at a propensity state of (1.0, 1.0). More concretely, even in a game as apparently straightforward as Harmony, trembles that occur on average in only 1 percent of all actions create enough misleading feedback to produce a steady-state distribution in which fewer than half of the pairs have cooperation propensities in the [.95, 1.0] interval (run 8.1).

So misleading feedback is clearly important. What, then, are the payoff conditions that allow misleading feedback to exist? We can see that if the payoff to cooperating in Harmony were always 3, regardless of what one's partner did, then there would be no misleading feedback in that game. Such a game would be *trivial* (Bendor and Swistak 1997)[23], both strategically and in terms of degree of adaptive difficulty.[24] Note that it follows immediately from Bendor and Swistak's definition that misleading feedback can occur in any nontrivial game. And since trivial games are indeed trivial in all important respects, this means that misleading feedback can be a factor in any game of any interest to political scientists.

#### 8.4.3.2 Endogenous Aspirations and Counterintuitive Comparative Statics/Dynamics

We have not come close to exhausting the empirical content of the model. An important type of prediction can be generated by varying the model's parameters—in particular, payoffs—and studying the effects on either the steady state (this is the stochastic process equivalent to doing comparative statics in an equilibrium rational choice model) or on the dynamics leading up to steady states. To some extent a comparison of behavior and outcomes in different games is part of this type of analysis, since one can go for instance, from Chicken to Prisoner's Dilemma by varying the relative magnitudes of the $P$ and $S$ payoffs. But payoffs can vary quantitatively even within the same type of game.

These comparative statics and dynamics will have to be reported and analyzed in future work. But we would like to briefly discuss here one type of counterintuitive effect that reveals the mediating power of endogenous aspirations. In general, one would expect that the average propensity to do action $x$, in either the steady state or along the way, would increase in the payoffs to $x$. This is intuitive, and often we do obtain this result. But not always. Consider the following example of a pair of Prisoner's Dilemma games (figure 8.4). In game 1, the payoff for exploiting one's partner is huge. Game 2 is exactly like game 1 except that the payoff for exploiting one's partner is much less. The result: the average propensity to defect is *higher* in game 2, both in the steady state and for almost all of the dynamics as well. (Compare runs 8.23 and 8.24, which use games 1 and 2, respectively.) Why? The result is driven by the mediating influence of dynamic aspirations. As we know, when $T$ is very high, aspirations rise to such high levels that only exploiting one's partner satisfices; all other outcomes are unsatisfactory. In particular, mutual defection gives unacceptably low payoffs, so the players do not settle down into the pure propensity state of always defecting. In contrast, if $T$ is much lower, as in game 2, then so are aspirations, which (combined with relatively good values of $P$) implies that the players are content with mutual defection. Hence, the average propensity to defect markedly increases in response to a big *decrease* in one of the action's payoffs.

This effect can be seen even more strikingly in a variant of Harmony (also in figure 8.4). This variant is even easier (less conflictual) than the original Harmony. Nevertheless, with a 1 percent chance of a tremble, only about 59 percent of the pairs lock into mutual cooperation in the steady state (run 8.25). Here game 2 is just like game 1 except that the payoff for mutual cooperation is much lower. The result: in game 2 almost everyone locks onto mutual cooperation in the steady state (run 8.26). This behavior is also more common dynamically, before the limiting distribution is reached. And if the payoff to mutual cooperation in game 2 were reduced *still* further, to

Two Prisoner's Dilemma Games

Game 1

| | C | D |
|---|---|---|
| C | 2,2 | 0,10 |
| D | 10,0 | 1.7,1.7 |

Game 2

| | C | D |
|---|---|---|
| C | 2,2 | 0,3 |
| D | 3,0 | 1.7,1.7 |

Intuitive prediction: Since defecting in game 1 yields better or equal payoffs than does defecting in game 2, the average propensity to defect should be higher in game 1.

Two Harmony-like Games

Game 1

| | C | D |
|---|---|---|
| C | 3,3 | 2,1 |
| D | 1,2 | 0,0 |

Game 2

| | C | D |
|---|---|---|
| C | 2.1,2.1 | 2,1 |
| D | 1,2 | 0,0 |

Intuitive prediction: Since (C, C) pays off more in game 1, and all else is equal, more players should lock onto (C, C) in game 1 than in game 2.

**Figure 8.4**
Counterintuitive Payoff Effects

2, then the game would become trivial and everyone would become completely disposed to cooperate, no matter how frequent trembles were.

This is more dramatic than the preceding Prisoner's Dilemma example because here there is obviously only one stable pure propensity state, $(C, C)$, and so surely, one thinks, reducing that state's payoffs would decrease its occurrence.[25] Yet the opposite occurs.

The effect is counterintuitive but not paradoxical. It makes sense once one recognizes the impact of endogenous aspirations. But if our intuitions overlook this mediating variable and focus instead on simpler input-output relations ("The more an action or an outcome pays off, the more it will occur"), then we will be surprised.

#### 8.4.3.3 Mixed Propensities versus Mixed Strategies

As noted earlier, in several of the games the process reached an apparently stable mixed propensity state. Indeed, in Win-Lose this was the only kind of stable state, just as the only Nash equilibrium in that game involves mixed strategies. It is now time to look at this apparent connection between mixed propensities and mixed strategies more closely. Win-Lose is a useful setting in which to explore this, since here every pure outcome gives one of the players the game's minimal payoff, whence all the pure outcomes are unstable. Thus the players must cope with some form of mixing.

Agents in our benchmark version of this game (run 8.7) appear to converge to the mixed Nash: the propensities are clustered fairly tightly around the optimal mixing probability of .5. Aspirations are consistent with propensities, and together they produce a balanced feedback pattern: when Row plays *up*, about half the time she gets positive feedback and half the time, negative feedback, and similarly for *down*.

But a more fine-grained analysis would reveal that the mixed propensities of these adaptive agents differ in several significant ways from the optimal mixed strategies of fully rational decision makers. First, although the average propensity for the *population* is almost bang-on, individual pairs are spread out around that value. And that is associated with a more important fact: adaptive trial-and-error can produce serially correlated behavior, which optimal decision makers will not exhibit. Consider a pair whose propensities happen to be at the optimum of $(.5, .5)$. Suppose Column wins today, with an outcome of (*up*, *right*). Then the very nature of Bush-Mosteller learning ensures that Row's probability of playing *up* tomorrow will fall while Column's will rise. Hence, seriality: the players' mixing in $t+1$ is not independent of what happened in $t$, even though the underlying stage game remains fixed.

Further, our adaptive agents do not respond to changes in stage game payoffs the way fully rational actors do. One of the most notorious predictions of classical noncooperative game theory is that in a mixed strategy equilibrium, player A does not respond to changes in her payoffs; instead, she responds to changes in her *partner's* payoffs. This seems counterintuitive to many people: it seems plausible that A would, in fact, respond to changes in her own payoffs. And our actors do. Consider run 8.27, in which Row wins big in the outcome of (*up*, *left*). Because Row fairly often gets this large payoff and because aspirations adjust to experience, her aspirations rise above 1. Thus *down* never evokes positive feedback, while *up* sometimes does. Hence Row becomes more predisposed to play *up*.[26] This is clearly not Nash behavior, which would require Row to keep Column indifferent between *left* and *right* by mixing at 50 percent. Further, although the payoff change does induce Column to move in the predicted direction—his propensity to play *left* falls, as it should—it does not go far enough. With the payoffs of run 8.27, Column should be playing *left* only 20 percent of the time, instead of the 38 percent that is predicted here.

## 8.5 Extensions and Conclusions

By analyzing several different types of games, we have tried to show that the domain of this model of aspiration-based learning is quite large. But the domain is much bigger than is indicated here. The model can be applied to any strategic situation that one might care to study, so long as each agent has only finitely many actions in the stage game and there are only finitely many decision makers—restrictions that are not very troubling.

We would like to sketch out three extensions that have strong political interpretations. The first one extends the model to circumstances in which the agents have more than two actions; the application is to two-party electoral competition. The second extends the model to hierarchical situations in which one agent has more authority than the other; the application is to floor-committee relations in legislatures. The third extends the model to *N*-person games; the application is to participation (turnout) in large electorates.

### *8.5.1 Electoral Competition*

In each of the seven stage games examined in this chapter, the agents had only two feasible actions. However, the model generalizes in a straightforward way to contexts in which the agents have any (finite) number of actions. One particularly important context is electoral competition, wherein the parties or candidates can adopt positions on a left-to-right spectrum or possibly in a multidimensional space.[27]

If the policy space is unidimensional and parties have aspirations over vote share, then we conjecture that they will converge to a pure propensity state in which each side aspires to half the vote and gets that share (which is its maxmin payoff); the median voter is the unique stable state.[28] What happens in multidimensional spaces is an open, and intriguing, question.

### 8.5.2 *Institutional Hierarchy: Floor-Committee Relations*

We began this project several years ago with a simple question: Would adaptively rational legislators learn to cooperate? In particular, under what circumstances would the floor median learn to defer to a committee, where the committee has the choice of acquiring or not acquiring expertise (Gilligan and Krehbiel 1987; Diermeier 1995)? The asymmetric roles of the floor and the committee require an asymmetric payoff matrix. Indeed, the actions available to the two sides are qualitatively very different: the floor chooses to defer to the committee or to retain control of the process itself, while the committee decides whether it should incur the costs of acquiring information (figure 8.5).

We have done some preliminary runs; they are encouraging. When conditions are favorable for cooperation—the committee is ideologically close to the floor median and the costs of acquiring expertise are low—the process tends to converge to a pure stable state of cooperation. But when the committee is ideologically distant from the floor or the costs of obtaining relevant information are high, then the only stable pure outcome seems to be an uninformed committee and a floor that keeps the reins in its own hands. Thus, if the legislature had a set of committees of varying ideological hue, then the floor median would tend to learn to defer to those committees with similar policy preferences but not to ideological outliers.

### 8.5.3 *Voter Turnout*

The "paradox of voting"—rational voters should not turn out in significant numbers in large electorates, but in fact voting is non-negligible in even the very largest national elections—has plagued the discipline for decades. Bendor, Diermeier, and Ting (n.d.) attack this problem by extending the present model to handle *N*-person games. Citizens learn to participate or to stay home, depending on

| | | Floor: Defer to committee | Floor: Retain control |
|---|---|---|---|
| Committee | Acquire information | a,w | b,x |
| | Remain uninformed | c,y | d,z |

Circumstances favorable to cooperation:

1. Floor and Committee are ideologically close: $x > w > z > y$.
2. Getting information is cheap: $a > c > d > b$.

Circumstances unfavorable to cooperation:

1. Players are ideologically far apart: $x > z > w > y$.
2. Information is expensive: $c > d > a > b$.

**Figure 8.5**
Committee-Floor Game

collective payoffs (whether their side won or lost), private costs (if they voted or not), and their dynamically adjusting aspirations. Preliminary simulation results indicate that even if the cost of voting is strictly positive for all voters, turnout is substantial. Most strikingly, participation is non-negligible (around 50 percent) even in an electorate of one million voters (Bendor, Diermeier, and Ting n.d.).

The preceding extensions suggest that a model of aspiration-based learning has considerable potential to shed light on important problems in the study of politics.

## Appendix

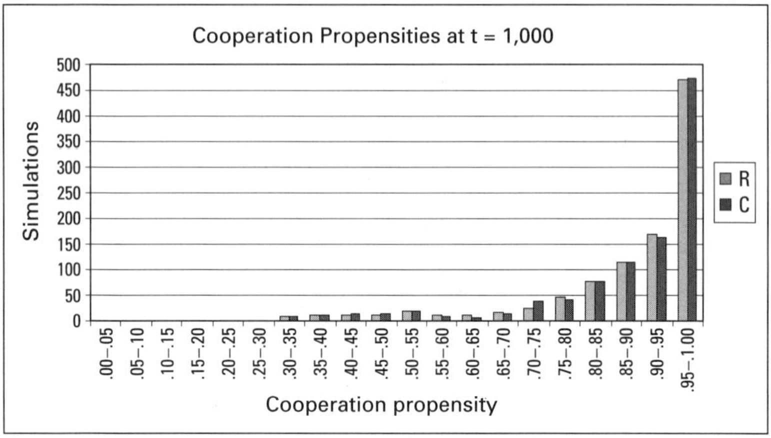


Payoff matrix:

| | |
|---|---|
| 3,3 | 1,2 |
| 2,1 | 0,0 |

Simulations: 1,000
Periods: 1,000
Tremble probabilities: $\rho = .001$, $\sigma = .001$, $\varepsilon = .001$
Adjustment parameters: $\alpha = 0.1$, $\beta = 0.1$, $\lambda = 0.95$, $\eta = 0.01$
Initial aspirations: (row) 1.5, (column) 1.5
Initial cooperation propensities: (row) .5, (column) .5

**Run 8.1**
Harmony

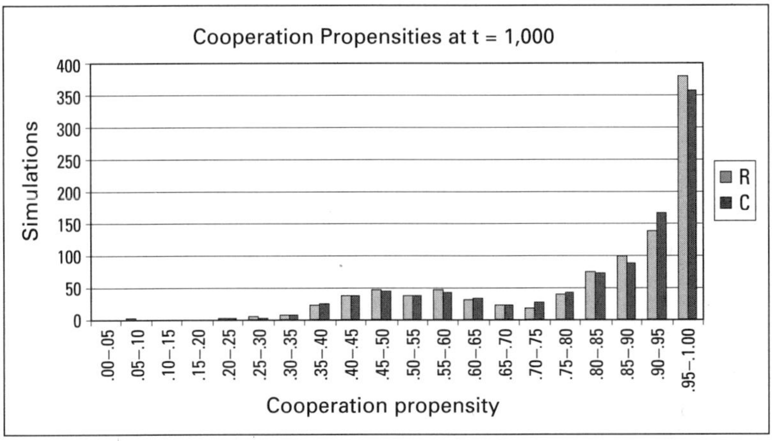


Payoff matrix:

| | |
|---|---|
| 3,3 | 0,2 |
| 2,0 | 1,1 |

Simulations: 1,000
Periods: 1,000
Tremble probabilities: $\rho = .001$, $\sigma = .001$, $\varepsilon = .001$
Adjustment parameters: $\alpha = 0.1$, $\beta = 0.1$, $\lambda = 0.95$, $\eta = 0.01$
Initial aspirations: (row) 1.5, (column) 1.5
Initial cooperation propensities: (row) .5, (column) .5

**Run 8.2**
Stag Hunt I

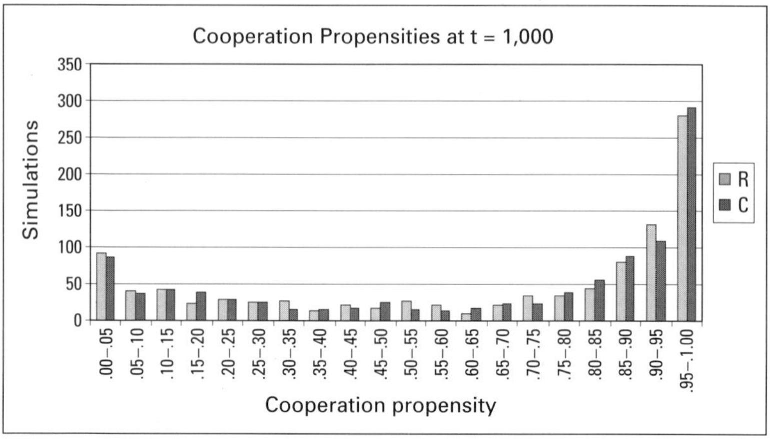


Payoff matrix:

| | |
|---|---|
| 3,3 | 0,1 |
| 1,0 | 2,2 |

Simulations: 1,000
Periods: 1,000
Tremble probabilities: $\rho = .001$, $\sigma = .001$, $\varepsilon = .001$
Adjustment parameters: $\alpha = 0.1$, $\beta = 0.1$, $\lambda = 0.95$, $\eta = 0.01$
Initial aspirations: (row) 1.5, (column) 1.5
Initial cooperation propensities: (row) .5, (column) .5

**Run 8.3**
Stag Hunt II

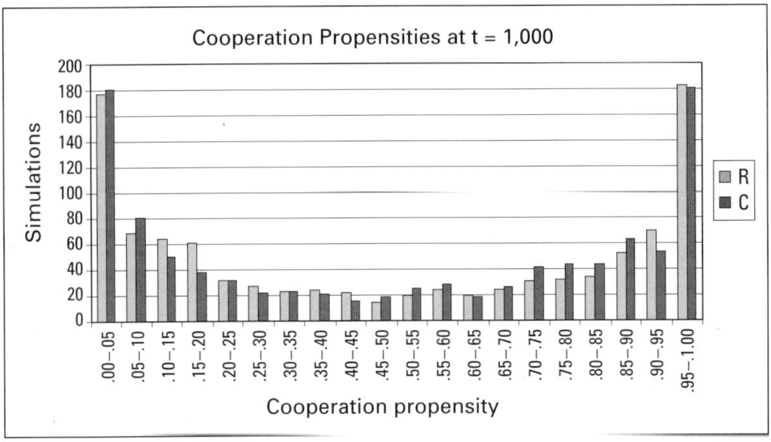


Payoff matrix:

| | |
|---|---|
| 1,1 | 2,3 |
| 3,2 | 0,0 |

Simulations: 1,000
Periods: 1,000
Tremble probabilities: $\rho = .001$, $\sigma = .001$, $\varepsilon = .001$
Adjustment parameters: $\alpha = 0.1$, $\beta = 0.1$, $\lambda = 0.95$, $\eta = 0.01$
Initial aspirations: (row) 1.5, (column) 1.5
Initial cooperation propensities: (row) .5, (column) .5

**Run 8.4**
Coordination

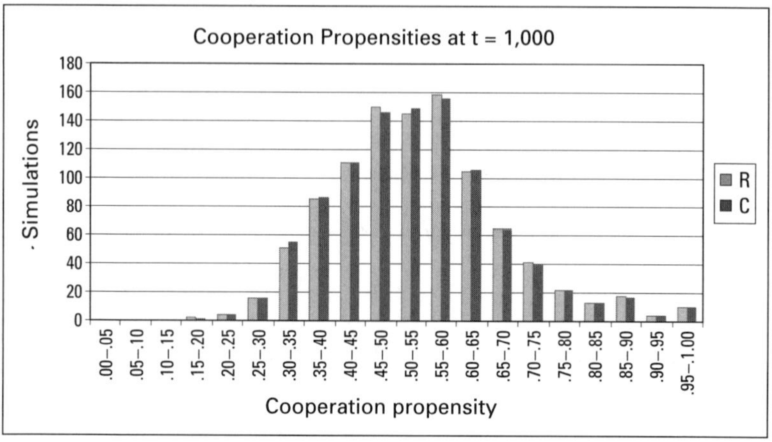


Payoff matrix:

| | |
|---|---|
| 2,2 | 1,3 |
| 3,1 | 0,0 |

Simulations: 1,000
Periods: 1,000
Tremble probabilities: $\rho$ = .001, $\sigma$ = .001, $\varepsilon$ = .001
Adjustment parameters: $\alpha$ = 0.1, $\beta$ = 0.1, $\lambda$ = 0.95, $\eta$ = 0.01
Initial aspirations: (row) 1.5, (column) 1.5
Initial cooperation propensities: (row) .5, (column) .5

**Run 8.5**
Chicken

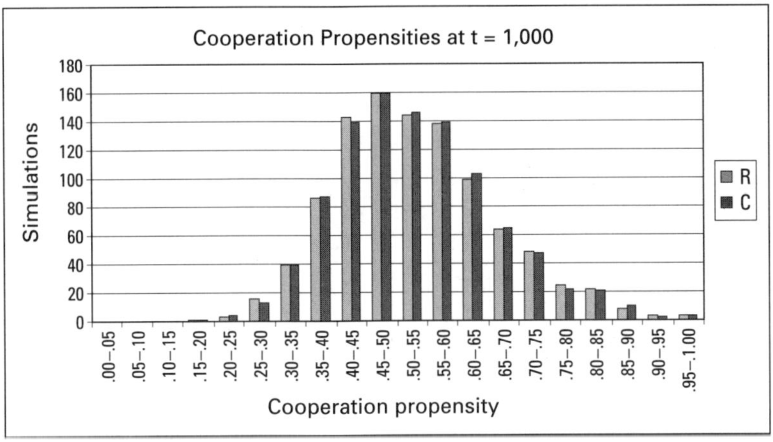


Payoff matrix:

| | |
|---|---|
| 2,2 | 0,3 |
| 3,0 | 1,1 |

Simulations: 1,000
Periods: 1,000
Tremble probabilities: $\rho = .001$, $\sigma = .001$, $\varepsilon = .001$
Adjustment parameters: $\alpha = 0.1$, $\beta = 0.1$, $\lambda = 0.95$, $\eta = 0.01$
Initial aspirations: (row) 1.5, (column) 1.5
Initial cooperation propensities: (row) .5, (column) .5

**Run 8.6**
Prisoner's Dilemma

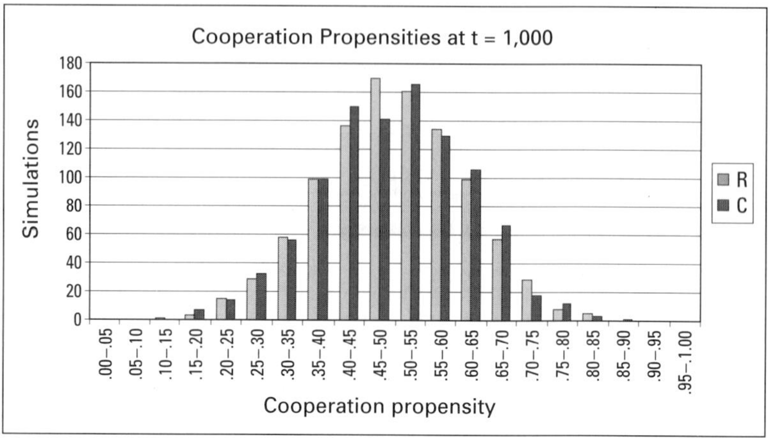


Payoff matrix:

| | |
|---|---|
| 1,0 | 0,1 |
| 0,1 | 1,0 |

Simulations: 1,000
Periods: 1,000
Tremble probabilities: $\rho = .001$, $\sigma = .001$, $\varepsilon = .001$
Adjustment parameters: $\alpha = 0.1$, $\beta = 0.1$, $\lambda = 0.95$, $\eta = 0.01$
Initial aspirations: (row) 1.5, (column) 1.5
Initial cooperation propensities: (row) .5, (column) .5

**Run 8.7**
Win-Lose

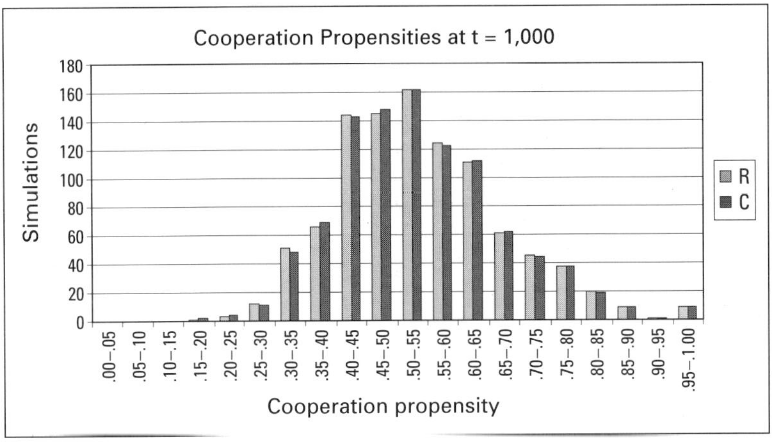


Payoff matrix:

| | |
|---|---|
| 2,2 | 0,3 |
| 3,0 | 1,1 |

Simulations: 1,000

Periods: 1,000

Tremble probabilities: $\rho = .001$, $\sigma = .001$, $\varepsilon = .001$

Adjustment parameters: $\alpha = 0.1$, $\beta = 0.1$, $\lambda = 0.95$, $\eta = 0.01$

Initial aspirations: (row) 0.5, (column) 0.5

Initial cooperation propensities: (row) 0, (column) 0

**Run 8.8**

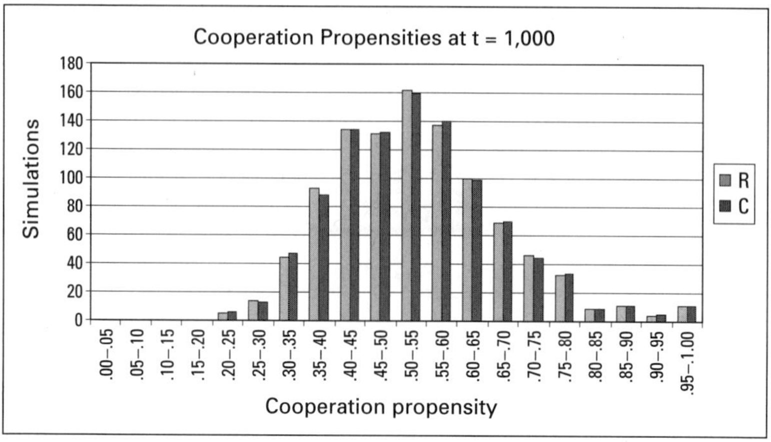


Payoff matrix:

| | |
|---|---|
| 2,2 | 0,3 |
| 3,0 | 1,1 |

Simulations: 1,000
Periods: 1,000
Tremble probabilities: $\rho = .009$, $\sigma = .009$, $\varepsilon = .009$
Adjustment parameters: $\alpha = 0.1$, $\beta = 0.1$, $\lambda = 0.95$, $\eta = 0.01$
Initial aspirations: (row) 1.5, (column) 1.5
Initial cooperation propensities: (row) .5, (column) .5

**Run 8.9**

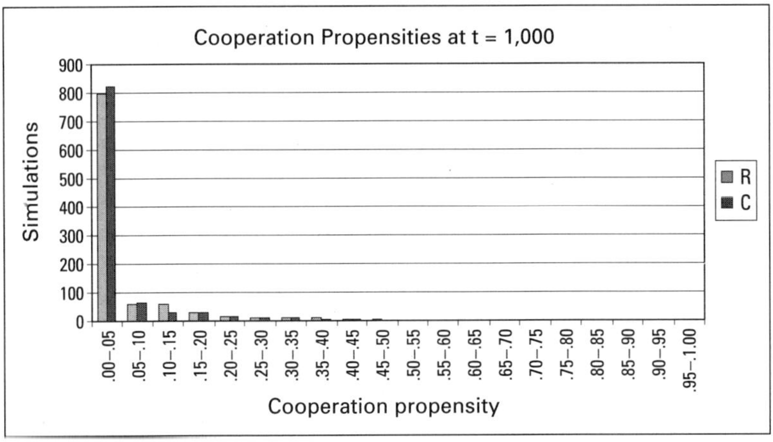


Payoff matrix:

| | |
|---|---|
| 3,3 | –5,2 |
| 2,–5 | 1,1 |

Simulations: 1,000
Periods: 1,000
Tremble probabilities: $\rho = .01$, $\sigma = .01$, $\varepsilon = .01$
Adjustment parameters: $\alpha = 0.1$, $\beta = 0.1$, $\lambda = 0.95$, $\eta = 0.01$
Initial aspirations: (row) 1.5, (column) 1.5
Initial cooperation propensities: (row) .5, (column) .5

**Run 8.10**

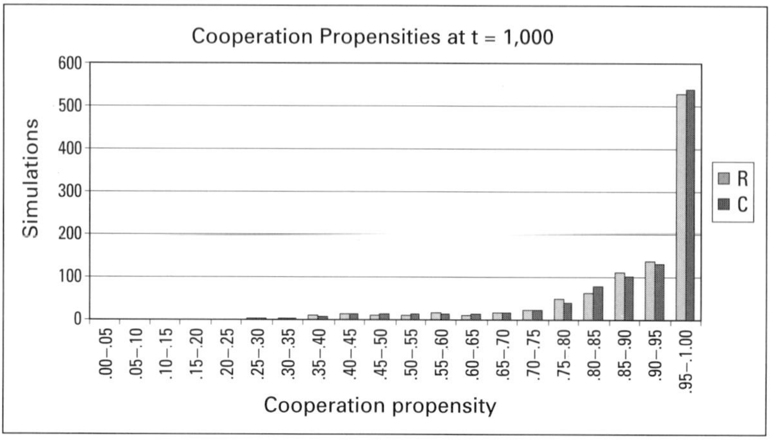


Payoff matrix:

| | |
|---|---|
| 3,3 | 1,2 |
| 2,1 | 0,0 |

Simulations: 1,000
Periods: 1,000
Tremble probabilities: $\rho$ = .001, $\sigma$ = .001, $\varepsilon$ = .001
Adjustment parameters: $\alpha$ = 0.1, $\beta$ = 0.1, $\lambda$ = 0.95, $\eta$ = 0.01
Initial aspirations: (row) 1.5, (column) 1.5
Initial cooperation propensities: (row) .5, (column) .5

**Run 8.11**

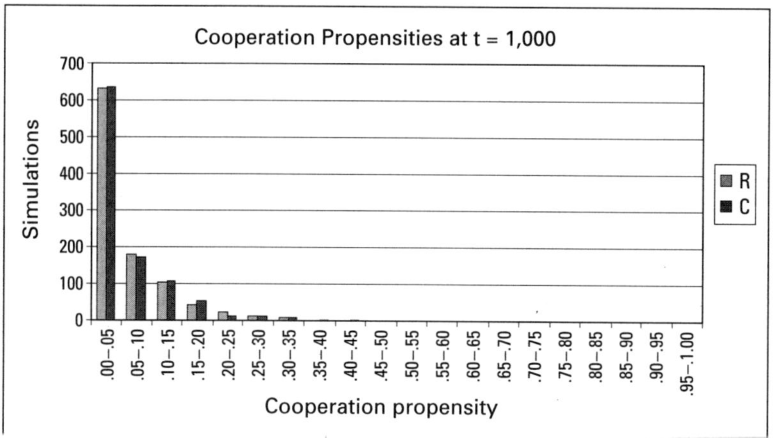


Payoff matrix:

| | |
|---|---|
| 3,3 | −5,1 |
| 1,−5 | 2,2 |

Simulations: 1,000
Periods: 1,000
Tremble probabilities: $\rho$ = .01, $\sigma$ = .01, $\varepsilon$ = .01
Adjustment parameters: $\alpha$ = 0.1, $\beta$ = 0.1, $\lambda$ = 0.95, $\eta$ = 0.01
Initial aspirations: (row) 1.5, (column) 1.5
Initial cooperation propensities: (row) .5, (column) .5

**Run 8.12**

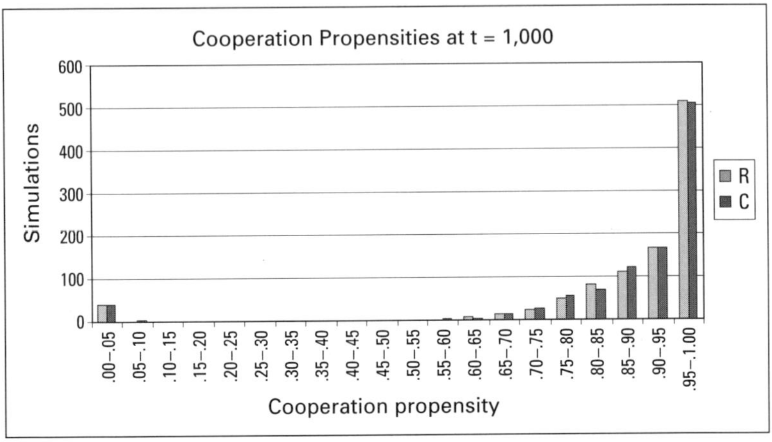


Payoff matrix:

| | |
|---|---|
| 100,100 | −10,2 |
| 2,−10 | 1,1 |

Simulations: 1,000
Periods: 1,000
Tremble probabilities: $\rho = .01$, $\sigma = .01$, $\varepsilon = .01$
Adjustment parameters: $\alpha = 0.1$, $\beta = 0.1$, $\lambda = 0.95$, $\eta = 0.01$
Initial aspirations: (row) 1.5, (column) 1.5
Initial cooperation propensities: (row) .5, (column) .5

**Run 8.13**

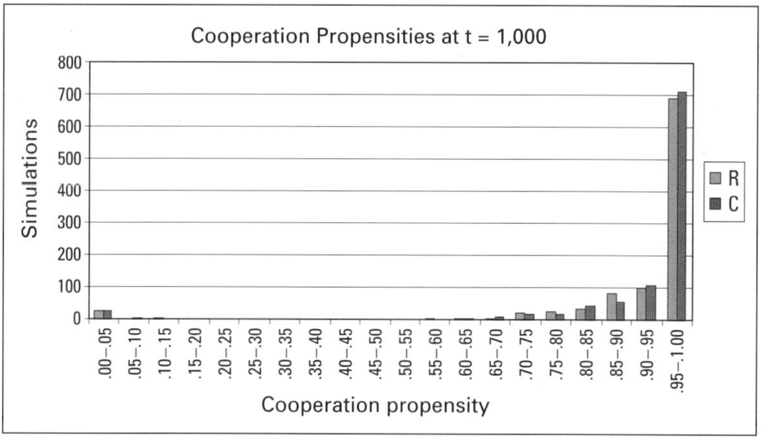


Payoff matrix:

| | |
|---|---|
| 100,100 | −10,1 |
| 1,−10 | 2,2 |

Simulations: 1,000

Periods: 1,000

Tremble probabilities: $\rho = .001$, $\sigma = .001$, $\varepsilon = .001$

Adjustment parameters: $\alpha = 0.1$, $\beta = 0.1$, $\lambda = 0.95$, $\eta = 0.01$

Initial aspirations: (row) 1.5, (column) 1.5

Initial cooperation propensities: (row) .5, (column) .5

**Run 8.14**

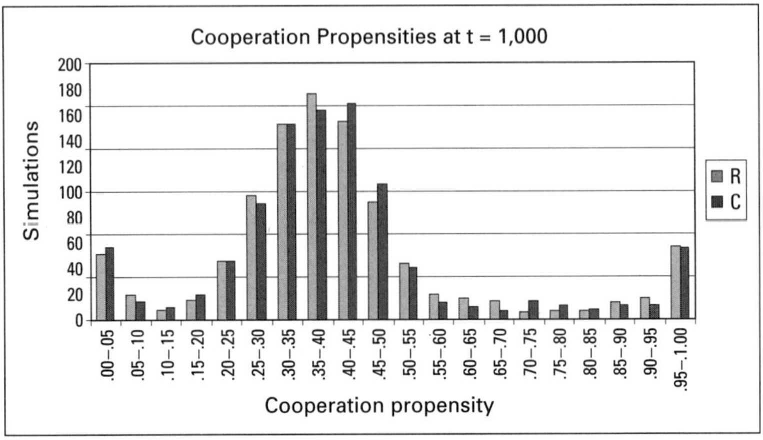


Payoff matrix:

| | |
|---|---|
| 1,1 | 2,10 |
| 10,2 | 0,0 |

Simulations: 1,000
Periods: 1,000
Tremble probabilities: $\rho = .001$, $\sigma = .001$, $\varepsilon = .001$
Adjustment parameters: $\alpha = 0.1$, $\beta = 0.1$, $\lambda = 0.95$, $\eta = 0.01$
Initial aspirations: (row) 1.5, (column) 1.5
Initial cooperation propensities: (row) .5, (column) .5

**Run 8.15**

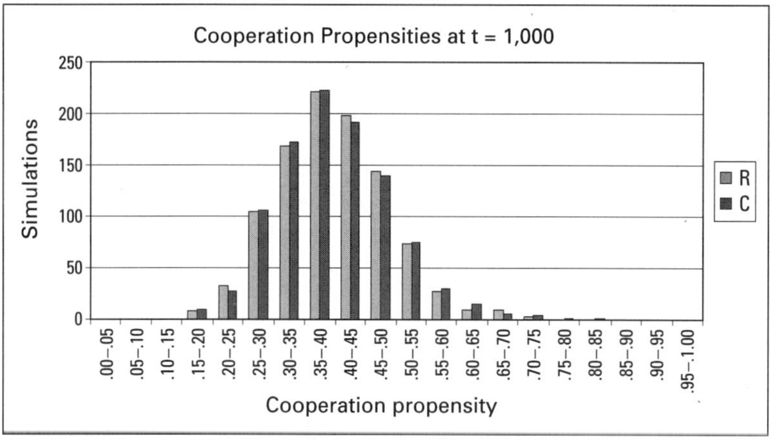


Payoff matrix:

| | |
|---|---|
| 2,2 | 1,10 |
| 10,1 | 0,0 |

Simulations: 1,000
Periods: 1,000
Tremble probabilities: $\rho = .001$, $\sigma = .001$, $\varepsilon = .001$
Adjustment parameters: $\alpha = 0.1$, $\beta = 0.1$, $\lambda = 0.95$, $\eta = 0.01$
Initial aspirations: (row) 1.5, (column) 1.5
Initial cooperation propensities: (row) .5, (column) .5

**Run 8.16**

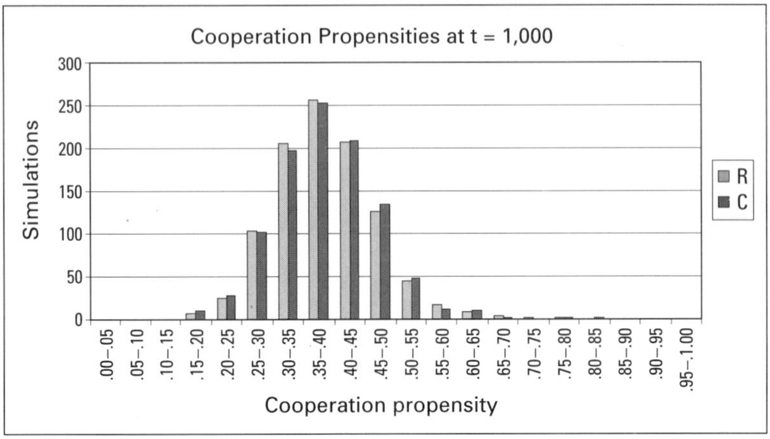


Payoff matrix:

| | |
|---|---|
| 2,2 | 0,10 |
| 10,0 | 1,1 |

Simulations: 1,000
Periods: 1,000
Tremble probabilities: $\rho = .001$, $\sigma = .001$, $\varepsilon = .001$
Adjustment parameters: $\alpha = 0.1$, $\beta = 0.1$, $\lambda = 0.95$, $\eta = 0.01$
Initial aspirations: (row) 1.5, (column) 1.5
Initial cooperation propensities: (row) .5, (column) .5

**Run 8.17**

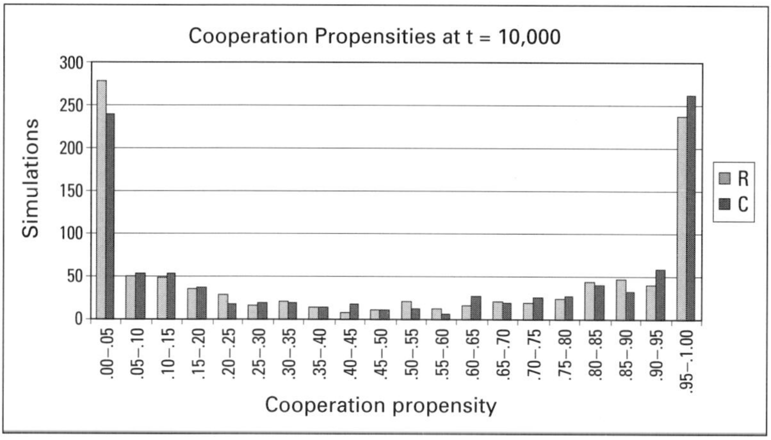


Payoff matrix:

| | |
|---|---|
| 1,1 | 2,3 |
| 3,2 | 0,0 |

Simulations: 1,000
Periods: 10,000
Tremble probabilities: $\rho = .001$, $\sigma = .001$, $\varepsilon = .001$
Adjustment parameters: $\alpha = 0.1$, $\beta = 0.1$, $\lambda = 0.95$, $\eta = 0.01$
Initial aspirations: (row) 1.5, (column) 1.5
Initial cooperation propensities: (row) .5, (column) .5

**Run** 8.18

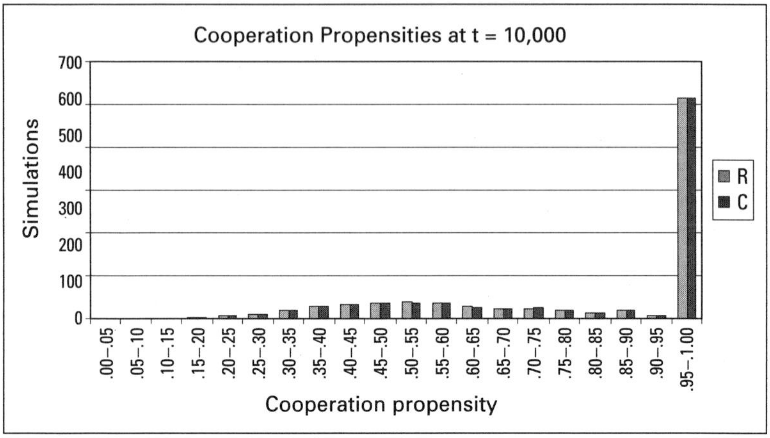


Payoff matrix:

| | |
|---|---|
| 2.7,2.7 | 1,3 |
| 3,1 | 0,0 |

Simulations: 1,000
Periods: 10,000
Tremble probabilities: $\rho = 0$, $\sigma = 0$, $\varepsilon = 0$
Adjustment parameters: $\alpha = 0.2$, $\beta = 0.2$, $\lambda = 0.95$, $\eta = 0.01$
Initial aspirations: (row) 1.5, (column) 1.5
Initial cooperation propensities: (row) .5, (column) .5

**Run 8.19**

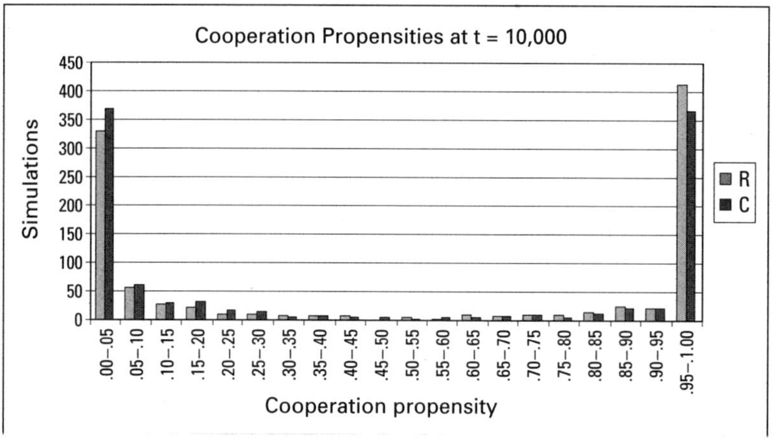


Payoff matrix:

| | |
|---|---|
| 1.01,1.01 | 1,3 |
| 3,1 | 0,0 |

Simulations: 1,000
Periods: 1,000
Tremble probabilities: $\rho = .001$, $\sigma = .001$, $\varepsilon = .001$
Adjustment parameters: $\alpha = 0.1$, $\beta = 0.1$, $\lambda = 0.95$, $\eta = 0.01$
Initial aspirations: (row) 1.5, (column) 1.5
Initial cooperation propensities: (row) .5, (column) .5

**Run 8.20**

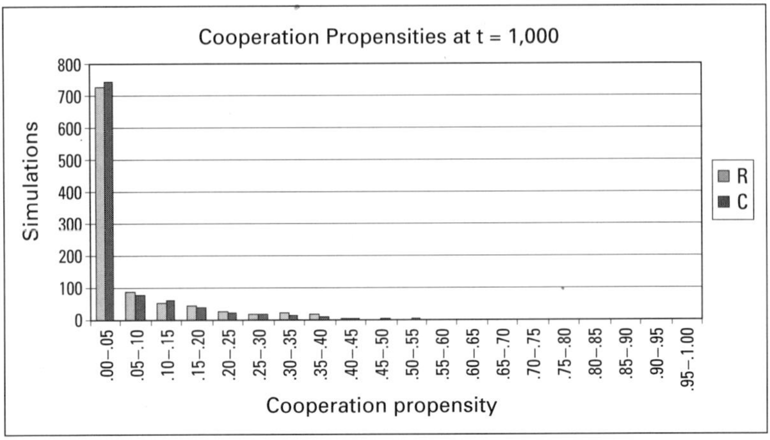


Payoff matrix:

| | |
|---|---|
| 2,2 | −5,3 |
| 3,−5 | 1,1 |

Simulations: 1,000
Periods: 1,000
Tremble probabilities: $\rho = .01$, $\sigma = .01$, $\varepsilon = .01$
Adjustment parameters: $\alpha = 0.1$, $\beta = 0.1$, $\lambda = 0.95$, $\eta = 0.01$
Initial aspirations: (row) 1.5, (column) 1.5
Initial cooperation propensities: (row) .5, (column) .5

**Run 8.21**

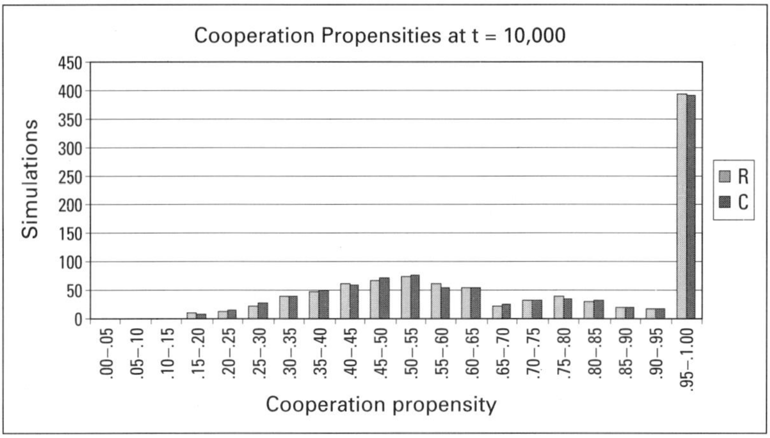


Payoff matrix:

| | |
|---|---|
| 2,2 | −5,3 |
| 3,−5 | −4,−4 |

Simulations: 1,000
Periods: 10,000
Tremble probabilities: $\rho = 0$, $\sigma = 0$, $\varepsilon = 0$
Adjustment parameters: $\alpha = 0.2$, $\beta = 0.2$, $\lambda = 0.95$, $\eta = 0.01$
Initial aspirations: (row) 1.5, (column) 1.5
Initial cooperation propensities: (row) .5, (column) .5

**Run 8.22**

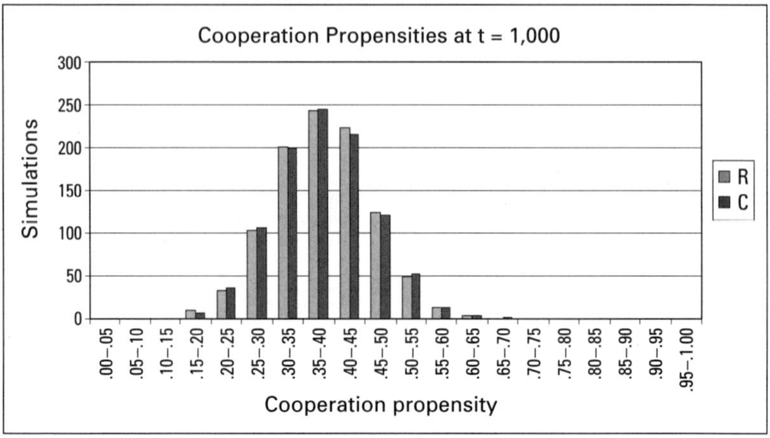


Payoff matrix:

| | |
|---|---|
| 2,2 | 0,10 |
| 10,0 | 1.7,1.7 |

Simulations: 1,000
Periods: 1,000
Tremble probabilities: $\rho$ = .01, $\sigma$ = .01, $\varepsilon$ = .01
Adjustment parameters: $\alpha$ = 0.1, $\beta$ = 0.1, $\lambda$ = 0.95, $\eta$ = 0.01
Initial aspirations: (row) 1.5, (column) 1.5
Initial cooperation propensities: (row) .5, (column) .5

**Run 8.23**

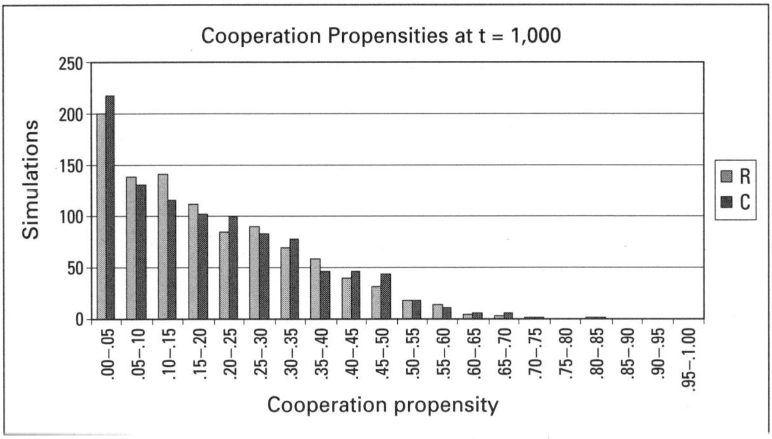


Payoff matrix:

| | |
|---|---|
| 2,2 | 0,3 |
| 3,0 | 1.7,1.7 |

Simulations: 1,000
Periods: 1,000
Tremble probabilities: $\rho$ = .01, $\sigma$ = .01, $\varepsilon$ = .01
Adjustment parameters: $\alpha$ = 0.1, $\beta$ = 0.1, $\lambda$ = 0.95, $\eta$ = 0.01
Initial aspirations: (row) 1.5, (column) 1.5
Initial cooperation propensities: (row) .5, (column) .5

**Run 8.24**

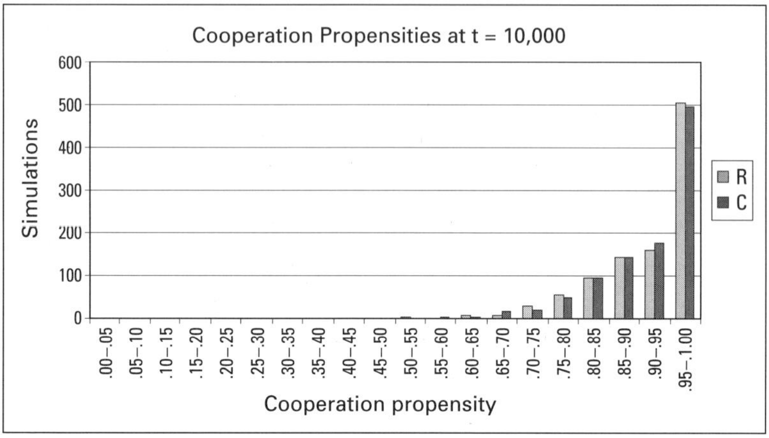


Payoff matrix:

| | |
|---|---|
| 3,3 | 2,1 |
| 1,2 | 0,0 |

Simulations: 1,000
Periods: 10,000
Tremble probabilities: $\rho = .01$, $\sigma = .01$, $\varepsilon = .01$
Adjustment parameters: $\alpha = 0.1$, $\beta = 0.1$, $\lambda = 0.95$, $\eta = 0.01$
Initial aspirations: (row) 1.5, (column) 1.5
Initial cooperation propensities: (row) .5, (column) .5

**Run 8.25**

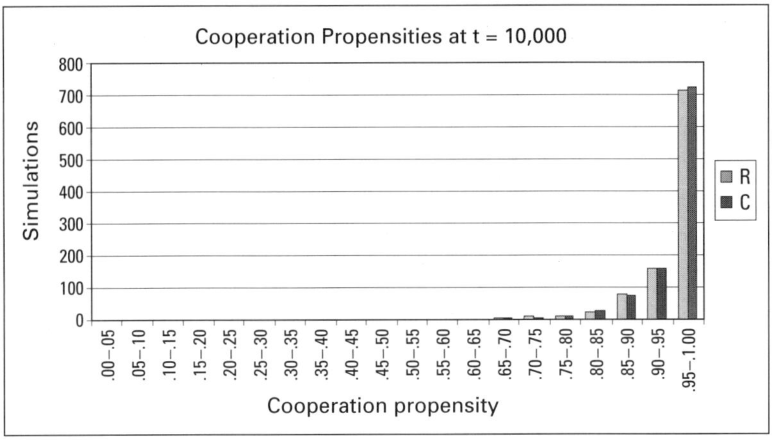


Payoff matrix:

| | |
|---|---|
| 2.1,2.1 | 2,1 |
| 1,2 | 0,0 |

Simulations: 1,000
Periods: 10,000
Tremble probabilities: $\rho = .01$, $\sigma = .01$, $\varepsilon = .01$
Adjustment parameters: $\alpha = 0.1$, $\beta = 0.1$, $\lambda = 0.95$, $\eta = 0.01$
Initial aspirations: (row) 1.5, (column) 1.5
Initial cooperation propensities: (row) .5, (column) .5

**Run 8.26**

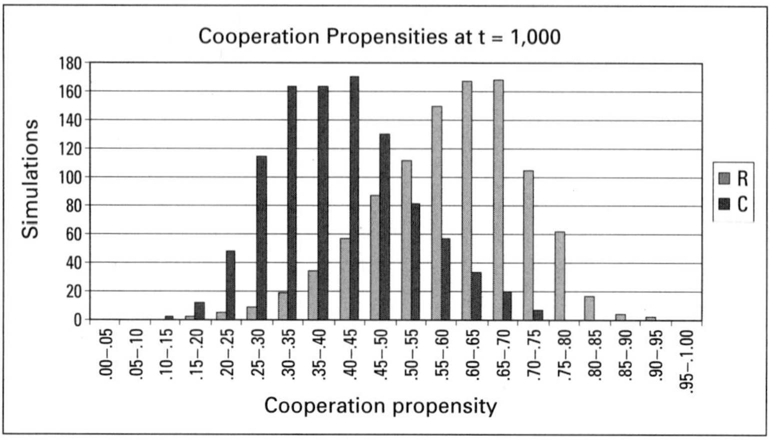


Payoff matrix:

| | |
|---|---|
| 4,0 | 0,1 |
| 0,1 | 1,0 |

Simulations: 1,000
Periods: 1,000
Tremble probabilities: $\rho = .01$, $\sigma = .01$, $\varepsilon = .01$
Adjustment parameters: $\alpha = 0.1$, $\beta = 0.1$, $\lambda = 0.95$, $\eta = 0.01$
Initial aspirations: (row) 1.5, (column) 1.5
Initial cooperation propensities: (row) .5, (column) .5

**Run 8.27**

## Notes

We thank panel participants at the 1999 annual meeting of the American Political Science Association for comments.

1. Thorndike long ago gave these assumptions the overly grand name of the law of effect, and so they are called in the psychological literature on learning.

2. See Estes (1962, 114–115, 131–135) for an assessment of both supporting and disconfirming evidence. For a more critical appraisal of the theoretical status of the law of effect, see Estes (1982, 77). For a detailed review of the evidence about one of the best-known implications of the reinforcement axioms—probability matching—see Myers (1976, 173–180).

3. In Simon's original satisficing theory, the aspiration level served as a stopping rule to terminate search. Our theory involves repeated interaction rather than search, so there is no natural end to this process. Consequently in our framework the aspiration level plays a different role: by leading to outcomes as satisfactory or unsatisfactory, it determines the sign of the feedback received by the agent and hence which actions are reinforced and which inhibited.

4. It is interesting to note that classical reinforcement theory was modified along essentially the same lines: "The rewards obtained over the past trials in a given context determine, by some averaging process, an internal standard or norm called the adaptation level. Each new reward is evaluated in relation to this adaptation level, having a positive influence on behavior if it is above the norm, a negative influence if it is below" (Hilgard and Bower 1966, 486).

5. We use *propensity* to underscore the psychological nature of the theory; mathematically, a propensity is a probability.

6. See Bendor, Mookherjee, and Ray (1998) for a more extensive discussion of the role of trembles in this kind of model.

7. The assumption of inertial adjustment ensures that the underlying stochastic process is aperiodic. This, together with the assumption about trembles on states, ensures that the process is ergodic. See note 9 for a brief discussion of ergodic stochastic processes.

8. This is obviously so for propensities, since they are bounded by 0 and 1. But it is also true of aspirations, since we have assumed that they too have lower and upper bounds. These bounds, together with the computer's truncation of decimals, ensure that there are only finitely many values of either parameter.

9. A limiting distribution is a kind of stochastic steady state: it is a probability distribution over the states such that if the process ever reached that distribution in date $t$, then it would have the *same probability distribution over the states* in date $t+1$. Clearly the predictive power of a stochastic model is enhanced if it has only one such limiting distribution. It is further enhanced if the process must *converge* to that unique distribution regardless of its initial probability distribution over states: in such cases one knows what the system's long-run probabilistic behavior looks like, no matter what the system's initial state was. (Such systems therefore display an important kind of history-independence.) Stochastic processes with unique limiting distributions to which they must eventually converge are called ergodic. Much is known analytically about the ergodicity of finite Markov chains with stationary transition probabilities, and we exploit that knowledge here.

10. For a purely computational use of aspiration-based models in sociological applications see Macy (1991a; 1991b), and Macy and Flache (2002). As we discussed in a related paper (Bendor, Diermeier, and Ting 2002), Macy's approach is subject to a "folk theorem," i.e., any outcome of the stage game can be supported as a stable outcome. The reason for this lack of predictive power is caused by the deterministic nature of those models, i.e., the lack of trembles or other stochastic shocks. See also Bendor, Mookherjee, and Ray (1998).

11. We slightly modify one of Snidal's properties, but the end result is the same.

12. Since many people are very familiar with Prisoner's Dilemma and its standard notation, it may be helpful to point out that in terms of this standard notation, what

is shared by these six games is $R > P$ (the reward to mutual cooperation beats the punishment of mutual defection) and $T > S$ (the temptation of exploiting beats the sucker's payoff of being exploited).

13. This misunderstanding—believing that the behavior of a single sample path will settle down as time goes to infinity—is so common that Feller (1967) devoted a good part of one chapter to dispelling it.

14. This procedure is reminiscent of Foster and Young's (1990) notion of "stochastically stable." However, Foster and Young investigate (myopic) best-response models rather than aspiration-based learning.

15. There *are* Prisoner's Dilemma simulations that reach such a population average, but the associated frequency distributions are not degenerate.

16. For fixed aspirations, Bendor, Mookherji, and Ray (1998) get the stronger result that in every pure stable outcome each player gets at least his maxmin payoff (proposition 2). For the games considered here, that is equivalent to excluding pure outcomes in which either player gets $\underline{\pi}$.

17. This may not generalize to $N$-person games, however. Our preliminary simulations on behavior in large $N$ settings suggest that certain inefficient mixed propensity states can endure for very long runs without any signs of breaking down.

18. Note, however, that because of the trembles, a particular pair never settles down indefinitely, so although in period 1,000 the Row player in simulation 5 may have lower aspirations and be inclined to cooperate while Column in this simulation has higher aspirations and be inclined to defect, by period 5,000 these roles could have reversed. Again, what settles down is the distribution of the population, not a particular pair.

19. Note, however, that in Stag Hunt the comparison was between two Nash equilibria. This is *not* true of Prisoner's Dilemma.

20. This result requires both that the tremble probability be set to zero and that $\alpha$ be sufficiently high (0.2 for this run). If the latter property did not hold, then the discreteness of the state space may stop players from converging to pure propensities. That is, a low $\alpha$ might make it impossible for players with propensities near 1 to adjust higher, since the program rounds the adjusted propensity to the nearest .001. This has the effect of creating "artificial" trembles as propensities approach 1.

21. Bendor, Mookherji, and Ray (1998) obtain a stronger result: when convergence is to inefficient Nash, it is only to inefficient equilibria that are also "protected." (Roughly, a protected Nash is one for which a deviation by Row does not hurt Column. Thus $(D, D)$ is a protected Nash in Prisoner's Dilemma.) This result holds, as usual, for fixed aspirations. With dynamically endogenous aspirations the restriction to protected Nash equilibria does not appear to hold: as noted, under certain parametric configurations the process converges to $(D, D)$ in Stag Hunt, and although this is Nash in both games, it is not protected in Stag Hunt II.

22. Note that since by assumption $(a, b)$ isn't Nash, either party could experiment away from $(a, b)$ and find the experimentation to be satisfying. This too makes a pure propensity state on $(a, b)$ vulnerable to destabilization.

23. They define a symmetric game as trivial if each player has an action that gives him the game's maximal payoff regardless of what his partner does.

24. Specifically, we would conjecture that in any trivial game, adaptation with dynamic aspirations will result in payoffs that converge to the game's maximal payoff, as $t \to \infty$.

25. In contrast, in the Prisoner's Dilemma example, although it is true that the effect was counterintutive in that reducing a *payoff* to an action made that action more common, we did not reduce the payoff to the *outcome* that became more common.

26. This tendency would be strengthened if we made the learning rule sensitive to payoff magnitudes, so that, for example, the more a payoff exceeded a current aspiration, the bigger the boost to the player's propensity to play the relevant action.

27. For adaptive models of Downsian competition in multidimensional policy spaces, see Kollman, Miller, and Page (1992; 1998) and Bendor, Mookherjee, and Ray (2001).

28. If aspirations are fixed throughout a game, then proposition 2 of Bendor, Mookherji, and Ray (1998) implies that the Downsian outcome is the only stable pure state, for a large class of learning rules (see, however, proposition 6 in Bendor, Mookherjee, and Ray 2001).

## References

Bendor, Jonathan, Daniel Diermeier, and Michael Ting. n.d. "A Behavioral Model of Turnout." *American Political Science Review* (forthcoming).

———. 2002. "The Empirical Content of Adaptive Models." Unpublished manuscript, Graduate School of Business, Stanford University.

Bendor, Jonathan, Dilip Mookherjee, and Debraj Ray. 1998. "Reinforcement Behavior in Repeated Games." Unpublished manuscript, Department of Economics, Boston University.

———. 2001. "Adaptive Political Parties in Downsian Competition." Paper, American Political Science Association Conference, San Francisco.

Bendor, Jonathan, and Piotr Swistak. 1997. "The Evolutionary Stability of Cooperation." *American Political Science Review* 91: 290–307.

Camerer, Colin. 1990. "Behavioral Game Theory." In *Insights in Decision Making*, ed. Robin Hogarth. Chicago: University of Chicago Press.

Cyert, Richard, and James March. 1963. *A Behavioral Theory of the Firm*. Englewood Cliffs, NJ: Prentice-Hall.

Diermeier, Daniel. 1995. "Commitment, Deference, and Legislative Institutions." *American Political Science Review* 89: 344–355.

———. 1998. "Explanatory Concepts in Rational Choice Theory." Unpublished manuscript, Northwestern University.

Estes, William K. 1962. "Learning Theory." *Annual Review of Psychology*, Vol. 13. Palo Alto CA: Annual Reviews, Inc.

———. 1982. *Models of Learning, Memory, and Choice: Selected Papers*. New York: Praeger.

Feller, William. 1967. *Introduction to Probability Theory and Its Applications*. New York: Wiley.

Foster, Dean, and H. Peyton Young. 1990. "Stochastic Evolutionary Game Dynamics." *Theoretical Population Biology* 38: 219–232.

Fudenberg, Drew, and David Levine. 1998. *The Theory of Learning in Games*. Cambridge, MA: MIT Press.

Gilligan, Thomas, and Keith Krehbiel. 1987. "Collective Decision-Making and Standing Committees: An Informational Rationale for Restrictive Amendment Procedures." *Journal of Law, Economics, and Organization* 3: 287–335.

Green, Donald, and Ian Shapiro. 1994. *Pathologies of Rational Choice*. New Haven: Yale University Press.

Hilgard, Ernest, and Gordon Bower. 1966. *Theories of Learning*. 3d ed. New York: Appleton-Century-Crofts.

Karandikar, Rajeeva, Dilip Mookherjee, Debraj Ray, and Fernando Vega-Redondo. 1998. "Evolving Aspirations and Cooperation." *Journal of Economic Theory* 80: 292–331.

Kemeny, John, and J. Laurie Snell. 1960. *Finite Markov Chains*. Princeton, NJ: Van Nostrand.

Kollman, Ken, John H. Miller, and Scott E. Page. 1992. "Adaptive Parties in Spatial Elections." *American Political Science Review* 86: 929–937.

———. 1998. "Political Parties and Electoral Landscapes." *British Journal of Political Science* 28: 139–158.

Macy, Michael. 1991a. "Learning to Cooperate: Stochastic and Tacit Collusion in Social Exchange." *American Journal of Sociology* 97: 808–843.

———. 1991b. "Chains of Cooperation: Threshold Effects in Collective Action." *American Sociological Review* 56: 730–747.

Macy, Michael, and Andreas Flache. 2002. "Learning Dynamics in Social Dilemmas." *Proceedings of the National Academy of Sciences* 99 (suppl. 3): 7229–7236.

Myers, Jerome. 1976. "Probability Learning and Sequence Learning." In *Handbook of Learning and Cognitive Processes*, Vol. 3, ed. W. K. Estes. Hillsdale, NJ: Lawrence Erlbaum Associates.

Myerson, Roger M. 1996. "Foundations of Social Choice Theory." CMSEMS Discussion Paper No. 1162. Northwestern University.

Shepsle, Kenneth. 1979. "Institutional Arrangements and Equilibrium in Multidimensional Voting Models." *American Journal of Political Science* 23: 27–59.

Simon, Herbert. 1955. "A Behavorial Model of Rational Choice." *Quarterly Journal of Economics* 69: 99–118.

Snidal, Duncan. 1991. "Relative Gains and the Pattern of International Cooperation." *American Political Science Review* 85: 701–726.

Young, H. Peyton. 1998. *Individual Strategy and Social Structure: An Evolutionary Theory of Institutions*. Princeton, NJ: Princeton University Press.

## Contributors

**Michael Bailey** is assistant professor in the Government Department at Georgetown University. His research on Congress, and on domestic sources of foreign policy, has appeared in *World Politics*, the *American Journal of Political Science*, and the *Journal of Law, Economics, and Organization*.

**David P. Baron** is the David S. and Ann M. Barlow Professor of Political Economy and Strategy at the Stanford Graduate School of Business, and professor of economics (by courtesy) and professor of political science (by courtesy) at Stanford University. He has published articles on the political economy of business and public policy in the *American Journal of Political Science*, the *Journal of Economics and Management Strategy*, the *American Political Science Review*, and the *Quarterly Journal of Economics*. His textbook *Business and Its Environment* is in its third edition.

**Jonathan Bendor** is the Walter and Elise Haas Professor of Political Economics and Organization at the Stanford Graduate School of Business. His research on theories of bounded rationality and organizational decision making has been published in the *American Political Science Review* and the *Journal of Law, Economics, and Organization*.

**Scott de Marchi** is assistant professor of political science at the University of North Carolina at Chapel Hill. He is also a fellow-at-large at the Santa Fe Institute. His research on strategic interaction and bounded rationality has been published in the *Journal of Politics*, the *Journal of Theoretical Politics*, and *Public Choice*.

**Daniel Diermeier** is the IBM Distinguished Professor of Regulation and Competitive Practice and professor of managerial economics and decision sciences at the Kellogg Graduate School of Management and professor of political science (by courtesy) at Northwestern University. His research focuses on game-theoretic models of political institutions and the foundations of formal political theory. His work has been published in the *American Economic Review*, the *American Political Science Review*, the *American Journal of Political Science*, the *Journal of Economic Theory*, and the *Quarterly Journal of Economics*.

**Joseph E. Harrington, Jr.,** is professor of economics at Johns Hopkins University. His research, which focuses on understanding electoral systems, organizations, and cartels, has appeared in the *American Economic Review, Management Science, Games and Economic Behavior*, and the *Journal of Political Economy*. His textbook with John Vernon and Kip Viscusi, *Economics of Regulation and Antitrust*, is in its third edition.

**Jude C. Hays** is assistant professor of political science and public policy at the University of Michigan, Ann Arbor. His research, which focuses on the interconnections between domestic politics, financial markets, and the international economy, has been published in the *American Journal of Political Science*.

**Michael Herron** is assistant professor of political science at Northwestern University. His research on legislatures and voting behavior, on ballot abnormalities in American presidential elections, and on theories of leadership has been published in the *American Political Science Review* and the *American Journal of Political Science*.

**John E. Jackson** is professor of political science and professor of business economics at the University of Michigan, Ann Arbor. His interests include the dynamics of party competition and the measurement of partisanship in new democracies. His research on political institutions and economic reform in Poland has been published in the *British Journal of Political Science, Political Analysis*, and the *Journal of Business Venturing*.

**Ken Kollman** is associate professor of political science, and senior associate research scientist at the Center for Political Studies, University of Michigan, Ann Arbor. His research interests include the study of party systems and electoral rules, the dynamics of electoral competition, and computational modeling of voting systems. His work has been published in the *American Political Science Review*, the

*American Economic Review*, the *British Journal of Political Science*, and the *Journal of Law, Economics, and Organization.*

**John H. Miller** is professor of economics and decision sciences, and professor in the Graduate School of Industrial Administration (by courtesy) at Carnegie Mellon University. He is also an external professor at the Santa Fe Institute. His research on economics and game theory and on complex adaptive systems has been published in the *American Economic Review*, *Econometrica*, the *Journal of Economic Behavior and Organization*, *Computational Economics*, *Management Science*, the *British Journal of Political Science*, *Journal of Economic Dynamics and Control*, and the *Journal of Evolutionary Economics.*

**Scott E. Page** is associate professor of political science, associate professor of complex systems, associate professor of economics (by courtesy), and senior associate research scientist at the Center for Political Studies, University of Michigan, Ann Arbor. He is also an external faculty member at the Santa Fe Institute. His research in economics and game theory, bounded rationality, computational economics, and complex systems has been published in the *Journal of Economic Theory*, the *American Economic Review*, the *Journal of Law, Economics, and Organization*, the *British Journal of Political Science*, *Complexity*, the *Journal of Urban Economics*, and *Computational Economics.*

**Diana Richards** is associate professor of political science at the University of Minnesota. Her research, which has focused on how cognitive knowledge structures create equilibria in social choice and coordination problems, has appeared in the *American Journal of Political Science*, the *Journal of Mathematical Psychology*, and the *Journal of Conflict Resolution.*

**Michael Ming Ting** is assistant professor of political science at the University of North Carolina, Chapel Hill. His research on bureaucracy and on elections has been published in the *American Journal of Political Science.*

# Index